Unprotected

Palestinians in Egypt since 1948

UNPROTECTED

Palestinians in Egypt since 1948

Oroub El-Abed

Institute for Palestine Studies
Beirut, Lebanon • Washington, DC

International Development Research Centre
Ottawa • Cairo • Dakar • Montevideo • Nairobi • New Delhi • Singapore

Library of Congress Cataloging-in-Publication Data

El-Abed, Oroub.
   Unprotected : Palestinians in Egypt since 1948 / Oroub El-Abed.
      p. cm.
   "Co-published by the Institute for Palestine Studies, Washington, DC and the International Development Research Centre, Ottawa, Ontario, Canada."
   Includes bibliographical reference and index.
   ISBN 978-0-88728-313-0 (pbk. : alk. paper) 1. Palestinian Arabs--Egypt. 2. Palestinian Arabs--Civil rights--Egypt. 3. Palestinian Arabs--Legal status, laws, etc.--Egypt. I. Title.

   DT72.P35E53 2008
   305.892'74062--dc22   2008044093

Institute for Palestine Studies
3501 M Street, N.W.
Washington, DC 20007
www.palestine-studies.org /
ipsdc@palestine-studies.org

International Development Research Centre
PO Box 8500
Ottawa, ON K1G 3H9
Canada
www.idrc.ca / info@idrc.ca
eISBN 978-1-55250-443-7

Printed in the United States of America

Contents

Abbreviations and Terms
Used in the Text

Abbreviations

AFSC:	American Friends Service Committee (Quakers)
AOGG:	Administration Office of the Governor of Gaza
AUC:	American University in Cairo
CAPMAS:	Central Agency for Public Mobilization and Statistics, the Egyptian government agency responsible for census data.
£E:	Egyptian pound
FMRS:	Forced Migration Refugee Studies Program
GAP:	Government of All Palestine
GBP:	British pound (pound sterling)
GUPS:	General Union of Palestinian Students
GUPW:	General Union of Palestinian Workers (generally referred to as "Labor Union")
GUPWom:	General Union of Palestinian Women (generally referred to as "Women's Union")
IDF:	Israel Defense Forces
NGOs:	Nongovernmental organizations
PLO:	Palestine Liberation Organization
PA:	Palestinian Authority
PLA:	Palestine Liberation Army
PRCS:	Palestine Red Crescent Society
PSU:	Palestinian Student Union
UAR:	United Arab Republic
UNCCP:	United Nations Conciliation Commission for Palestine
UNHCR:	United Nations High Commissioner for Refugees
UNRWA:	United Nations Relief and Works Agency

Interview Codes

(See the section "Conducting the Interviews" in Appendix 1 for details)

   PP: Pilot visits/interviews by the author
   P: Pilot visits/interviews by research team (author and
         assistants) in Cairo Governorate
   AP: Visits/interviews conducted after termination of
         fieldwork
   7:    Regular interviews conducted in Sharqiyyah
         Governorate
   8:    Regular interviews conducted in Qalyubiyyah
         Governorate

Note: Throughout the text, each quotation from an interview is followed by a code indicating the category of visit, the governorate, the number of the household visited within the category, the name of the town or district within the governorate, and the date the interview was conducted. "P12, 'Izbit al-Nakhal, 29 May 2002," for example, indicates the twelfth household visit by the research team in Cairo Governorate, the district of 'Izbit al-Nakhal, on 29 May 2002; "7/43, Hehya, 15 July 2002" indicates the forty-third regular interview conducted by the research team, in Sharqiyyah Governorate, the district of Hehya, on 15 July; "PP9, Port Said, 18 June 2002 indicates the ninth pilot visit by the author, in Port Said Governorate, the city of Port Said, on 18 June; and so on. It should be emphasized that the number refers to the *household* visited, and in many cases a number of persons were interviewed within the household. The same household number, then, may be used for various family members; this will generally be indicated in the text.

Arabic Terms

arzuki: wage laborer

'ashwa'iyyat: unplanned urban settlements, built without proper permits

azhari: religious schools

basta or *farsha* in the Egyptian dialect: the pushcart of street vendors

bahth ijtima'i: Social worker visit to a family to assess its socioeconomic conditions

gama'iyyah: cooperative

gharib: stranger

ghurbah: in exile

ishash: simple houses made of hay

kafil: guarantor

Maktab Wafidin: general administration for foreign students

markaz: the administrative division below the level of governorate (plural: *marakiz*); the governorate comprises *marakiz*

Mugamma': the administrative body that processes bureaucratic documents and papers

Muhafazah: Governorate

qism: the administrative division below that of *markaz* within a governorate (plural: *aqsam*)

tawtin: permanent resettlement of Palestinians in Arab host countries

tijarat shanta: bag trade

wafid: immigrant, foreigner

Other Information

Land is measured in dunams and feddans; 1 feddan = 4,074 square meters; and 1 dunam = 1,000 square meters.

During the period in which this research was conducted (2001–3), the value of one Egyptian pound (£E) fluctuated between $0.15 and $0.22. In 1960, £E 1 = $2.00.

Acknowledgments

This manuscript was written during 2003, when I was still based in Cairo. Many individuals helped me as I researched and wrote the book. I thank Barbara Harrell-Bond, then-acting director of the Forced Migration and Refugee Studies Program (FMRS) at the American University in Cairo and supervisor of my project, for her support. I would not have been able to study the livelihoods of refugee communities in Egypt without her assistance. I also gratefully acknowledge the help of Anita Fabos, the former director of FMRS, whose persistence and energy gave me the chance to work in the program as a researcher and adjunct lecturer.

This study would not be what it is today without my team of assistants. I thank Elizabeth Frantz, who believed in the study and the validity and importance of what we were doing. Arwa al-Burei, Islam Ghirbawi, Sahar Mansour, Ali Barghouti, and Rania Yousef helped conduct the field interviews. Arwa helped update the research in preparation for publication; I am so proud to see that she was able to get a scholarship to study human rights in the Netherlands and that she completed her degree and currently is applying to a masters program in the United Kingdom. Bisan Aidwain, Samy al-Aidy, and Sherifa Shafie helped collect articles, newspapers clippings, regulations, and laws.

I thank Ron Wilkinson, the first editor of this manuscript, for his help, support, and advice. Matar Saqer, the editor/translator of the Arabic version, approached this project with dedication and passion. Matar, himself a refugee and the spokesperson of the United Nations Relief and Works Agency for Palestine Refugees, got so immersed in the work that I often felt he was with us in Cairo, conducting the interviews and analyzing the setup. I very much appreciate his input, his generous giving of his time, and his efforts.

This book might not have been published had it not been for Dr. Joseph Massad, who brought my manuscript to the Institute of Palestine Studies in Washington, DC. Linda Butler, who edited it, did an amazing job filling in historical gaps, shaping the text, and enhancing its cohesiveness. I cannot thank her enough for her work and patience. I would also like to thank Rasmi Jebril in

Amman and Marc Lavergne, director of CEDEJ (Centre d'Etudes et de Documentation Economiques, Juridiques et Sociales) in Cairo, for their help in preparing the maps.

I would also like to acknowledge the team at FMRS, including Alia Arafa, Kasia Grabska, Marwa Hassan, and Etab Adel Saad, for their help in administrative and technical matters. I appreciate the moral support of Fateh Azzam, the director of the program just before I left. I thank American University in Cairo professors Nadine Naber and Jean Allain who helped me when I first started my research proposal.

The research was made possible with funding from Canada's International Development Research Centre (IDRC). I was very happy to know and work with the center's Middle East Special Initiatives senior specialist, Roula El-Rifai; she was amazingly supportive throughout the two years in Egypt with all the difficulties I faced and through the editing and production of the book. I would also like to thank her team, Eileen Alma, Claire Fitzpatrick, and Michael Atalla, for their help in matters relating to the grant.

I thank my Palestinian interviewees for so generously sharing their time and experiences with me and my assistants. Their input has been invaluable. I sincerely hope that this report adequately voices their concerns. I also thank Abdul Qader Yassin, a Palestinian refugee living in Egypt and a resource person on the situation of Palestinians in Egypt; Amal al-Agha al-Farra, an active and enthusiastic member of the Palestinian Women's Union; Muna (from Madinet al-Salam) and Fathieh (from Wailey), the Palestinian social workers who were very helpful to me when I first started the pilot field visits; and Ali Jawhar, the head of the Palestinian Businessmen's Council and the Palestinian Charitable Association, who was generous with his time, meeting with my research assistants and hearing our ideas about how better to serve Palestinians in Egypt. H.E. Zuhdi al-Qudwah, the Palestinian ambassador to Egypt, provided information on the status and numbers of Palestinians in Egypt.

I owe sincere thanks to Abbas Shiblak, his mother, and his sister Raeiseh for having hosted me in Oxford during my visit in summer 2002 to the documentation center of the Refugee Studies Centre at Queen Elizabeth House. We built on the social capital that our families had established when they lived in Palestine before the exodus. Sincere thanks are due to Dawn Chatty of Oxford University for her constructive comments on a draft of this study and to Elia Zureik of Queens University, Canada, who reviewed my proposal and my manuscript and suggested ideas to incorporate in the final report and encouraged me in my work. I thank Aage Tiltnes of the Fafo Institute for Applied Social Science for his insight and interest in the research. He offered many helpful comments based on his own experience conducting quantitative and qualitative research in the region.

I would like to express my gratitude to the team at the Centre d'Études et de Recherches de Moyen Orient Contemporain (CERMOC) in Amman, Jordan (now called the Institut Francais de Proche Orient), to which I am affiliated. Hana Jaber, who was then the head of CERMOC, hosted me as a researcher for three months so that I could use the library, which specialized in Palestinians in exile. Librarian Aida Bin Saad Maraka was always available to offer assistance and regular updates on information relevant to the research.

Finally, I thank my immediate family for their constant love and support: my brother Samer, whose care and regular phone calls made me laugh as I dealt with the ongoing culture shock of living in Egypt; my brother Khaldoun, who never stopped encouraging me to take risks, to stick to my principles, and to learn from each step in my professional development; and not least, my mother, whose patience, strength, and support have been vital. My sincere thanks and love are due to the three of them and to the memory of my father, Anwar, for having stood by me through this experience.

Timeline

September 1918: Palestine is occupied by British forces following the Ottoman defeat in World War I.

July 1922: The League of Nations approves Britain's Mandate over Palestine, incorporating the Jewish National Home project, without the consent of the Palestinian inhabitants. The Mandate officially comes into force in September 1923.

October 1922: The first British census of Palestine shows the population distribution as 78 percent Muslim, 11 percent Jewish, and 10 percent Christian.

August 1929: Militant Zionist demonstrations at the Wailing Wall precipitate Palestinian rioting in Jerusalem that spreads to other towns, especially Hebron. (This episode is known as the Buraq crisis.)

November 1931: The second British census of Palestine already shows the effect of unrestricted Jewish immigration, with the population now 73 percent Muslim, 17 percent Jewish, and 9 percent Christian.

May 1936: An Arab general strike is called to protest Britain's pro-Zionist policies. The strike, which lasts six months, evolves into the Arab rebellion.

1936–39: The "Great Arab Rebellion" continues, during which the British authorities ban the Arab Higher Committee (the highest Palestinian political body), exile the Palestine leadership, and totally disarm the Palestinian population.

May 1939: Britain issues a White Paper restricting Jewish immigration and land sales.

1945–47: As World War II ends, Zionists escalate their campaign (including military) against Britain to lift restrictions on Jewish immigration.

February 1947: Britain turns the Palestine problem over to the United Nations; the date for the end of the Mandate is later set for 14 May 1948.

29 November 1947: UN General Assembly Resolution 181 recommends the partition of Palestine into an Arab state and a Jewish state. Skirmishes begin between Zionist forces and Arab irregulars.

2 April 1948: The Haganah, the fighting force of the Yishuv (the Jewish community in Palestine), launches Plan Dalet, a series of thirteen military operations, to conquer those parts of Palestine assigned to the Jewish state under UN General Assembly Resolution 181.

24 April 1948: Massive shelling of Jaffa by the Irgun, a militant offshoot of the Haganah, is followed by an all-out offensive by the Haganah, triggering the first wave of Palestinians to Egypt in boats. Jaffa falls to the Zionists on 10 May.

9 May 1948: The Egyptian government creates the Higher Committee for Palestinian Immigrant Affairs to handle the influx of Palestinians into Egypt; temporary refugee camps are set up in 'Abbasiyyah (a Cairo suburb), Qantara Sharq in Sinai, and Azarita near Port Said.

14 May 1948: The British Mandate over Palestine ends; Israel declares statehood.

The UN General Assembly creates the position of UN Mediator for Palestine, tasked with promoting a truce between the parties and working toward "a peaceful adjustment of the future situation in Palestine." Count Folke Bernadotte, named to the position, arrives in Palestine shortly thereafter.

15 May 1948: Arab state armies enter those parts of Palestine assigned to the Arab state under the UN partition plan, marking the start of the "regular" phase of the 1948 war. Egyptian forces cross into Gaza and deploy up the coast to Isdud, with lesser force sent through the Negev and Hebron to the Bethlehem area.

September 1948: The Government of All Palestine (GAP) is established to govern the parts of Palestine remaining in Arab hands (and as a counter to Transjordanian ambitions). The GAP effectively becomes a shell under Egyptian control.

Palestinian refugees housed in 'Abbasiyyah and Azarita camps are moved to Qantara Sharq.

17 September 1948: UN Special Mediator Count Bernadotte is assassinated by the Zionist "dissident" Stern gang, one day after presenting his Progress Report to the UN General Assembly calling, inter alia, for the right of the refugees to return to their homes.

Mid-October 1948: The Israel Defense Forces (IDF; replacing Haganah) launch Operation Ten Plagues against Egyptian troops holding Gaza.

October 1948–February 1949: 4,000 Egyptian troops (including the battalion in which Gamal Abd al-Nasser was a staff officer) are surrounded by the IDF in the "Faluja pocket" but manage to hold out until the armistice.

11 December 1948: UN General Assembly Resolution 194 (III), based largely on Bernadotte's recommendations, is passed. Paragraph 11 calls for the right of Palestinian refugees to return to their homes and for the establishment of the UN Conciliation Commission (UNCCP).

January 1949: Under an agreement with the United Nations, the American Friends Service Committee (AFSC, also known as the Quakers) assumes responsibility for relief operations in the Gaza Strip.

24 February 1949: An Egyptian-Israeli armistice agreement is signed at Rhodes; Article IV places the "Gaza Strip," a small part of the Gaza district (1.3 percent of Palestine) held by Egyptian forces at the end of the war, under Egyptian military and administrative rule.

August 1949: The Clapp Commission (the Economic Survey Mission) of the UNCCP is formed to tour the Arab countries (including Egypt) to investigate ways to alleviate refugee suffering.

September 1949: Some 7,000 Palestinian refugees still remaining in Qantara Sharq camp in Sinai are transferred to the Maghazi camp in the Gaza Strip.

December 1949: The United Nations Relief and Works Agency (UNRWA) is created on the recommendation of the Clapp Commission; it takes over responsibility for Gaza refugees from the AFSC in mid-1950.

December 1950: The United Nations establishes the Office of the High Commissioner for Refugees (UNHCR), mandated to represent refugees with state governments to assure their protection.

July 1951: The Convention Relating to the Status of Refugees, the most comprehensive document on refugee rights, is adopted by the United Nations in Geneva. Palestinian refugees are implicitly excluded from its purview under Article 1D.

1952: The League of Arab States, based in Cairo, establishes the Administrative Office of Palestine.

23 July 1952: The Free Officers, led by Gamal Abd al-Nasser, overthrow the Egyptian monarchy in the July Revolution. General Muhammad Naguib becomes the figurehead president of the Egyptian republic.

September 1952: Yasir Arafat is elected president of the Palestinian Student Union (PSU) in Cairo, the only Palestinian organization at the time having free elections. Salah Khalaf (Abu Iyad) is elected vice president.

23 February 1954: President Naguib is forced to resign; Gamal Abd al-Nasser becomes president of Egypt.

1954: Nasser opens Egyptian universities to qualified Palestinian students tuition-free; relaxes restrictions on Palestinian ownership of businesses in

Egypt; passes regulations allowing licensed Palestinian refugee doctors, dentists, veterinarians, and midwives to practice in Egypt; and loosens restrictions to allow some Gazans to work as teachers in Egypt. These are the first measures relaxing the Egyptian ban on Palestinian employment.

28 February 1955: An Israeli raid on Egyptian military posts in Gaza kills thirty-nine Egyptian troops, marking a turning point in Egyptian foreign policy and the beginning of Nasser's focus on the wider Arab-Israeli conflict. Mustafa Hafiz commando units in the Strip are authorized to conduct cross-border raids into Israel.

September 1955: Egypt concludes the "Czech arms deal," alarming Western powers and Israel.

26 July 1956: Nasser nationalizes the Suez Canal Company, in which France had been the majority shareholder.

29 October–2 November 1956: The Suez war begins with the tripartite (Britain, France, and Israel) invasion of Egypt; Israel occupies the Sinai Peninsula and Gaza Strip.

February–March 1957: Israel withdraws first from the Sinai Peninsula and finally from the Gaza Strip under strong U.S. pressure.

September 1958: Egypt and Syria form the United Arab Republic (UAR). The union is seen as the first step toward wider Arab unity and the liberation of Palestine.

1959: The General Union of Palestinian Students (GUPS), a diaspora-wide Palestinian organization whose nucleus was the PSU (led by Arafat and Khalaf from 1952 to 1957), is established in Cairo with Nasser's support. The GUPS becomes part of the PLO in 1969.

Fatah is established as a secret organization in Kuwait by Yasir Arafat, Salah Khalaf, and others.

The Egyptian Foreign Ministry orders that Palestinians in Egypt be given access to jobs.

February 1961: Syria secedes from the union with Egypt; Egypt retains the name UAR (until the Sadat period).

March 1962: Law 66 permits the recruitment of Palestinians in the Egyptian public sector and government bodies and treating them on equal footing with Egyptian nationals. This law is considered the beginning of the "Golden Era" for Palestinians in Egypt.

1963: The diaspora-wide General Union of Palestinian Workers (GUPW) is established in Helwan, Egypt, becoming part of the newly created PLO in 1965. Also in 1963, the Palestinian Women's League is established in

Cairo and is absorbed into the PLO's General Union of Palestinian Women (GUPWom) in 1965.

January 1964: The Arab League Summit in Cairo, acting at the behest of Nasser, charges Palestinian diplomat Ahmad Shuqayri with initiating contacts aimed at establishing a Palestinian entity.

2 June 1964: The first Palestine National Council meeting in (East) Jerusalem formally proclaims the establishment of the Palestine Liberation Organization (PLO) under the auspices of the Arab League and Nasser's patronage. In the months that follow, Palestine Liberation Army (PLA) units are established in Syria, Jordan, and Gaza ('Ayn Jalut Brigade).

11 September 1965: The Arab League adopts the Casablanca Protocol on the treatment of Palestinian refugees in the Arab host countries. Egypt (along with Algeria, Iraq, Jordan, North Yemen, Sudan, and Syria) ratifies the protocol without reservation.

5 June 1967: Israel launches a surprise attack first on Egypt and then on Jordan and Syria, occupying the remaining Palestinian territories (Gaza Strip and West Bank), Syria's Golan Heights, and Egypt's Sinai Peninsula. Hundreds of thousands of Palestinians are displaced. Several thousand Palestinian fighters are captured by the IDF (along with Egyptian forces) and deported to Egypt as part of the second major influx of Palestinians into the country.

The massive defeat of the Arab armies discredits Arab nationalism and spurs the popularity of Palestinian guerrilla organizations, especially Fatah.

November 1967: Nasser meets with Fatah leaders in Cairo and begins supplying the movement with training facilities and arms.

December 1967: Shuqayri is ousted as head of the PLO and an interim leadership is established.

February 1969: Arafat becomes chairman of PLO, which is now dominated by the Palestinian guerrilla organizations led by Fatah.

November 1969: Nasser brokers the "Cairo agreement" between Yasir Arafat and the Lebanese army, legitimizing the Palestinian fedayeen's foothold in Lebanon.

July 1970: Nasser accepts the second Rogers plan for an Israeli-Arab settlement based on the implementation of UN Security Council 242 (rejected by the Palestinians), prompting massive anti-Nasser demonstrations in Jordan and elsewhere. Nasser closes down PLO and Fatah radio stations broadcasting from Cairo.

September 1970: Civil war ("Black September") between the Palestinian guerrilla organizations and the Hashemite forces breaks out in Amman.

The confrontation ends with the expulsion of the fedayeen from Jordan in July 1971.

28 September 1970: Nasser dies of a heart attack after negotiating a truce between Arafat and Jordan's King Hussein. Vice President Anwar Sadat succeeds him as Egypt's president.

January 1972: GUPS joins student demonstrations protesting the no-war, no-peace stalemate of President Sadat, who singles out Palestinians for censure.

6 October 1973: Egypt and Syria launch a war against Israel to recapture their territories occupied in 1967; the PLO's 'Ayn Jalut Brigade participates under Egyptian command.

28 October 1974: At the Arab League Summit in Rabat, Morocco, Egypt co-sponsors a resolution recognizing the PLO as the sole, legitimate representative of the Palestinian people.

September 1974: Egypt and Israel conclude the "Sinai I" disengagement agreement brokered by U.S. Secretary of State Henry Kissinger.

March 1975: Civil war breaks out in Lebanon, with heavy involvement of PLO fighters.

September 1975: Egypt and Israel conclude the Sinai II disengagement agreement, effectively removing Egypt from the Arab-Israeli conflict. Palestinian students of GUPS hold protest demonstrations; many are deported.

19 November 1977: Egyptian president Anwar Sadat visits Jerusalem and addresses the Israeli Knesset, launching a peace plan and exacerbating tensions with the PLO. In Cairo, widespread student demonstrations are held to protest the government's moves; the PLO-affiliated GUPS is closed permanently. Sadat launches the "Egypt First" slogan.

December 1977: The PLO joins the anti-Egyptian "Steadfastness and Confrontation Front" with Syria, Algeria, Libya, and South Yemen at the Arab summit in Tripoli.

18 February 1978: Egyptian Minister of Culture Yusif al-Siba'i is assassinated in Cyprus by the renegade Palestinian Abu Nidal faction; Egypt launches an anti-Palestinian media campaign and new laws affecting Palestinians.

Spring 1978: Laws 47 and 48 annul all regulations treating Palestinians on a par with Egyptian nationals. Palestinian access to public sector jobs and to free public education at all levels ends. Severe restrictions on private sector employment follow.

17 September 1978: Israel and Egypt sign the Camp David framework for peace.

17 March 1979: Israel and Egypt sign a peace treaty. The PLO "freezes" relations with Egypt; all PLO offices and affiliates are closed except the Labor Union and two offices handling routine business.

6 October 1981: President Sadat is assassinated by Egyptian Islamists in Cairo; Husni Mubarak assumes the presidency. Egypt's Emergency Law, in force intermittently since 1958, is reimposed and remains in force to this day.

1981: Egypt ratifies the 1951 UN Convention Relating to the Status of Refugees, with reservations concerning a number of articles that effectively absolve it from obligations concerning the rights to residency, education, work, and public assistance to refugees within its borders.

6 June 1982: Israel invades and occupies Lebanon up to and including Beirut; Beirut is under siege throughout the summer, provoking outrage in Egypt. The events in Lebanon lead to a PLO-Egyptian thaw.

September 1982: PLO/PLA forces are expelled from Beirut under a deal brokered by the United States to end the siege of Beirut; some Palestinian fighters return to Egypt. Lebanon's president-elect is assassinated days after the PLO departure, triggering massacres of Palestinian civilians in Beirut's Sabra and Shatila refugee camps by Christian rightist militias under Israeli watch.

Late 1982: The headquarters of the Palestine Red Crescent Society is transferred from Lebanon to the Cairo suburb of Heliopolis; construction of the Palestine Hospital begins.

December 1983: The PLO-Egyptian thaw is consecrated by a meeting between Arafat and Mubarak.

Summer 1985: Law 104 bars foreign (including Palestinian) ownership of agricultural properties or fertile lands in Egypt.

December 1987: The first intifada breaks out in the Israeli-occupied Gaza Strip and the West Bank.

2 August 1990: Saddam Hussein's Iraqi forces occupy Kuwait. In the ensuing crisis, the PLO makes statements in support of Iraq; the Gulf states cut off funding to the PLO, precipitating a financial crisis. The PLO budget in Egypt is slashed, and activities and welfare programs are reduced.

February 1991: A U.S.-led coalition that includes Egypt launches the Gulf war, ousting Iraqi troops from Kuwait. Hundreds of thousands of Palestinians are expelled from Kuwait and other Gulf states. Some holders of Egyptian travel documents return to Egypt, but tens of thousands of others are stranded.

12 September 1991: An amendment to a resolution passed at the 46th Session of the Arab League Conference of Supervisors of Palestinian Affairs held in August allows member states to observe the 1965 Casablanca Protocol in accordance with their national laws.

30 October–1 November 1991: The Madrid Conference, aimed at achieving Arab-Israeli peace, is launched. Palestinians from inside the occupied territories (under the unofficial direction of the PLO) begin negotiations with Israel.

1992: In a move related to the ongoing peace negotiations, Egyptian Ministerial Decision No. 24/722/92 reduces university fees paid by the children of PLO and Palestinian public sector employees to 10 percent of the full amount.

January 1993: Direct secret negotiations between the PLO and Israel begin in Oslo.

13 September 1993: The Oslo Declaration of Principles between the PLO and Israel is signed in Washington, DC.

May 1994: The PLO and Israel sign the Gaza-Jericho agreement, which formally establishes the "Palestinian Authority" in the Gaza Strip and Jericho (in the West Bank). The jurisdiction of the Palestinian Authority is later expanded under subsequent agreements.

1995: The Palestine National Fund shifts its focus to state-building. The PLO budget in Egypt is further reduced; the Palestine Red Crescent Society and a number of health facilities are transferred from Egypt to Gaza. Thousands of Palestinians, mainly with PLO connections, begin to relocate to Gaza.

September 1995: Libyan president Muammar Qadhafi calls on Arab states to expel Palestinian residents to areas under PA control; expels 1,000 Palestinian holders of Egyptian travel documents to no-man's land on Libyan-Egyptian border. Stalemate lasts until 1997.

28 September 2000: The second intifada breaks out in the occupied territories.

October 2002: The UNHCR issues a "Note on the Applicability of Article 1D of the 1951 Convention on Refugees" in an effort to clarify circumstances under which Palestinians can be eligible for UNHCR coverage.

July 2004: The Egyptian National Assembly passes Law 154 amending Egypt's 1975 Nationality Law. The revised law allows Egyptian women married to foreigners to pass their citizenship on to their children, automatically for those born after the law's adoption and upon formal application for those born before. With regard to Palestinians, the law has been implemented only for children born *after* 2004; under an unwritten policy, the great majority of applications filed on behalf of persons born to Egyptian mothers and Palestinian fathers before 2004 have been rejected.

Maps

NORTHERN EGYPT

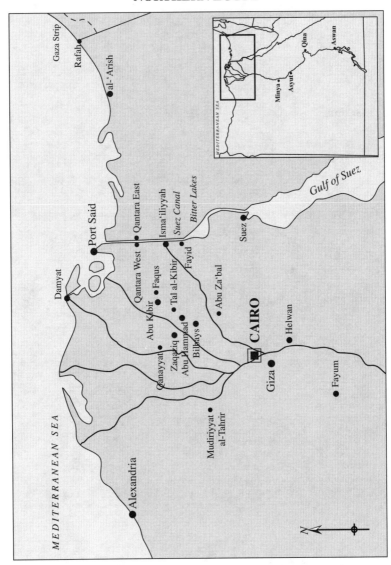

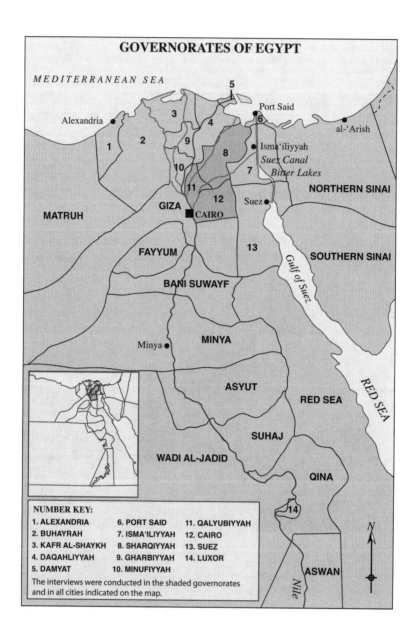

GOVERNORATES OF EGYPT

MEDITERRANEAN SEA

Alexandria

Port Said

al-'Arish

Isma'iliyyah
Suez Canal
Bitter Lakes

NORTHERN SINAI

GIZA
CAIRO

Suez

MATRUH

SOUTHERN SINAI

FAYYUM

Gulf of Suez

BANI SUWAYF

Minya

MINYA

ASYUT

RED SEA

RED SEA

SUHAJ

WADI AL-JADID

QINA

NUMBER KEY:

1. ALEXANDRIA	6. PORT SAID	11. QALYUBIYYAH
2. BUHAYRAH	7. ISMA'ILIYYAH	12. CAIRO
3. KAFR AL-SHAYKH	8. SHARQIYYAH	13. SUEZ
4. DAQAHLIYYAH	9. GHARBIYYAH	14. LUXOR
5. DAMYAT	10. MINUFIYYAH	

The interviews were conducted in the shaded governorates
and in all cities indicated on the map.

Nile

ASWAN

N

CAIRO

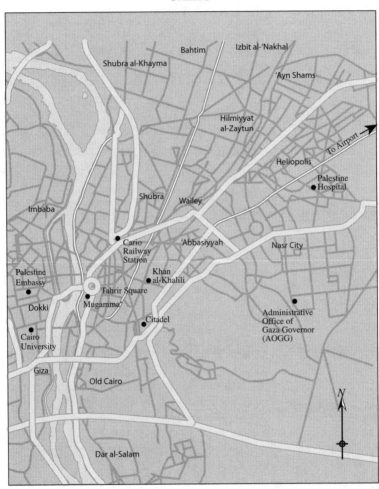

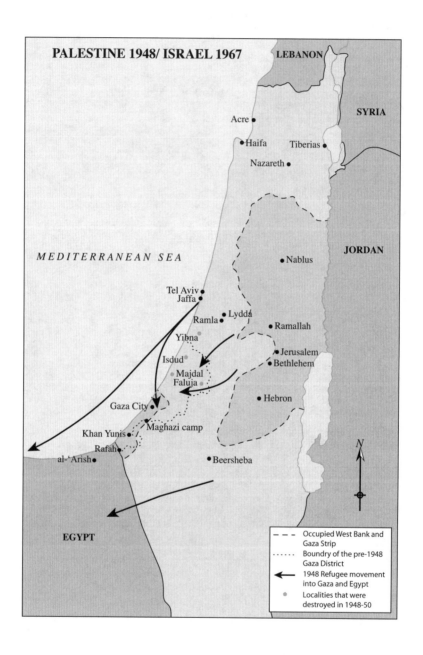

PALESTINE 1948/ ISRAEL 1967

LEBANON

SYRIA

MEDITERRANEAN SEA

Acre

Haifa Tiberias

Nazareth

Nablus

JORDAN

Tel Aviv
Jaffa

Ramla Lydda

Ramallah

Yibna

Isdud

Majdal
Faluja

Jerusalem
Bethlehem

Hebron

Gaza City

Maghazi camp

Khan Yunis

Rafah

al-'Arish

Beersheba

N

EGYPT

- – – Occupied West Bank and
         Gaza Strip
- · · · · Boundry of the pre-1948
         Gaza District
- ◀—— 1948 Refugee movement
         into Gaza and Egypt
- ●   Localities that were
         destroyed in 1948-50

Introduction

Although much has been written about Palestinian refugees in general, the origins and history of the Palestinian refugee problem, and the conditions of Palestinians living in what is known as the Arab "host countries," little has been written about the Palestinians in Egypt. This is perhaps not surprising: Egypt never hosted anything like the huge influx of refugees that poured into Jordan, Lebanon, Syria, the West Bank, or the Gaza Strip during the 1948 war. The Palestinians who entered Egypt in 1948 probably did not exceed 13,000, many of whom did not remain, and a similarly small number entered in 1967 from Gaza. The community today remains small, probably not more than 75,000 persons dispersed among 15 of Egypt's 27 governorates.

Furthermore, the Palestinians of Egypt were never served by the United Nations Relief and Works Agency (UNRWA), a body that has become virtually synonymous with Palestinian refugees. They do not live in camps and have not been a subject of study by social researchers. Finally, the scholarly attention paid to the political relationship between Nasser's Egypt and the Palestine issue overall completely overshadowed the social and economic conditions of the small community of Palestinians actually living in the country.

Yet a study of the Palestinian community in Egypt not only fills a gap in the literature on the Palestinian refugees, it also provides insights into the survival strategies of a vulnerable group in a host country that itself faces daunting poverty, overpopulation, and enormous pressures on scarce employment opportunities and resources—in other words, a host population scarcely better off than the refugees. The difference, of course, is that although the Egyptian hosts are citizens with all the rights available to citizens, even those Palestinians who were born in Egypt and have spent all their lives there face tight restrictions on their access to education, to work, to own land or property, to benefit from government services, and to secure residency.

This was not always the case. From the late 1950s up to the late 1970s, the community enjoyed a special legal status whereby its members were treated like Egyptian nationals in most domains.

1

These privileges were abruptly canceled in 1978, following the assassination in Cyprus of a close associate of Egyptian president Anwar Sadat by a renegade Palestinian faction. Although the assassination was the trigger, however, the sudden policy change in fact had more to do with the peace process that was unfolding at the time between Egypt and Israel. At all events, the Palestinians in Egypt were overnight subjected to all the restrictions applicable to foreigners, and from then on Egypt's pledges under Arab League protocols to protect Palestinian rights have been largely ignored. Thus, with the community not covered by any international agency, the Palestinians in Egypt have been left virtually unprotected.

The Arabic word for stranger is "*gharib*," from which is derived the word "*ghurba*," meaning exile, a place where one is made to feel a stranger. Since the tightening of regulations and the curtailment of their rights, Palestinians in Egypt are acutely aware of living in the "*ghurba*," a key concept that underpins this entire project.

Refugees, Displaced Persons, and Migrants

This study was carried out under the auspices of the Forced Migration and Refugee Studies (FMRS) Program at the American University in Cairo (AUC), with funding from the International Development Research Centre—Canada (IDRC). The FMRS Program has also analyzed the livelihoods of other refugee groups in Egypt, such as Sudanese and Somalis. These projects, like this one on Palestinian refugees, explore social networks, grassroots associations, legal protection, income generation, and all aspects of coping strategies refugees have adopted in Egypt. With such research, FMRS hopes to have an impact on improving the refugee policies of government agencies and nongovernmental organizations while the refugees await the day they can return to their homelands.

Most refugee groups in Egypt are entitled to seek protection from the United Nations High Commissioner for Refugees (UNHCR), which the Egyptian government has charged with the task of determining the refugee status of asylum seekers under a 1959 bilateral agreement. Political and economic definitions and categories are important for such purposes, as well as in international law. For the Palestinians in Egypt, who, as mentioned, are not covered by any UN agency, and who are unlikely to be part of any refugee negotiations that may eventually be held between the Israeli government and the Palestinian Authority (PA), such categories have little practical relevance.[1]

Nevertheless, the majority of the Palestinian refugees living in Egypt would qualify as "refugees" under the definition devised by UNRWA for the purpose of determining eligibility for its assistance programs.[2] According to UNRWA, Palestinian refugees and their descendants "shall mean any person whose normal place of residence was Palestine during the period 1 June 1946 to 15 May 1948 and who lost both home and means of livelihood as a result of the 1948 conflict."[3] This definition obviously applies to the Palestinians who entered Egypt in 1948 and remained there; it also applies to most of those who entered in the wake of the 1967 war from the Gaza Strip, which had been under Egyptian administration since 1949. Indeed, the majority of the Palestinians who entered in 1967 were already registered with UNRWA, having been among some 200,000 refugees who had crowded into the Strip after fleeing or being driven out of their homes during the 1948 war.

As a general rule, however, the hundreds of thousands of people who left or were pushed out of the Gaza Strip and the West Bank in the 1967 war are not accorded an unqualified "refugee" classification. Rather, under established UN definitions, they fall into two groups: "refugees-displaced" and "displaced."[4] The "refugees-displaced" are those who had been forced to flee twice—the first time in 1948 to Gaza or the West Bank, and the second time in 1967 to neighboring countries. The "displaced," on the other hand, are original inhabitants of these territories uprooted for the first time by the 1967 war. Initially, "displaced persons" did not qualify for UNRWA assistance, but because of the magnitude of the humanitarian crisis following the 1967 war, the UN General Assembly expanded the definition of eligibility for UNRWA relief to include "other persons in the area [served by UNRWA] who are at present displaced and are in serious need of immediate assistance as a result of the recent hostilities."[5] Because UNRWA did not operate in Egypt, however, neither the already-registered "refugees-displaced" nor the "displaced persons" entering the country were eligible to receive the assistance they would have received elsewhere.[6]

Finally, while the great majority of the Palestinians in Egypt came as a result of war (especially the 1948 and 1967 wars), thousands entered during the 1950s and 1960s who could be categorized as "socioeconomic migrants." The Gaza Strip, which, as mentioned, was administered by Egypt following the 1949

Israeli-Egyptian armistice agreement, suffered daunting economic problems and unemployment under the strain of a refugee influx that outnumbered the indigenous population almost three to one. Starting from the late 1950s, Egyptian president Gamal Abd al-Nasser, in an attempt to alleviate the hardship conditions, began calling on Palestinians from Gaza with high school diplomas or college degrees to apply for work in Egypt's public sector, relaxing government regulations accordingly. Meanwhile, Nasser also opened Egyptian universities to qualifying Palestinian students on an unprecedented scale, and large numbers of Gazans took advantage of the opportunity. When the 1967 war broke out and Israel occupied the Gaza Strip, an unknown but significant number of students, teachers, employees in various Egyptian government departments, and small businessmen and traders were unable to return to Gaza and remained in Egypt permanently.

Project Aims

The primary research data on which this monograph is based derive from in-depth interviews with Palestinian families and individuals in rural and urban areas of Egypt. These interviews focus in particular on the multiple survival strategies they deployed to secure or renew legal residency, obtain an education or vocational skills, find employment, hold on to property that had been acquired before land ownership by Palestinians in Egypt was prohibited, and in general to support themselves in adverse socioeconomic conditions and the increasing legal constraints after 1978. These strategies encompassed reliance on social and family networks, partnerships, and close relations with the host community, including intermarriage, as well as a range of specific tactics and stratagems. Field research foregrounded conditions prevailing at the time, but the interviews revealed information from across time, shedding light on how the Palestinians arrived in Egypt, what determined where they settled, the impact of shifts in government policies, and the fallout of larger regional and local events and how that fallout affected their lives and relationships.

The study as conceived therefore had two broad aims. The first was to provide a window on how Palestinians mobilized their tangible and intangible assets to pursue income-generating opportunities, secure education and services, and generally plan for the future. The second was to provide a sense of the shape of the community, its broad history, and the general setting in terms of host country policies, laws, and public attitudes.

Whereas the ultimate aim of the interviews was to convey a cross-section of the community, it was my conscious decision to focus on the "hidden Palestinians"—the poor and vulnerable segment that struggles to get by, eking out a living, scrambling for residencies and schooling. Contrary to a widespread myth in Egypt that the Palestinian community is wealthy,[7] the great majority of the community is in fact poor and highly vulnerable. Though official data are not available, a study dating to 1997 put forward estimates that are consistent with anecdotal evidence and our own research findings: 78 percent of the community was estimated to be living under the poverty line, 18 percent was classified as having average salaries, and 4 percent was seen as wealthy.[8] The vast majority of the Palestinians in Egypt are found among the lower-middle, lower, and poorest classes.

A few general definitions are in order. *Livelihood* in this study refers to the means, activities, entitlements, and assets used to make a living. *Assets* in this context are natural and physical (housing and/or land tenure, common property resources, schools, health clinics), social (community, family, social networks), political (participation in civil society, associations, and community organizations), human (e.g., education, labor, health, skills), or economic/financial (e.g., jobs, savings, regular remittances, pensions).[9] In examining the livelihoods of a population, especially a refugee population, vulnerability is a key consideration. Assessing vulnerability requires identifying the various resources (physical, economic, and social) needed to maintain the adequate provision of shelter, health, education, social services, and legal protection. With such a baseline, the impact of changes in resources, economic performance, and socio-political conditions can be assessed.[10]

Looking at the coping strategies and networks on which the Palestinians relied to "reconstruct" their lives in the *ghurba*, I consider livelihoods and vulnerabilities from the viewpoint of the Palestinians themselves. Rather than reducing refugees to mere victims of political circumstances and an economic burden, I see them as dynamic agents capable of making a real contribution to the host society if the legal framework allows them to do so, and of fending for themselves and generating their own resources even if it does not.

Research Methodology

The research for this project was conducted over two years, from 2001 to 2003. (Details about the research methodology are provided in Appendix 1.) Published material on the Palestinians in Egypt is limited to a relatively small number of articles, monographs, and chapters of books, many of which are several decades old. The present monograph used the available published resources as well as archived articles from the Egyptian press. For the general context, literature on the Palestinian exodus, Arab host state policies relating to the Palestinians, Arab League positions on the issue, and Palestinian status under international refugee law was reviewed in libraries in Jordan, Egypt, and Britain. Egyptian government administrative and legislative regulations relating to Palestinians in the *Jaridah Rasmiyyah* (Official Gazette) were also collected and reviewed.

Finding authoritative statistical data on the Palestinians in Egypt was far more difficult. While in the case of the Sudanese and Somali refugees in Egypt, at least partial population data exist with the UNHCR, no reliable statistics can be found for the Palestinians. The Egyptian government either does not have records on Palestinians, as some officials have claimed, or (what is more likely) it considers the disclosure of such data to impinge on state security. Off the record, I was told by officials in the Foreign Ministry that there were approximately 70,000 Palestinians in Egypt in 2000; the population had been larger several years earlier, but tens of thousands of Palestinians, mainly associated with the PLO, left for Gaza after the establishment of the Palestinian Authority in 1994. Indicative of the imprecision concerning population data, the World Refugee Survey 2002 Country Report of the U.S. Committee for Refugees stated that the Palestinian population in Egypt "was believed to number 50,000 or more persons at the end of 2001, with some estimates placing the number as high as 70,000."[11] The Palestinian Central Bureau of Statistics estimated the number to be 57,000 for the same year.[12]

Given the dearth of reliable population data, which ruled out statistical sampling and quantitative data collection, the project was designed as a qualitative study based on the interviews. Preparatory work involved the identification of the areas and governorates where significant numbers of Palestinians live, the selection and training of research assistants, and the design and testing of an open-ended questionnaire to serve as a guide for conducting the interviews. As the principal researcher, I visited—sometimes with a member of the research team—various regions where Palestinians were known to live in order to map out an interviewing strategy. I also conducted pilot interviews, mainly in the Cairo area. In light of the pilot interviews, the questionnaire was reviewed and some adjustments were made.

It bears mention that locating Palestinians outside Cairo, where certain quarters are known to have Palestinian residents, is not always easy. The fact that they are not registered with UNHCR and are not served by any of the faith-based or other humanitarian groups assisting other refugee groups in Egypt complicates the task. Palestinians are dispersed among most of Egypt's northern governorates (see Map 2). Only very rarely does one find a largely Palestinian village or neighborhood. Palestinians are mostly scattered in small towns or in mixed urban neighborhoods. They are intermingled with middle-class and poor Egyptians, in *'ashwa'iyyat* (unregulated urban settlements, built without proper permits), and even in prosperous residential quarters. Finding them is made more difficult by the fact that they are often virtually indistinguishable physically and culturally from Egyptians, and most have adopted the Egyptian dialect. Generally, our research team located Palestinians by word of mouth. After finding the first Palestinian household in an area, we used a snowball method to locate other households in the vicinity.

Project Redirection by *Force Majeure*

Conducting field research on any refugee or minority population in Egypt is politically sensitive, but this is particularly so in the case of the Palestinians. Palestine and Palestinians remain volatile and high-profile issues, arousing passions and fierce debate to this day. Egypt's long and intense political engagement with the Palestine problem and the PLO, and its ongoing mediating role between the Palestinians and Israel, make the topic even more sensitive, with justifiable concerns that data could be politicized or used in ways that could conflict with Egypt's national interests. Emergency laws are still in force in Egypt, requiring security clearance for all social research. Even with such clearance, fears and insecurities can lead to suspicions, even when the field research is conducted completely in the open.[13]

In May 2002, the team—consisting of five research assistants and myself—began our visits and interviews in Palestinian households. Working in pairs, we conducted one-on-one, face-to-face interviews with as many members of each household as was possible, using as a guide the above-mentioned open-ended questionnaire (Appendix 2). Our plan envisaged that the process would continue until mid-December, by which time we hoped to have covered 15 of Egypt's 27 governorates and to have conducted interviews in some 300 households.

In mid-July, however, after only two and a half months of interviews, our field work was abruptly halted for "security reasons," in spite of the fact that we had obtained all the necessary documentation and clearance and had in no way strayed beyond the limits of the study. By the time the team was stopped, we had visited 80 households and interviewed 401 persons, mainly in the governorates of Cairo, Qalyubiyyah, and Sharqiyyah, with a small number in Port Said, Isma'iliyyah, and Northern Sinai.[14]

The premature interruption of the field research, which left us with less than a third of our intended sample, raised a number of problems. The sample could no longer be regarded as representative: No members of the tiny wealthy segment of the population had been interviewed, and the middle class was underrepresented. Most of the interviews we conducted had been with the struggling segment of the community. Even though, as already noted, this group represents the majority of the Palestinians in Egypt, the smaller number of interviews meant that we had fewer examples, and therefore far less detail than we had anticipated, of the range of strategies and coping mechanisms employed.

These issues caused us to reconsider the presentation of the findings. Certainly, the social networks and livelihood strategies of the Palestinians in Egypt still form the core of the monograph; its primary purpose remains to highlight the precariousness of the community in general and the struggle of individuals to navigate their lives within a shifting framework. However, it was decided to expand the historical setting and overall context beyond what we had initially envisaged, and beyond what is normally required or expected in a social science project of similar scope. This made particular sense given the fact that little has been written about the Palestinian community in Egypt as a whole in recent years. No additional on-site research into regulations and relevant conditions was possible in light of the decisions and rulings taken by the security apparatus,[15] but the original material has been supplemented through an array of secondary sources. All of the chapters are illustrated, where relevant, with material from our interviews.

It should be emphasized that while the historical and background sections have been expanded, this monograph by no means pretends to be a history of the Palestinian community in Egypt or of the Egyptian government's Palestine policies or relations with the PLO. Neither is it a comprehensive survey of the changing laws and regulations that shaped their lives, or of their status under international refugee law. Still, I hope that the monograph succeeds in providing a broad, useful overview of the community, and that it perhaps (if only indirectly) may suggest areas worthy of further study.

Finally, while recognizing that the interviews that form the core of the monograph are now more than five years old, I am assured by my friends and colleagues in Egypt that the material is as relevant today as it was when it was collected. I very much wish that this were not the case.

Notes

1. The importance of refugee definitions for final-status negotiations was demonstrated in 1993, when eligibility rules for registration with UNRWA were expanded. Initially, only persons in need of assistance could apply to UNRWA. The reformulation of the rules allowed previously unregistered persons who had left Palestine during the requisite time period to apply for refugee status. This constituted an acknowledgment of the political implications of refugee status for the right of return in eventual final-status negotiations. The amended rules applied only to Palestinians residing in areas served by UNRWA, and therefore did not apply to Palestinian refugees in Egypt or elsewhere. See Lex Takkenberg, *The Status of Palestinian Refugees in International Law* (Oxford: Clarendon Press, 1998).

2. UNRWA's five areas of field operations are Jordan, Syria, Lebanon, the West Bank, and the Gaza Strip. The West Bank having been annexed by Jordan in 1950, the two areas were both served by UNRWA's Jerusalem Office. The exclusion of the Palestinian community in Egypt from its mandate is discussed in chapter 2.

3. UN document, Consolidated Eligibility Instructions, document Rev. 7/83, January 1984, quoted in Elia Zureik, *Palestinian Refugees and the Peace Process* (Washington, DC: Institute for Palestine Studies, 1996), p. 9.

4. *Population displacement* is defined as the process of collective dislocation and/or settlement of people away from their normal habitat by a more powerful force; see Seteney Shami, "The Social Implications of Population Displacement

and Resettlement: An Overview with a Focus on the Arab Middle East," *International Migration Review* 27, no. 101 (1993), pp. 4–33.

5. UN General Assembly Resolution 2252 (ES-V) of 4 July 1967. It should be noted, however, that although UNRWA expanded its assistance to those displaced by the 1967 war, it never changed its working definition of a Palestine refugee.

6. Between 1982, when Israel completed its withdrawal from the Sinai Peninsula, and 2000, UNRWA provided "hardship assistance" to up to 4,500 Palestinian residents of "Canada Camp," established by Israel on the Egyptian side of the border with Gaza in the early 1970s. The last of these refugees were transferred to Gaza in 2000. The Canada Camp is not dealt with in this study, but for a brief background of how it came about, see Appendix 1 under the section "Locating Palestinians—Northern Sinai."

7. According to a United Nations Development Program (UNDP) Country Report for Egypt in 2004, "Egyptians say there are many rich Palestinians. There may be a few rich Palestinians, but much of this is myth" (http://hdr.undp.org/en/reports/nationalreports/arabstates/egypt/name,3282,en.html). This myth was propagated by the Egyptian press at times of political tension, sometimes at the clear instigation of the government.

8. Quoted in *al-Ahram Hebdo*, 22 October 1997.

9. See http://hdr.undp.org/en/humandev/hdi/.

10. André Le Sage and Nisar Majid, "The Livelihoods Gap: Responding to the Economic Dynamics of Vulnerability in Somalia," *Disasters: The Journal of Disaster Studies, Policy and Management* 26, no. 1 (2002), pp. 14–15.

11. See www.refugees.org/countryreports.

12. See www.pcbs.gov.ps.

13. Emergency Law 162 of 1958. The law gives the authorities extensive powers to suspend basic liberties. Authorities can arrest suspects at will and detain them without trial for prolonged periods; refer civilians to military or state security courts whose procedures fall far short of international standards for fair trials; and prohibit strikes, demonstrations, and public meetings.

14. Twenty-six households were visited in the Cairo Governorate (the neighborhoods of 'Ayn Shams, Dar al-Salam, Wailey, Madinat al-Salam, Faysal), 44 in Qalyubiyyah and Sharqiyyah, and 5 in Port Said, Isma'iliyyah, and Northern Sinai.

15. I was allowed to remain in Egypt until the end of my contract with AUC, but I was subsequently unable to obtain a re-entry permit.

Chapter 1

Arriving in Egypt

The Palestinian presence in Egypt is largely the product of trauma and war, expulsion and dispossession. Apart from those who arrived in the late 19th and early 20th centuries, and the several thousands who entered during the 1950s and 1960s as part of President Gamal Abd al-Nasser's efforts to alleviate the dire economic situation of the Gaza Strip (then under Egyptian administration), those who came to Egypt from Palestine did not come seeking a better life. Rather, they came as refugees fleeing their country in 1948 in boats, or on foot or camelback across the desert, or as part of the wave pushed into Egypt in the wake of the 1967 war, often as captives trucked to the border by Israeli troops.

This first chapter focuses on the successive waves of Palestinian refugees[1] and the political context of each. It also sets out the political situation of Gaza from 1948 to 1967, which had a crucial impact both on Egyptian policy and on the nature of the influx following the 1967 war. Particular attention will be paid to the 1948 war and its background, not only because the war triggered the first large wave of refugees, but especially because it constitutes the defining event of the entire Palestinian experience.

Before the Nakba

Palestine and Egypt, although separated by desert, have been linked by millennial trade routes, shared history, and culture. Palestine historically served as Egypt's gateway to the Arab East, and at various times it fell within Egypt's political sphere of influence. In the late 19th century, when Egypt was experiencing an economic boom fueled by the cotton trade, the opening of the Suez Canal, and other factors, *Shawam* (inhabitants of *Bilad al-Sham*, the Syrian provinces of the Ottoman Empire, including present-day Syria, Lebanon, and Palestine) gravitated to Egypt to seek their fortunes. In 1927, some 8,000 *Shawam*, many of them Palestinians, were living in Egypt and engaged in commerce[2]; a number of these had their own businesses. Meanwhile, the Palestine railway system, which had been linked to Egyptian cities in the first decades of the 20th century, facilitated still further travel and trade between the two countries.

Although some earlier migrants to Egypt were well-off and indeed did make their fortunes there, many had only modest economic means:

> My father-in-law worked in the railway station. He often traveled to Suez City, where he married an Egyptian. When the war started in 1948, he went with his wife to stay with her family in Egypt. (P14, 'Ayn Shams, 1 June 2002)

A considerable number of Egyptians also lived in Palestine, particularly the Jaffa region. The commercial back and forth served to strengthen social networks linking the two peoples. In the northern and eastern parts of Egypt, intermarriage between Palestinians and Egyptians had been common since the beginning of the 20th century:

> My grandparents [mother's side], who are Egyptian, lived in Bataynah Sharqiyyah, near Jaffa, in Palestine. My grandfather was a camel trader and worked between Jaffa and Sharqiyyah [Egypt]. When the war broke out, the Jews invaded their house and attacked them. They fled on foot along with many others in a mass exodus toward Gaza. (7/30, Bilbays, July 2002)

Beyond economic and family ties as factors in pre-1948 Palestinian emigration to Egypt, politics began to intrude after World War I and the Ottoman defeat, when Great Britain assumed the Mandate over Palestine. Given Britain's imposition on Palestine of its Jewish National Home policy, which facilitated Jewish immigration and land transfers to Jews, tensions were inevitable. The most important outbreak of violence in the early years of the Mandate was the 1929 Buraq Rebellion ("the Wailing Wall incident"), when Zionist demonstrations at the Western Wall of the al-Aqsa mosque triggered Arab rioting targeting Jewish communities, which spread well beyond Jerusalem. As a result of the clashes, during which 133 Jews and 116 Arabs were killed, a number of Palestinian families left for neighboring countries, including Egypt.

As soon as the fighting stopped, most returned to their homes. Far more serious was the 1936–39 Palestinian Arab rebellion against British rule, which began as a general strike protesting Britain's pro-Zionist policies and demanding a representative government that reflected the country's overwhelming Arab majority. The turmoil during that period, and the brutal British suppression of the revolt, caused additional numbers of Palestinians, especially from the Hebron region, to seek refuge in Egypt.[3] A number of these acquired Egyptian citizenship,[4] but many others returned to Palestine. Egypt was also favored by a number of Palestinian political figures as a place of exile during and after the Mandate period.

The 1948 War and the First Wave of Refugees

Following World War II, tensions between the Arab and Jewish communities in Palestine mounted. Already in 1942, the Zionist movement had approved the Biltmore program, which openly declared the establishment of a Jewish state in all Palestine as the Zionist goal. As soon as the war ended, Zionist groups launched a major campaign of violence against the British aimed at forcing them to lift the restrictions on Jewish immigration into Palestine imposed by the 1939 White Paper.[5] Unable to resolve the contradiction between its promises to the Jewish minority under its Jewish National Home policy and its obligations to the Arab majority, Britain in February 1947 decided to refer the Palestine problem to the United Nations and to end its Mandate over Palestine. The result was that on 27 November 1947, the UN General Assembly passed a resolution recommending the partition of Palestine into two states, a Jewish state comprising 55.5 percent of the country (including almost all the rich coastal area) and a Palestinian state on the remainder, at a time when Jews constituted less than a third of the population and owned less than 7 percent of the land.[6]

In light of the demographic and land ownership realities, the Zionists had long recognized that a Jewish state could not be secured without force of arms. Thus, starting from the late 1930s, the Haganah, the fighting force of the Yishuv (the Jewish community in Palestine), was built up, trained, and armed. As soon as World War II ended, a massive arms acquisition program was launched.[7]

With the passage of the UN partition resolution, the outbreak of war between Jews and Arabs was just a matter of time.[8]

Almost immediately after news of the UN partition resolution spread, skirmishes broke out between the Haganah and Arab irregular forces and volunteers. A number of Palestinians, especially those with economic resources and family or other ties in neighboring countries, began to leave the country until the situation clarified. As had been the case for those who left in 1936–39, they viewed their exile as temporary and fully expected to return. This first "exodus" of mainly upper and middle-class Palestinians from the cities took place between December 1947 and March 1948, and is estimated at approximately 75,000 people.[9]

A number of these Palestinians went to Egypt, mainly to Alexandria or Cairo, renting hotel rooms or apartments or staying with relatives or friends. Hala Sakakini, the daughter of the well-known Palestinian historian and educator Khalil Sakakini, wrote in her diary on 16 May 1948 that Heliopolis, the middle-class Cairo suburb where she was staying with her family, "has become a Palestinian colony. Every other house is occupied by a Palestinian family."[10] While this is certainly an exaggeration, there is no doubt that many Palestinians of means made their way to Egypt on their own before the first big wave of refugees.

The Palestine war began in earnest in early April 1948, when the Haganah launched its massive Plan Dalet, a series of thirteen operations aimed at militarily securing the areas designated for the Jewish state. After the fall of the mixed Arab-Jewish city of Haifa on 22 April, the Jewish forces prepared to launch Operation *Chametz* (Operation "Passover Cleansing") to conquer the villages surrounding Jaffa.[11] On 25 April, the eve of the Haganah's planned assault, the Zionist "dissident" group Irgun began a massive mortar assault on the city of Jaffa itself, triggering the first important wave of Palestinian refugees into Egypt. According to Israeli historian Benny Morris, over 1,100 refugees arrived in Port Said from Jaffa and Haifa between 25 and 29 April, mostly in small steamers and fishing boats, some in open row boats without sails.[12] Another wave arrived in Port Said by boat between 2 and 8 May[13] as the Haganah and Irgun tightened the siege of Jaffa, completely surrounding it by land, with only the sea route open for escape. When the city finally fell on 10 May, the remaining civilians fled, many to Egypt. In all, at least 3,000 Palestinians arrived in boats from Jaffa during April and May, disembarking in Port Said and Alexandria.[14] Many of the Palestinians in Egypt today are descendants of refugees from Jaffa.[15]

Many of those we interviewed mentioned the 1948 exodus, mostly in passing, within the context of where they settled or how they arrived in Egypt (see chapter 3). Others, however, dealt with the exodus more directly:

> We are originally from Jaffa. My father used to own a fish market. [When the fighting started,] my father's family fled to Gaza. There, they had a summer house overlooking the sea. When his family left, my father refused to leave and remained in Jaffa to fight with the other *shabab* [young men]. Their dignity prevented them from leaving. Some weeks later, when the shelling intensified throughout the city, my father was forced to leave and joined his family. They left with a friend of the family and arrived in Fayid, Egypt. (7/26, Abu Hammad, 10 July 2002)

Immediately following the withdrawal of the last British troops from Palestine and the official end of the Mandate, Israel declared statehood on 14 May 1948. The next day, the regular armies of Transjordan, Syria, Iraq, and Egypt entered Palestine in an attempt to save what was left of the areas allotted to the Arabs under the UN partition plan. By that time, over 300,000 refugees had already fled or been driven out, and important areas earmarked for the Arab state by the United Nations had been seized, including (as already mentioned) Jaffa and the Arab villages of the Jerusalem corridor. The Haganah launched an assault on the Arab town of Acre, also allotted to the Arab state, on 14 May, and the town fell on 17 May.

Egypt, though woefully ill-prepared for war (the final decision to enter had not been taken until 14 May[16]), initially sent only nine battalions (probably not more than 5,000 men) into Palestine. The main force was deployed up the Gaza coast as far north as Isdud, while a smaller, lighter force moved across the Negev through Beersheba and Hebron to Bethlehem. Suffering from long lines of communication across the Sinai desert, inadequate supplies, and poor central command,[17] the Egyptians fought bravely under the circumstances[18] but were progressively dislodged from their positions as the Israeli forces turned in earnest to the southern front with the launch of Operation Ten Plagues in mid-October. As the Israelis advanced, thousands of refugees poured into the shrinking areas held by the Egyptians from the more than 40 villages occupied and destroyed by the Israeli forces in the Gaza district alone, as well as from the occupied villages of the adjacent Hebron and Ramla districts. The following testimony of a refugee from Yibna (also called Yubna) in the Ramla district gives a sense of how the refugees tried to keep one step ahead of the fighting:

> We are originally from Yubna. When the 1948 war started, Yubna inhabitants, including my own family, fled to Isdud. We had to leave all of our belongings [and property], including wheat fields. We later arrived in Majdal and then Khan Yunis.[19] As the fighting approached, we moved to another area. We bought camels and left Khan Yunis for Faqus [in Egypt], where my cousins were living. When crossing Sinai, people either walked or traveled on camels to Faqus and lived in tents. (7/35, Faqus, 14 July 2002)[20]

By the time the armistice agreements between Israel and the warring Arab states were signed in Rhodes during the first half of 1949, Israel was in possession of 78 percent of Palestine (compared to the 55.5 percent allotted by the UN partition plan). The great bulk of what was left in Arab hands was the West Bank, held by Transjordan, with a tiny band along the southern coast of Gaza held by Egypt. Into this minuscule territory, a mere 1.3 percent of Mandate Palestine, at least 200,000 refugees—over 25 percent of the total refugee population of the 1948 war—had crowded. The refugees thus vastly outnumbered the indigenous population of that area, estimated at some 75,000, most of whose agricultural lands had been seized by the Israeli forces and incorporated into the new state.[21] This was the territory—now officially known as the Gaza Strip—that was placed under Egyptian administration in Article VI of the Egyptian-Israeli armistice agreement signed on 24 February 1949.[22]

Under the terms of the armistice, the Egyptian force trapped in the "Faluja pocket," which had withstood an Israeli siege for more than three months,[23] was given safe conduct; a number of Palestinians who had fought alongside them in the enclave withdrew with them and were allowed to enter Egypt. Before the armistice, in the late stages of the war, other Palestinians had entered Egypt with retreating Egyptian forces.[24] Notable among these were Palestinian fighters from Abdel-Qadar Husseini's guerrilla force, *al-Jaysh al-Muqaddas*, who had been trapped with Egyptian irregulars in Hebron and cut off from retreat since October, and who withdrew with the Egyptians when they were finally allowed to leave.[25] In both these cases, some of the Palestinian fighters entering Egypt were accompanied by their families.

Between the influx from Jaffa in April–May 1948 and the entry into Egypt of Palestinian fighters in the late stages of the war, additional refugees, especially after the first and second truces of summer 1948, crossed the Sinai by camelback, taking the road from Gaza to Zaqaziq or Faqus (in Sharqiyyah Governorate).[26] No official figures on the size of the 1948 influx are available, but credible estimates range from 11,000 to 13,000 people.[27]

The Government's Immediate Response

Compared to the refugee flow into the other Arab countries bordering Palestine, the influx of refugees into Egypt was very small, the numbers limited by the natural barrier of the Sinai desert, population distribution in Palestine, and Egyptian government policies. Even so, the Egyptian government, like the other Arab governments, had been as ill-prepared for the arrival of the refugees as it had been for its own military participation in the war. When large numbers began to arrive in April 1948, the Ministry of Social Affairs prepared an emergency camp at a former British army barracks in 'Abbasiyyah, Cairo. A number of our interviewees speak of this camp:

> We left Jaffa when the war started and went to Lydda. We rested at the mosque there, washed, slept, and ate. We then walked through the hills to Gaza, where we stayed in a camp. Later, we decided to go to Egypt. We went to Rafah, then to Sinai, and arrived in 'Abbasiyyah, near the "English camp" and the rails in Cairo. The authorities gave out tents divided with sheets and delivered food to us. (Um Ahmad, PP1, Madinat al-Salam, Cairo, 17 January 2002)

As the influx of refugees swelled with the intensification of the fighting in Palestine, the Egyptian government on 9 May created the Higher Committee of Palestinian Immigrant Affairs to take responsibility for the health and the social, religious, and cultural welfare of the newcomers.[28] That same month, two additional camps were created to accommodate the flow: Qantara Sharq, in northeastern Egypt, on the east (Sinai) side of the Suez Canal, and

Azarita (also known as Mazarita) at the southeast end of Port Said.
Qantara was the main camp, and in September 1948 the refugees
who had been housed in the 'Abbasiyyah camp were moved there;
by this time, Qantara alone housed some 11,000 refugees.[29] The
camp even provided military training for young men who wanted
to join the army to liberate Palestine.[30]

Conditions were harsh, even prisonlike, and many refugees
tried their utmost to get out.[31] The following describes the ordeal
of a refugee who ended up in Kuwait:

> Khayriddin Abuljubayn, a teacher who was forced out of Jaffa,
> took refuge in Egypt on 27 April 1948. To his total dismay, he
> and his family, his fiancée and her family, and many friends,
> relatives, and acquaintances were all put in an Egyptian
> "concentration camp" called 'Abbasiyyah. His father, who
> traveled to Egypt by sea, was incarcerated in another camp
> called Qantara. Almost all the Palestinians coming from the
> Jaffa area and south Palestine were placed in such camps
> under the pretext that they need not go to Cairo, since they
> could return to their villages and cities [in Palestine] shortly.
> The actual reason rested in the government's fear of an angry
> reaction if the refugees reached Cairo and told the Egyptians
> there of the events in Palestine.
>
> While in the camp, Abuljubayn realized certain facts. First,
> he was now a refugee, and his return to his native city was
> blocked by the victorious Israelis. From now on, he had to
> cope with statelessness and exile. His first priority in camp
> was to get out. After ten days, he escaped and was able to find
> help that resulted in the release of his family. Once free, he
> received a letter from a friend, Nijim ... who was in the Qantara
> "concentration camp." In the letter, he asked Abuljubayn "to
> go to the director of the Kuwaiti house in Cairo" and tell him
> that Nijim needs help to get out of the camp and wants to go
> to Kuwait. Through this contact Nijim was released. When he
> arrived in Kuwait in fall 1948, he immediately sent visas to
> Abuljubayn and other Palestinian teachers.[32]

At the time of the Palestine war, Egypt was already beset
with population pressures and economic problems, and the
determination of King Farouk's government to limit the refugee
influx (to the extent this was possible) only hardened as the scope
of the Palestinian disaster became apparent. In late summer 1949,
the Clapp Commission (officially the Economic Survey Mission)

was established by the United Nations Conciliation Commission of Palestine (UNCCP) to investigate ways to improve the situation of the refugees, including by resettlement in the region.[33] When the commission arrived in Cairo for discussions, the government stated its position unambiguously: According to *al-Ahram* (21 May 1950), "The Egyptian government was keen to abide by the resolutions of the United Nations concerning repatriation and the mandate of the Conciliation Commission of Palestine (CCP), and has informed the Clapp Commission that Egypt is too crowded with its own people and cannot receive the refugees on its territories." Indeed, in September 1949, just over six months after the signing of the armistice agreement that put Gaza under Egyptian administration, the government issued a decree to send the some 7,000 residents still remaining in the Qantara camp to the Gaza Strip,[34] where the Maghazi camp, near Dayr al-Balah, had been built to house them.[35] Already, Egypt's policy of concentrating the Palestinians to the extent possible in Gaza, and of maintaining a strict separation between Egypt proper and the Gaza Strip under its administration, was clear.

Meanwhile, a special committee had been formed in Egypt proper to consider the applications of people who had the financial means to support themselves outside the camps and who had an Egyptian guarantor (*kafil*) to sponsor their stay. Most of those who had neither an Egyptian guarantor nor proven financial means were transferred to Gaza. At the same time, the refugees were openly encouraged to leave for other countries, especially if they had family elsewhere. In some cases, Egypt paid their fare.[36]

Through these various means, of the thousands of Palestinians who had entered Egypt in the wake of the 1948 war, only a few thousand remained by 1950.[37]

The Gaza Strip, 1948–67: Setting the Stage for the 1967 Wave

Egypt did not witness another large influx of Palestinians until the 1967 war, when Israel seized the Gaza Strip. Nevertheless, thousands of Palestinians entered Egypt from Gaza between 1948 and 1967.[38] Some of the refugees who had been sent from Qantara Sharq to the Gaza Strip in 1949 managed to slip back into Egypt early on,[39] and a small number entered in the wake of the tripartite

Suez invasion of 1956 (see below). But by far the largest influx of Palestinians, who would have been classified as "socioeconomic migrants," entered as a result of policies adopted by the new regime established by the Free Officers who overthrew the Egyptian monarchy in 1952. Even while maintaining the old regime's strict separation between Egypt and the Gaza Strip, the new government enacted measures that allowed for a certain back-and-forth movement between the two areas. These included the creation of a free trade zone for industrial and consumer goods in Gaza, where many luxury and other items unavailable in the now-socialist Egypt of the late 1950s could be purchased.[40] More important, in the early 1960s, the new regime also adopted liberalizing policies concerning education and employment that resulted in a significant influx of Gazans into Egypt as students, workers, teachers, government employees, and traders. While many of these, especially those who came to study, did not remain, and many others had no intention of immigrating to Egypt permanently, many did end up staying, either because of marriage or because they were there during the 1967 war and were unable to return.

Gaza's main importance for the present study, however, does not derive from the immigration that took place in the 1950s and 1960s. Rather, its importance lies in the political events unfolding there—as well as its place in the Arab-Israeli conflict during those years—which were crucial to shaping the next big wave of Palestinian migration to Egypt during and after the June 1967 war. Indeed, Gaza early on became an important "flash point" in growing tensions between Egypt and Israel.

One of the principal sources of Egyptian-Israeli tensions was the "infiltration" of Palestinians from Egyptian-administered Gaza into Israel that began even before the end of the 1948 war. According to reports from Gaza by UN officials and relief workers with the American Friends Service Committee (AFSC, the Quakers), which had taken over refugee relief efforts in the Strip in January 1949,[41] the refugee population in the aftermath of 1948 was virtually starving and for several years did not have shelter beyond tents. Yet within view, just across the border in the newly established State of Israel, lay the lands and ruined villages of the destitute refugees now crammed together in intolerable conditions in the tiny Strip. It was in such circumstances that the "infiltrations" from Gaza into Israel began, with refugees sneaking across the border back to their villages to reclaim possessions, harvest crops, or just for a "glimpse of their abandoned houses."[42] In the early 1950s, according to Benny Morris, some 10,000 to 15,000 instances of "infiltration" occurred annually, and between 1949 and 1956 (mostly in 1949–51), the Israel Defense Forces (IDF) killed between 2,700 and 5,000 Arab infiltrators, the "vast majority" of them unarmed.[43] But increasingly, there were also armed infiltrators—revenge operations in response to IDF actions, as well as cross-border raids organized by the Muslim Brotherhood and the Communists. This guerrilla activity had been strongly discouraged by the Egyptian government, first by the monarchy and then by the Free Officers, which both sought to avoid confrontation with Israel at all costs. The Israeli government, while well aware of Egyptian opposition to the raids, used the guerrilla activity as an excuse to launch disproportionately deadly retaliatory strikes.

On 28 February 1955, the IDF carried out an attack on Egyptian forces stationed in Bir al-Safa near the Gaza city railway station, killing 39 Egyptian soldiers. According to Moshe Sharrett, Israel's prime minister at the time (at odds with preeminent Israeli leader David Ben-Gurion, then defense minister, and his deputy, Moshe Dayan), the attack was largely unprovoked.[44] Morris calls the raid a "clear watershed," after which the Egyptian authorities not only ended their opposition to the guerrilla raids, but themselves became involved in sponsoring them.[45]

These new government-sponsored activities were organized by Mustafa Hafiz, chief of the Palestine branch of Egyptian military intelligence in Gaza, who formed a commando unit whose nucleus was a group of Palestinians who had been utilized by the Egyptians to conduct unarmed reconnaissance missions inside Israel since 1949.[46] Following the February 1955 raid, Hafiz was authorized by the Egyptian high command to transform his fedayeen—who were paid out of the Egyptian administration in Gaza—into a formal military unit called the 141 Battalion.[47] The special force, which was commonly known as the Mustafa Hafiz Brigades,[48] figures in a number of our interviews, especially those relating to the 1967 refugee wave (as described in the next section). In addition to the Mustafa Hafiz fedayeen, other Palestinian battalions were formed as part of the Egyptian forces in Gaza. Palestinians also made up the Palestine Border Guard.[49]

Although the infiltrations and growing tensions on the Sinai/Gaza front were undoubtedly a factor in setting the stage for the Suez war—the October–November 1956 "tripartite" invasion of Egypt by Britain, France, and Israel—it was Nasser's conclusion of the Czech arms deal in September 1955 and his nationalization of the Suez

Canal Company in July 1956 that constituted the most immediate triggers. On 29 October 1956, Israeli forces occupied the Sinai and the Gaza Strip, and several days later a combined Anglo-French force launched an attack along the Suez Canal. Contemporary UNRWA reports described the "screening operations" throughout the Gaza Strip conducted by the Israeli military "to find persons who were members of the so-called 'Palestine Brigade' or who participated in fedayeen operations."[50] During these screening operations, close to 500 Palestinian civilians were killed.[51] Thousands of fedayeen, Palestinian border guards, and Palestinian and Egyptian soldiers were taken prisoner by the IDF,[52] and scores of Palestinian fighters were summarily executed.[53] Hundreds managed to escape to Jordan, and subsequently either returned to Gaza following the Israeli withdrawal or went to Egypt. A Palestinian woman now living in Cairo recounts:

> My husband was the first to arrive in Egypt. During the 1956 tripartite invasion, he was arrested by the Israelis because he was part of Mustafa Hafiz's 141 forces in Gaza. Eventually, he managed to escape to Jordan and from there he came to Egypt. (P25, al-Zawiyyah al-Hamra, 25 June 2002)

A number of fedayeen managed to escape through the Sinai and the Canal Zone into Egypt proper with the retreating Egyptian troops, though Morris adds that some of these, "like thousands of Egyptian troops," must have "died of thirst and hunger on the trek westwards."[54] Israel withdrew from the Gaza Strip only in March 1957, and then only under very strong U.S. pressure.[55]

The next chapter explains how the Suez invasion provided the final element in the crystallization of Nasser's pan-Arabist policies, an important component of which was the Palestine issue. As part of these policies, Nasser in May 1964 presided over the establishment of the Palestine Liberation Organization (PLO), headed by Palestinian lawyer Ahmad Shuqayri, as a means of maintaining control over the Palestinian national movement that was beginning to emerge. The significance of this move with regard to Gaza and the subsequent (1967) influx of Palestinians into Egypt is that the PLO's regular armed forces, the Palestine Liberation Army (PLA), were also established in 1964: The PLO's Egyptian-sponsored 'Ayn Jalut Brigade was set up with its headquarters in Cairo, but most of its manpower was in Gaza. The new organization soon opened training camps, recruiting especially among refugee youth, where support for the PLO was strongest.[56] A great many of these fighters, along with the men associated with the Mustafa Hafiz Brigades, the Palestine police, and the Palestinian personnel of the Gaza administration, ended up in Egypt after the 1967 war.

In the Wake of the 1967 War

Israel's surprise attack on Egypt, Syria, and Jordan was launched on 4 June 1967 in response to Nasser's insistence on the withdrawal of the UN Emergency Force stationed in the Sinai and his closure of the Straits of Tiran to Israeli navigation in May. The war resulted in the capture in six days of the entire Sinai Peninsula from Egypt, the Golan Heights from Syria, and the last areas of Mandate Palestine not taken by Israel during the 1948 war: the West Bank, seized from Jordan, and the Gaza Strip, seized from Egypt.

The 1967 war probably produced the largest single wave of Palestinian immigration into Egypt; many if not most of those who immigrated were originally 1948 refugees and thus twice displaced.[57] A substantial number of the 1967 influx had some relationship to the Egyptian military. In the debacle of the war, some 6,000 PLA officers, soldiers, and reservists fighting under Egyptian command were captured by the Israelis[58] along with tens of thousands of Egyptian soldiers. (Some PLA forces fought until the surrender of Gaza City on 7 June, with 120 dead.) According to the Israeli commanding officer of the southern front, 5,000 of the captured PLA fighters were deported to Egypt, with the remaining 1,000 being imprisoned at Atlit, in Israel proper.[59] The usual procedure was for the captives to be turned over to the Red Cross:

> I was then part of the PLO's Liberation Army and was taken hostage until being released to the Red Cross. The other hostages and I were interned in Isma'iliyyah before being taken to Fayid to join the Egyptian army. (P9, Wailey, 24 June 2002)

Of the 5,000 PLA personnel deported to Egypt, 2,000 were reorganized by the Egyptian command and deployed under its direct authority to Bitter Lakes (al-Buhayrat al-Murra) bordering on the newly occupied Sinai Peninsula. According to Palestinian military expert Yezid Sayigh, the remaining PLA personnel—some 3,000 or 4,000 men—were "diverted into a 'surplus'" or reserve and allowed to resettle in the Tahrir district (province) northeast of Cairo on the road to Alexandria.[60] An undetermined number of Mustafa Hafiz fighters also entered Egypt. Operating underground, these men were not so much captured en masse as hunted down, with hundreds managing to escape to Egypt or Jordan.[61] Many people in our interviews refer to family members who entered Egypt with the Mustafa Hafiz forces, often without details concerning how they arrived:

> We originally come from Abraj, and my family used to work in agriculture. In 1948, we were expelled to Gaza. I was four [years old] then. We moved from one place to the other until staying in Shati refugee camp [Beach Camp] in Gaza. My father joined the Mustafa Hafiz 141 fedayeen. After 1967, he came to Cairo with the Egyptian army. (P9, Wailey, 24 June 2002)

In addition to the Palestinian forces fighting with the Egyptians, members of the police forces in Gaza were also allowed to settle, as were the Palestinian employees of the various departments of the Egyptian Administrative Office of the Governor of Gaza (AOGG).

In line with Egyptian policy, arrangements were subsequently made for the families of these men to be brought to Egypt to join them.[62] The following quote recounts the role played by the Red Cross in some of these family reunifications:

> Several years after the 1967 war, the Red Cross provided buses to take some families, mainly women and children, from Gaza to Egypt. We rode a bus with red-curtained windows that had a curtain between the driver and the passengers to prevent them from seeing the Israeli military bases on the road. At the Suez Canal, we rode a boat to cross the canal. The Egyptian forces received us and took us to clinics to be vaccinated. (P10, 'Ayn Shams, 23 May 2002)

The 1967 war resulted in massive dislocation. According to UNRWA, which had taken over responsibility for the refugees from the AFSC in 1950 and which was "on the ground" in most of the occupied areas during and after the hostilities, at least 350,000 persons were newly displaced from the West Bank, Gaza, the Syrian Golan Heights, and the Sinai, some 175,000 of them made refugees for the second time.[63]

While Israel wanted to retain both the West Bank and Gaza, it was not keen to inherit their large refugee populations.[64] In the aftermath of the war, Israel "encouraged" several hundred thousand Palestinians to leave the West Bank and Gaza Strip. Some of our interviews allude to Israel's policy of requiring exiting individuals to sign forms stating that they were leaving voluntarily and understood they would not be allowed to return.[65] A Gaza woman whose husband, a truck driver, had been trapped in Egypt when the war broke out, had this to say about leaving Gaza with her three children to join him:

> I came to Egypt from Gaza via Jordan. When leaving Palestine, the Jews [i.e., the Israeli forces] made us sign/fingerprint a blank white paper to let us pass. I had to sign. All I wanted was to run away with my children to a safe place. (31/7, Bilbays, 11 July 2002)

The most significant influx of nonmilitary personnel into Egypt in 1967 resulted from Israel's massive sweep of the Gaza Strip in search of men with possible connections to Palestinian resistance groups. Israel soon set about rounding up men of fighting age, loading them onto buses or trucks, and transporting them to the Egyptian border. A number of the interviews describe the process:

> On one of the nights following the Israeli invasion of Gaza City in 1967, the [Israeli] forces called on all men between the ages of 16 and 50 to go out to the playground of a school. To my knowledge, no one responded. Later, a masked man with several Israeli soldiers came to my family's house and pointed at me, so I had to go with them to the schoolyard, where I saw many men from the city. We were taken to a military camp at Beersheba. Some of us were taken to be interrogated. We were then taken in a truck to Qantara West. There, the Red Cross registered our names and permitted us to enter. (P16, 'Ayn Shams, 8 June 2002)

The same scene was re-enacted repeatedly throughout Gaza. A number of our interviews refer to Egypt's reluctance to go along with Israel's forced transfer by accepting the "hostages." Some testimonies, as the one below, tell how Israel compelled Egypt to allow the men to enter by threatening to kill them. A number of the interviews also allude to the Red Cross being called upon to facilitate the process:

> On 18 June 1967, I was 20 or 21 years old, and the Jews were going around the houses in Khan Yunis calling on men between the ages of 12 and 40 to go to Cinema *al-Hurriyyah*. "Those who do not respond or run away will be killed." I went to the cinema with my brother-in-law, who was an old man. Soldiers asked us to hurry to the center. The leader was selecting people, and whoever did not respond was killed. I was selected among many. We were put in buses with curtained windows. We expected them to ask us to dig our own graves and then bury us alive, like they did in the 1956 war. On the bus, we were given dry bread, which made us thirsty. In the Muthalath area, buses stopped and the Jews asked the Red Cross to negotiate with Egyptian forces to take us. Egypt at that time was opposed to receiving Palestinians. The Israelis threatened to kill us because they did not want us to go back to Palestine. Israeli soldiers forced the passengers on the first bus to step off of the bus in order to be executed. In response, Egypt permitted us to enter the country. We were taken to Ramda and were asked to walk on a sandy road to the canal. There, we were received by an Egyptian lieutenant. (23/7, Salhiyyah, 7 July 2002)

Forced to accept the refugees, the Egyptian government decided to induct able-bodied young men suitable for military service into their armed forces, which had been seriously depleted by the war, during which tens of thousands had died. Processing the "hostages" took place at several temporary camps that were set up, including Qantara on the *western* side of the Suez Canal. A number of our interviewees referred to the selection process:

> Thousands of other Palestinians and I were taken hostage during the 1967 war. The Israeli forces took us to Beersheba. From there, after Egypt accepted us, we were taken to the Red Cross, which was waiting for us. We were taken in buses to Qantara. The Egyptian security forces divided the Palestinians into military and civilian groups. Civilians were transferred to Mudiriyyat al-Tahrir to work in agriculture. Soldiers were transferred to the Tal al-Kibir military camp to verify their military numbers with the PLO office at Nasr City. There, we were divided into sub-groups (*kata'ib*) and trained by Egyptian forces. Our group was later taken to A'miriyyah,

where we took part in the War of Attrition [1969–70]. (P5, Dar
al-Salam, 18 May 2002)

Another person captured by the Israelis and sent to Egypt, also
classified as suitable for recruitment into the military, recounts the
following:

A Palestinian friend of mine lived in Shubra, Cairo. I stayed
with him until I was called to join the army at Tal al-Kibir
military camp. We were later taken to A'miriyyah and then to
al-Buhayrat al-Murra [Bitter Lakes] military bases. (P16, 'Ayn
Shams, 8 June 2002)

The camp mentioned most often in our interviews was
Mudiriyyat al-Tahrir,[66] where the men classified as "civilians"
remained temporarily. Some worked in agriculture in the area and
eventually self-settled, while others were hired for government
service:

I was among those Palestinians taken hostage by the Israelis
on 20 June 1967. In Egypt, we arrived in Mudiriyyat al-Tahrir,
where we stayed for three weeks in a village called Abd al-
Salam Amir. There were 6,000 of us. Some members of the
group with whom I was staying were asked to take jobs in the
government, so we went to Cairo and lived in a flat together.
When each of us took his post, and some were posted
around the republic, we lost contact with each other. (AP3,
Alexandria, August 2002)

Hadi, a young man from Bayt Hanun in Gaza who was among those
classified as a civilian at Mudiriyyat al-Tahrir, described how he
was hired from the camp for the legal and administrative affairs
department at the Ministry of Interior (8/5, Bahtim, 3 July 2002).

Needless to say, not all those who were captured by the Israeli
forces and expelled to Egypt in 1967 were connected with the
Egyptian military or were men of fighting age. It is clear from a
number of our interviews that some families simply took advantage
of the chaos of the situation to cross into Egypt:

My husband's family arrived with masses of other Palestinian
families in 1967. They came walking to Abu Za'bal [city in
Qalyubiyyah Governorate]. My father-in-law became a truck

driver. His wife and children soon left Gaza to join him with the help of the Red Cross. (8/3, Abu Za'bal, 30 June 2002)

As mentioned earlier, Gaza's status as a free trade zone under Nasserist socialism had fostered extensive commercial ties, and a number of people who had business interests in Egypt or who had been involved in transport or trade were able to enter the country. These included wealthy Gaza businessmen, who transferred not only their capital but also their businesses to Egypt.[67] This category also included traders of far more modest means:

My husband arrived in Abu Kabir in 1967 with his family. They had been involved in the *tijaret shanta* [bag trade] between Gaza and Egypt. (7/29, Abu Kabir, July 2002)

Numbers, once again, are elusive. The Gaza section of UNRWA's report on the 1967 war quoted the official Egyptian estimate that some 13,000 refugees and displaced persons had entered Egypt during and in the wake of the conflict.[68] This number did not include the thousands of Gazan students, teachers, or other employees hired under Nasser's liberalization and other persons stranded in Egypt who were allowed to stay. According to Egyptian government estimates, the number of Palestinians in the country by 1969 had reached 33,000, compared to its 1960 estimate of 15,500.[69]

Post-1967 Immigration and Emigration

Although the influx of 1967 was the last major wave of Palestinians into Egypt, the size of the community has continued to ebb and rise.

After Israel's invasion of Lebanon and siege of Beirut in 1982, the PLO apparatus and fighters in the Israeli-occupied areas of Lebanon were forced to leave the country under a deal brokered by the United States. Egypt was not among the countries where PLO fighters were sent as units, although the 'Ayn Jalut Brigade still had its headquarters in Egypt, and a good number of PLA fighters who had previously been stationed there did return.[70] Again, it is impossible to offer figures with any confidence, but according to *al-Ahram* (16 July 1985), there were more than 100,000 Palestinians in Egypt in 1985.[71]

The largest post-1967 influx of Palestinians into Egypt followed the Gulf war of 1991. An estimated 450,000 Palestinians had been living in Kuwait at the time it was occupied by Iraq in August 1990, and an estimated 70–80 percent of these were either expelled in the wake of the war or had fled after the Iraqi invasion as the crisis heated up.[72] Most of these had originally come from Jordan or the West Bank, or were descendants of those who had. Tens of thousands, however, held Egyptian travel documents, and many had never had Egyptian residence permits (see chapter 4). The number of those with valid residency permits who were allowed back into Egypt is unknown, but certainly there were many. Far greater numbers, however, did not even attempt to enter, knowing that their travel documents excluded the possibility of residency.

Finally, a substantial outflow—estimated by the PLO ambassador to Egypt in 2001 at 45,000[73]—followed the establishment of the Palestinian Authority (PA) in the West Bank and Gaza in 1994 as a consequence of the September 1993 Oslo accords signed by Israel and the PLO. Throughout this study, numerous interviews refer to those who left for Gaza in the 1990s; this emigration will be discussed in chapter 6.

Notes

1. Notwithstanding the formal distinction between *refugees* and *displaced persons* under United Nations definitions, as set out in the introduction, this study uses *refugees* to refer to both groups.

2. Nadera Sarraj et al., *Arab Palestinians in Egypt* [in Arabic] (Cairo: Dar El Mustakbal, 1986), p. 9.

3. A longstanding tradition links Hebronites to Egypt; Cairo's famed Khan al-Khalili derives its names from Hebronite merchants who established themselves in the city.

4. Abdul Qader Yassin, "Palestinians in Egypt" [in Arabic], *Samed al-Iqtisadi Magazine* 18, no. 106 (1996), p. 2.

5. The White Paper represented Britain's proposed solution to the Palestine problem: conditional independence for a unitary Palestinian state after 10 years, a maximum of 15,000 Jewish immigrants annually for 5 years, and protection of Palestinian land rights against Zionist acquisition.

6. For details, see Walid Khalidi, "Revisiting the UNGA Partition Resolution," *Journal of Palestine Studies* 27, no. 1 (Autumn 1997), p. 11.

7. See Ricky-Dale Calhoun, "Arming David: Haganah's Arms Procurement Network in the United States, 1945–49," *Journal of Palestine Studies* 36, no. 4 (Summer 2007), pp. 22–32.

8. Although the borders of the two states had been drawn under the resolution in an attempt to include a minimum of Arabs in the Jewish state, virtually nowhere did the Jews have more than a bare majority or own but a fraction of the land. Whereas the proposed Arab state had 818,000 Palestinians and 10,000 Jews, the proposed Jewish state had about 499,000 Jews and 438,000 Palestinians. Khalidi, "Revisiting the UNGA Partition Resolution," p. 11.

9. Benny Morris, "Critical Analysis of the Birth of the Palestinian Refugee Problem" (2001), accessed at http://www.palestineremembered.com/Acre/Palestine-Remembered/Story562.html.

10. Quoted in Laurie Brand, *Palestinians in the Arab World: Institution Building and the Search for a State* (New York: Columbia University Press, 1988), p. 44.

11. See Walid Khalidi, "Plan Dalet: Master Plan for the Conquest of Palestine," *Journal of Palestine Studies* 18, no. 1 (Autumn 1988), 4–33.

12. Benny Morris, *1948 and After: Israel and the Palestinians* (Oxford: Clarendon Press. 1994), p. 291.

13. Ibid., p. 292.

14. Brand, *Palestinians in the Arab World*, p. 43.

15. Yassin, "Palestinians in Egypt," *Samed al-Iqtisadi*.

16. See Gamal Abdul Nasser, "Memoirs of the First Palestine War." *Journal of Palestine Studies* 2, no. 2 (Winter 1973), pp. 3–32.

17. Ibid.

18. See Edgar O'Balance, *The Arab-Israeli War 1948* (Westport, CT: Hyperion Press, 1981), pp. 184, 200, 205.

19. Yibna was occupied by Israeli forces in early June; Isdud was held by the Egyptians until dislodged in late October; Majdal was captured from the Egyptians in November. Khan Yunis remained in Egyptian hands.

20. For another firsthand account giving a sense of the extreme dislocation during the fighting in the Gaza area, and the efforts to get to areas held by the Egyptians, see Um Jabr Wishah, "The 1948 War and its Aftermath," *Journal of Palestine Studies* 35, no 4 (Summer 2006), pp. 54–62.

21. An estimated 80 percent of the original inhabitants had lost livelihoods after the war. Of approximately 1 million dunams planted in barley and grains in the Gaza district, only 71,000 remained in the Gaza Strip. Brand, *Palestinians in the Arab World*, p. 49.

22. Egypt was the first Arab state to sign an armistice, largely to free its soldiers trapped in the "Faluja pocket," where they had held out for months; they were evacuated as one of the terms of the agreement.

23. Gamal Abd al-Nasser was a staff officer in the 6th battalion, which fought at Faluja, and during a truce in the long siege was designated by his command to meet the representative of the Israeli forces to discuss terms.

24. Brand, *Palestinians in the Arab World*, p. 43.

25. The Egyptian forces trapped in Hebron were mainly irregulars, members of the Muslim Brotherhood, under the command of Egyptian regular officers. The Hebron area was held by the Arab Legion of King Abdallah, bitterly opposed to the Husseini-led forces, which is why these men would have been eager to leave with the Egyptians.

26. Brand, *Palestinians in the Arab World;* this was confirmed also in our interviews.

27. Brand (*Palestinians in the Arab World*, p. 43) puts the number at 11,000, as does Sari Hanafi; see Hanafi, *Entre Deux Mondes: Les Hommes d'Affaires Palestiniens de la Diaspora et la Construction de l'Entité Palestinienne* (Cairo: CEDEJ [Centre d'Etudes et de Documentations Economique, Juridique et Sociale], 1997). Sarraj et al. (*Arab Palestinians in Egypt*) state that the Qantara Sharq temporary camp housed 12,000 persons in 1949; if the figure is accurate, the 1948 influx would have been at least that large. Yassin, citing a 1994 document issued by the Egyptian Department of Immigration, Passports, and Nationality on categories of travel documents that year on the basis of arrival date, lists 13,032 arrivals in 1948; see Abdul Qader Yassin, *Palestinians in Egypt* [in Arabic] (Ramallah Shaml, 1996), p. 6.

28. The Committee was composed of members from the ministries of interior, social affairs, health, agriculture, defence, foreign affairs, the railway department, and borders department, in addition to the Red Crescent. A budget was set by the government of Egypt for £E 300,000. The Arab League's High Council contributed £E 4,000; Yassin, "Palestinians in Egypt," *Samed al-Iqtisadi*.

29. Report of the Egyptian Ministry of Social Affairs on the activities of the Higher Committee, cited in Maha Dajani, *The Institutionalisation of Palestinian Identity in Egypt* (Cairo: American University in Cairo Press), p. 16.

30. Sarraj et al., *Arab Palestinians in Egypt.*

31. Yassin, *Palestinians in Egypt* (Shaml).

32. Shafeeq Ghabra, *Palestinians in Kuwait* (Boulder, CO: Westview Press, 1987), p. 36.

33. See chapter 7.

34. Yasin, in Terry Rempel, *The United Nations Conciliation Commission for Palestine, Protection, and a Durable Solution for Palestinian Refugees,* Information and Discussion Brief No. 5 (Bethlehem, West Bank: BADIL, 2000), p. 44.

35. Laurie Brand, "Nasir's Egypt and the Re-emergence of the Palestinian National Movement." *Journal of Palestine Studies* 17, no 2 (Winter 1988), p. 43; see also p. 31 regarding the transfer to Gaza effected under an agreement concluded between Egypt and the American Friends Service Committee.

36. Brand, *Palestinians in the Arab World*, p. 45; Yassin, *Palestinians in Egypt* (Shaml), p. 5.

37. Brand, *Palestinians in the Arab World*, p. 45. Dajani (*Institutionalisation of Palestinian Identity in Egypt*, p. 16) puts the figure at 4,000. Whatever the case, by 1954 the number must have been at least 7,000: An October 1954 meeting of the Higher Committee concerning relief for the refugees set as an initial target

assistance for 5,000, with the ultimate target to be 7,000. Brand, *Palestinians in the Arab World*, p. 45.

38. We found no reference to entry data, but official Egyptian statistics put the Palestinian population in Egypt in 1960 at 15,493 (Brand, *Palestinians in the Arab World*, p. 46), so it seems safe to assume that the number was in the thousands.

39. Brand, *Palestinians in the Arab World*, p. 45.

40. See Sara Roy, *The Gaza Strip: The Political Economy of De-Development*, 2d ed. (Washington, DC: Institute for Palestine Studies, 2001), p. 90.

41. See Julie Peteet, "The AFSC Refugee Archives on Palestine, 1948–1950," in Salim Tamari and Elia Zureik, eds., *Reinterpreting the Historical Record: The Uses of Palestinian Refugee Archives for Social Science Research and Policy Analysis* (Jerusalem and Washington, DC: Institute for Jerusalem Studies and Institute for Palestine Studies, 2001), pp. 109–28.

42. Benny Morris, *Israel's Border Wars 1949–1956* (Oxford: Clarendon Press, 1993), p. 30.

43. Ibid., p. 427. The annual number of infiltrations gradually fell to about 4,500 by the mid-1950s, as the IDF's shoot-on-sight "free fire" policy increasingly had a deterrent effect.

44. Roy, *Gaza Strip*, pp. 69–70.

45. Morris, *Israel's Border Wars 1949–1956*, p. 86. Morris also notes (pp. 92–93) that the "radical change" in Egypt's policy toward Israel triggered by the raid was evidenced even at the rhetorical level: infiltrators, whom Egypt previously called "thieves," were now called fedayeen (men of sacrifice).

46. Yezid Sayigh, *Armed Struggle and the Search for State: The Palestinian National Movement 1949–1993* (Oxford and Washington, DC: Oxford University Press and the Institute for Palestine Studies, 1997), p. 63.

47. Ibid., pp. 63–64. Hafiz himself was assassinated by Israel in mid-1956.

48. By December 1955, the Mustafa Hafiz brigade, officered by Egyptians, comprised some 700 Palestinians.

49. These reached a total strength (not including the Mustafa Hafiz brigade) of 4,000 by 1956. All but five of the officers were Egyptian. Sayigh, *Armed Struggle and the Search for State*, p. 62.

50. UNRWA, *Special Report of the Director of the UNRWA for Palestinian Refugees in the Near East Covering the Period 1 November 1956 to mid-December 1956*, Official Records of the General Assembly, Eleventh Session, Supplement No. 14 (A/3212), New York: United Nations (1957).

51. Morris, in *Israel's Border Wars 1949–1956*, quotes a UN source as saying that 447 to 455 Arab civilians were killed by Israeli troops in the first three weeks of occupation. He cites a UN report as specifying that 140 refugees and 135 local residents were killed on a single day (3 November 1956) in Khan Yunis by the IDF as they searched for weapons (p. 424).

52. Sayigh, *Armed Struggle and the Search for State*, p. 65.

53. Morris, *Israel's Border Wars 1949–1956*, p. 424, reports that dozens of the fedayeen who were rounded up were summarily executed without trial and that

another 66 ("probably fedayeen") were executed in an number of other incidents during screening operations in the Gaza Strip between 2 and 29 November. Sayigh states that between 930 and 1,200 Palestinians were estimated to have been killed by the IDF before it withdrew on 7 March 1957; see *Armed Struggle and the Search for State*, p. 65.

54. Morris, *Israel's Border Wars 1949–1956*, p. 423.

55. It is very unlikely that many Palestinians entered as a result of the 1956 tripartite aggression. Most of those who escaped with the Egyptian troops after Israel occupied the Gaza Strip would have returned after the Israeli withdrawal four months later. A 1994 document on the number of Egyptian travel documents according to entry date, obtained by Abdul Qader Yassin from the Egyptian foreign ministry, shows only 142 arriving in 1956; Yassin, *Palestinians in Egypt* (Shaml), p. 6; Brand, *Palestinians in the Arab World*, p. 46.

56. Roy, *Gaza Strip*, p. 73.

57. In all likelihood, the 1967 wave included refugees in Egypt's Qantara Sharq camp, whose occupants were transferred to Gaza in September 1949.

58. Sayigh, *Armed Struggle and the Search for State*, p. 169.

59. Ibid., p. 170.

60. Ibid. In a rare error in his monumental work, Sayigh wrote that the 3,000–4,000 men "diverted into a 'surplus'" were resettled in the "Tahrir district of Cairo." In fact, they were resettled in the Tahrir district (province) of the Gharbiyyah governorate on the desert fringes of the delta, an area of extensive land reclamation projects.

61. Sayigh, *Armed Struggle and the Search for State*, p. 170.

62. Brand, *Palestinians in the Arab World*, p. 46.

63. UNRWA, *Report to the Secretary General Covering 1 July 1967–30 June 1968*, Official Records of the General Assembly, Twenty Third Session, Supplement No. 13 (A/7213) (New York: United Nations. 1968), p. 1.

64. See Tom Segev, *1967: Israel, the War, and the Year that Transformed the Middle East* (New York: Metropolitan Books, 2007), chapter 21.

65. Ibid., p. 536.

66. *Al-Ahram* (5 October 1967) mentions the creation of three new camps— Omar ben al-Khattab, Othman Bin Affan, and 'Ayn Jalut—in all likelihood specifically connected to the PLA personnel.

67. Dajani, *Institutionalisation of Palestinian Identity in Egypt*, p. 92. According to Dajani, businessmen from Gaza henceforth dominated the Palestinian business community in Egypt.

68. UNRWA, *Report to the Secretary General Covering 1 July 1967–30 June 1968*, p. 7. The same section also stated that 40,000–45,000 registered refugees were believed to have left the Gaza Strip since the hostilities, though most of these probably went to Jordan.

69. Brand, *Palestinians in the Arab World*, p. 46.

70. Dajani, *Institutionalisation of Palestinian Identity in Egypt*, p. 16, cites a PLO official as stating that in September 1984 the Palestinian population of Egypt had expanded following the 1982 invasion.

71. This figure is almost certainly high; the Egyptian policy establishment at the time was eager to exaggerate the sacrifices it had made for the Palestinians and the burden they constituted to the state.

72. Many Palestinians had been living and working in the Gulf states since the late 1950s and especially since 1967. However, when the labor market contracted, they were confronted with a basic dilemma. They were not able to return to their homeland and in many cases were not able to return to the first country of refuge or to the state that issued them their travel documents. This dilemma was highlighted during the Gulf war, when thousands of Palestinians were collectively expelled or forced to flee from Arab countries. Palestinian sources estimate that around a quarter of a million did not reach a place of secure residency during this time.

73. Interview with PLO ambassador Zuhdi al-Qudwah, 23 September 2001.

Chapter 2

Politics, Policies, and Attitudes in the Host State

In the previous chapter, we dealt with the successive waves of Palestinian refugees into Egypt in their political context, with the discussion of government policy largely confined to the immediate response to the influx in terms of emergency measures and efforts to limit the numbers allowed entry. The present chapter, by contrast, deals with the host government's broad policies toward the Palestinian community that remained—whether in Egypt proper or, up to 1967, in the Gaza Strip—as reflected in its legislation or administrative orders. These policies have undergone changes according to the regime in place, the evolving political situation, and developments in the Arab-Israeli conflict. Thus, regulations concerning the Palestinians in Egypt, as announced in the *Jaridah Rasmiyyah* (the Official Gazette), fluctuated over time, reflecting a constellation of factors both international and local.

Palestinians in Egypt were vulnerable not only because of changing policies and legislation, but also because of swings in public opinion most often entirely beyond their control. Thus, the present chapter, in addition to providing an overview of government policy from the monarchy to the "Golden Era" under Nasser, through the low ebb during Sadat's last years, and finally to the uneasy stalemate under Mubarak, will also look at the shifts in public attitudes toward the Palestinians that both reflected and influenced government policy.

Egyptian Policy under the Monarchy

While doing its best to provide emergency aid to the refugees, the Egyptian government was determined to keep to a minimum the number of Palestinians allowed to remain in the country. This was primarily a practical response to Egypt's own overpopulation and poverty, but the proposition of Palestinian "separateness" implied in the policy dovetailed with a political justification fully embraced by the refugees themselves: the Palestinians were soon to return to their homes, as called for by UN General Assembly Resolution 194 (III) of December 1948.

Thus, starting from the signing of the armistice agreement in February 1949, Egypt had two "distinct" Palestinian populations under its control: the small population that had managed to remain in Egypt proper, and the population of the Egyptian-administered Gaza Strip, massively expanded by an influx of more than 200,000 refugees from elsewhere in Palestine. The premise of separateness was to have considerable influence on Egyptian policy toward both communities.

The Refugee Community in Egypt

In line with the government's preoccupation with limiting the Palestinian presence in the country, there was never any question of granting them citizenship (as Jordan had done for its own purposes in 1954) or of absorbing them in any way, though the government did flirt with international projects to settle some of them in the Sinai Peninsula. Unlike the other states bordering Israel, Egypt had not requested UN relief when the refugees began to arrive in significant numbers in April 1948. Not wanting to create conditions suitable for the refugees to remain, the government had also not wanted assistance in Egypt proper from UNRWA when it began operations in 1950. Instead, it transformed the Higher Committee for Palestinian Immigrants that had been created to take charge of the refugees in May 1948 (see chapter 1) into an aid agency, which classified Palestinians according to economic need and established strict eligibility criteria for assistance.[1]

To receive aid (limited though it was), Palestinians had to prove their status as refugees, defined by the Higher Committee as persons who sought refuge in the country from 1948 to 1950. They did this by showing the residency cards recording refugee status that had been issued by the Egyptian Department of Passports and Nationality. Those who did not have proof of refugee status, or who lacked the other qualifications required to obtain temporary residency permits (i.e., proven financial resources and an Egyptian sponsor), were left to fend for themselves when the temporary camps were dismantled in 1948–49. A ministerial decision concerning the issuance of temporary residence identity documents to Palestinian refugees stipulated that the documents could not be renewed for more than one year and should indicate the material assistance being received by the holder. Subsequently, as of 1950, travel documents (as well as birth certificates) for Palestinians in Egypt became the province of the Government of All Palestine (GAP), the Cairo-based shadow government sponsored by Egypt (see section below). The GAP passports, or travel documents, required the same proof of refugee status as the residence cards issued by the government. Holders of GAP passports could obtain one-year residence permits provided they could meet the other requirements.

The consequences of not having a residence permit were dire: Without legal residency, there was no access to government assistance or services. In the realm of education, for example, the Higher Committee had provided schooling in the temporary camps set up for Palestinians in 1948, but after the camps were dismantled in 1949 and Palestinians began moving to Egyptian towns, a ministerial decision was issued stating that

> non-Egyptians are not to be admitted in Egyptian schools unless their passports indicate possession of a residence permit from the Ministry of the Interior. Those who do not have residence permits are required to apply to the Ministry of the Interior. The school will renew the residency accordingly. (*al-Ahram*, 13 April 1949)

Even with legal residency, however, life for the refugees was harsh. Travel was extremely difficult, especially because the GAP documents were recognized by practically no other state. But the restriction that caused the greatest hardship was the prohibition on work. Written directly on the residence permit were the words "work for or without wages is forbidden."[2] As a result, even those Palestinians who had some money when they arrived in Egypt soon saw their savings depleted. Unemployment was rife among Egyptians as well, but Egyptians at least could seek work without fear of deportation.

The Gaza Strip and the Refugees

Just as there had been no question of granting Egyptian citizenship to Palestinians, so there was never any question of

Egypt's annexing the Gaza Strip, as Jordan had done with the West Bank. Although Egypt maintained a very tight grip on the territory, with military rule and an extensive intelligence network, ideologically, for the Egyptian regime, the Gaza Strip was *Palestine*, the part of the country that had been preserved pending Palestine's liberation as promised by the rhetoric of the Arab regimes.

During the 1948 war, Egypt had been the prime mover behind the Arab League Political Committee's creation in September 1948 of the GAP, initially headed by Hajj Amin al-Husseini, which was declared the official government of Palestine.[3] Though the GAP had officially rejected the 1947 UN partition plan, it was in fact set up to govern those parts of Palestine assigned to the Arab state under that plan, or, more accurately, the parts of Palestine that would remain in Arab hands when the war ended. After Jordan's King Abdallah annexed the West Bank in 1950, however, the GAP's only "sovereign territory" was the Gaza Strip. Furthermore, by that time, its "rule" was already a façade: From the signing of the Egyptian-Israel armistice in February 1949, the Gaza Strip was run entirely by the Egyptian Military Government established there. With its headquarters transferred to Cairo, the GAP became a largely fictional body whose main function was to represent Palestine on the Arab League Council and to issue travel documents to Palestinians in Egypt and Gaza. The GAP continued its virtually paper existence until the death of its president, Ahmad Hilmi Abd al-Baqi, in 1963.[4]

As already noted, Egypt had not requested UNRWA assistance for the Palestinian refugees in Egypt proper. The Gaza Strip, however, was another matter: There was no way that Egypt could have provided for the Gaza Strip's more than 200,000 refugees.[5] In January 1949, the AFSC (the Quakers) had assumed responsibility for organizing relief in the Strip under an agreement with the United Nations, which had charged them with this task pending more permanent arrangements. The Quakers, in coordination with the Egyptian government, had set up camps and provided other forms of relief until mid-1950, when UNRWA took over.[6] In September 1950, UNRWA signed an agreement with Egypt setting the terms for its operation in the Gaza Strip. Under the agreement, UNRWA and its personnel were granted freedom of movement inside Egypt and the Gaza Strip and between the two areas, diplomatic immunity for the UNRWA director and members of its Advisory Commission, and exemption from customs duties and taxes of all goods and equipment imported into Gaza in connection with its mission; the Egyptian government also agreed to provide without charge services relating to the goods and equipment in transit through Egypt for the refugees (including loading and unloading, transport, storage, and safe conduct).[7] The task of providing food, health care, housing, and education to this destitute population was staggering. Although UNRWA (and the Quakers before them) performed admirably in terribly difficult conditions—by 1953, it had moved most of the refugees out of tents and into more permanent shelters in some eight camps and created twenty-six UNRWA schools[8]—the refugees long remained suspicious of the Agency and of the UN in general, believing that the international community intended to settle them rather than promote their right under UN General Assembly Resolution 194 (III) to return to their homes.

These same suspicions also applied to the Egyptian government, which in fact had been exploring development schemes from early on, especially in the Sinai, where refugees might be settled. Officially, the Egyptian government, like the other Arab states, rejected the idea of permanent refugee resettlement on the grounds that Israel, having created the refugee problem, now had an obligation to permit the refugees to return to their homes as called for in UN General Assembly Resolution 194. In practice, however, the government could hardly ignore the dire situation in the tiny Gaza Strip, which had by far the highest refugee concentration in the Arab world and few land resources to sustain them. The gap between declared and actual policy is implicit in a 5 June 1950 letter sent from Beirut to the Foreign Office by Sir Henri Knight, the United Kingdom Delegate to the UN Advisory Commission on Refugees: "Would there be any fear that the Egyptian government may wish to hold to Gaza refugees as a bargaining counter in peace negotiations [it should be noted that] the suggestion that something may be done for the refugees in Sinai came from the Egyptians themselves and the problem is how to get the Egyptians to revert to this tentative suggestion and to translate it into a more positive form."[9] Knight elsewhere mentions that the Middle East representative of the AFSC reported that the Egyptian foreign minister had "spoken in general terms of resettling a number of refugees in Sinai, particularly along the coastal strip."[98] Long-term projects discussed included the Sinai Irrigation Project, which was intended to resettle 50–60,000 refugees in agricultural settlements through the construction of an irrigation system diverting water from the Nile through irrigation channels.[11] Funds for the projects were to be raised by UNRWA in order to settle and provide employment for Palestinian refugees and thereby (it was believed) foster peace in the region.

As for Egypt's actual policies toward the population of Gaza, military rule was strict, the border between Egypt and Gaza was closely monitored, and little if anything was done to alleviate their plight in any way.[12]

Nasser and the Golden Era

Points of Continuity with the Old Regime

On 23 July 1952, the monarchy was overthrown by the "Free Officers," led by Nasser. Though the July revolution, and the popular enthusiasm it generated, was at least partly the result of Egypt's humiliating defeat in Palestine,[13] the policies of the new republic toward the Palestinians under its rule initially changed little. General Muhammad Naguib, whom the Free Officers had chosen to be the first president of the Egyptian republic, sent a clear message that he would not accept refugees from the Gaza Strip in Egypt, including even the Sinai (although in fact the new regime, like the old, discreetly pursued resettlement projects there). The bureaucracy set up to deal with the Palestinians remained in place: The Higher Committee of Palestinian Immigrant Affairs continued as an aid agency; residency continued to be strictly controlled and was based on the same criteria established under the monarchy; and travel between Gaza and Egypt, and between Egypt and abroad, continued to be subject to difficult-to-obtain permits. At no time under Nasser was the requirement for an entry permit into Egypt lifted.

Even after the policies began to be liberalized, bureaucratic issues such as passports and residence permits did not significantly change. In 1960, for example, Egypt, by then called the United Arab Republic (UAR) to reflect the establishment of the Egyptian-Syrian union in 1958,[14] issued its first major decision (number 28) concerning the provision of travel documents for Palestinians. Under the decision, the same proof of refugee status and legal residence as under the monarchy was required to obtain the travel documents. Furthermore, the continuing difficulty of travel is shown in Article 2 of the decree, which bars the travel document holder from traveling even between the northern and the southern regions (i.e., Syria and Egypt) of the "united" republic without both a visa and a return visa. Similarly, Decision 181 of 1964, while stipulating that Palestinian refugees should be given temporary travel documents upon request, required exactly the same proof of refugee status and possession of valid Egyptian residence permits. It also specified that the travel document did not permit entry into or transit through Egypt without a transit visa or a visa and return visa.

Indeed, two basic premises of monarchical Egypt were never to change. First, the separate Palestinian identity was to be safeguarded. The aforementioned Decision 28 of 1960 concerning travel documents, for example, was accompanied by instructions from the Interior Ministry to the Department of Immigration, Passports, and Nationality emphasizing the need to preserve the Palestinian nationality for Palestinian residents of the UAR because they would be returning to their original homeland after its liberation (*al-Ahram*, 20 April 1960). Second, the notion of Gaza as an entirely separate, Palestinian entity—however illusory in practice, given Egypt's total control over the territory—was strictly adhered to and remained a mainstay of Egyptian policy until Israel seized the Strip in 1967.

Finally, despite Naguib's opposition to refugee resettlement projects, the new regime also continued to explore such projects: The British embassy in Beirut reported that the "younger officers concerned with the matter had spoken of UNRWA producing large projects to settle them in Egypt."[15] At the same time, Nasser, from the beginning the strong man of the regime and as of February 1954 the president of Egypt after having pushed Naguib aside, had demonstrated sympathy with the Palestinians and had already initiated projects and increased the provision of services to refugees in the Gaza Strip. According to a British diplomat in Cairo, "His [Nasser's] principal concern was to improve the feeding of the refugees, which he thought was deplorable and demoralizing. To this end, he hoped to get more money devoted to relief and if necessary to divert to this purpose some funds from the UN resettlement programme."[16] None of these projects reached fruition, however, at least partly because of refugee hostility or suspicion of any plans that could be seen to compromise their right of return.

"Nasserism and Palestinianism: Two Sides of the Same Coin"

As mentioned in chapter 1, Israel's raid on the Gaza Strip in February 1955 had marked a turning point in the new government's foreign policy in general and its Palestine policy in particular: It was this raid that convinced President Nasser to shift his priorities from the domestic arena to inter-Arab politics and the wider conflict with Israel. The policy shift was greatly accelerated by the autumn 1956 Israeli-Franco-British tripartite invasion of Egypt, after which the country's "raison d'être, as Nasser defined it, was, for practical and ideological reasons, linked to its mission as leader of the Arab nation. Thus, Arabism and the Palestinian issue became inseparable—they were natural allies in Nasser's quest for a special role for Egypt to play."[17] In the words of Maha Dajani, from that time forward "Nasserism and Palestinianism became two sides of the same coin."[18]

There is no doubt that the main thrust of Nasser's "Palestine policy" concerned the Palestinian *political* problem and was aimed at the wider Arab world. It was within that framework that Nasser opened Egyptian universities to qualifying Palestinian students from all Arab countries, waiving fees and offering subsidies and grants to help defray their living costs. Egyptian universities had always been a magnet for Arab students, but as of 1954 the number of Palestinian students studying in Egyptian institutions of higher learning surged dramatically; medicine and engineering faculties were especially favored. Nasser also allowed the Palestinian student organization, which not infrequently participated in and even led demonstrations against his regime, to thrive.[19] It was also within that framework that he sponsored the creation of the PLO in 1964.

With Palestine a central plank in Nasser's pan-Arabism, it was only natural that he should take a more active interest in the welfare of Palestinians both in the Gaza Strip and at home. Accordingly, Nasser in 1958 approved a budget of £E 100,000 to create work opportunities in Gaza, mainly in agricultural projects and the packaging and export of oranges.[20] As for Palestinians in Egypt proper, given the enormous hardship imposed on resident Palestinians by the prohibition against work, the first changes he introduced involved an easing of restrictions on employment (though Egypt itself continued to suffer economic instability and high unemployment). However, the initial changes concerned only a very small class of professionals, mainly in the medical field. Thus, in July 1954, Laws 415 and 416 permitted, respectively, licensed refugee doctors and veterinarians to practice in Egypt. These laws were followed in September by Law 481 permitting certified midwives to practice, and in October by Law 537 authorizing the licensing of Palestinians with degrees in dentistry.[21] Far more important for the Palestinian community as a whole was the gradual relaxation of the no-work regulations for resident Palestinians that began in the mid-1950s.[22]

The real watershed, however, concerned employment in the public sector, without doubt the most important in the Egyptian economy. Responding to poor economic conditions in the Gaza Strip, in 1954 President Nasser loosened restrictions so as to allow some Gazans to work as teachers in Egypt, although he issued no official regulation to formalize the policy. In 1959, the Ministry of Foreign Affairs required the Ministry of Social Affairs to make jobs accessible to Palestinians in Cairo and other Egyptian cities,[23] and in the early 1960s Nasser called upon high school graduates and diploma holders in Gaza to apply for work with the Egyptian government.

But it was not until March 1962 that the Egyptian president formalized these new employment practices by issuing Law 66, which permitted the recruitment of Palestinians in government bodies and gave them the same employment options as Egyptian nationals. Article 1 of Law 66 reads as follows:

> Article 1—As an exception to Section 1 of Article 6 (Law 210 of 1951), concerning public sector employees, it is permitted for Palestinians to work in government and public sector jobs and to be treated as nationals of the United Arab Republic. (*Jaridah Rasmiyyah*, No. 58, 10 March 1962)

Law 66 marked the beginning of what Palestinians in Egypt continue to this day to call the "Golden Era." The law was followed by a May 1963 decision exempting Palestinians from the requirement to obtain work permits issued by the Egyptian Minister of Labor.[24] Further confirmation of the "new era" came with Law 46 of 1964, concerning civil servants in government, which explicitly reasserted the exemption of Palestinians from "foreign status."[25] The importance of these laws cannot be overstated. Their impact is made clear in a number of our interviews:

> I am originally from Khan Yunis. When the 1948 war started, my family and I were living in Jaffa. We were forced to move back to Khan Yunis. My family used to travel quite often to Egypt when Gaza was under Egyptian rule and the road was open for travel. After I finished my high school exams in agriculture in 1962, Abd al-Nasser called on young Palestinians to work in Egypt. I went to Cairo and I started working as a teacher of science at a government school in Ataba. (P21, Giza, Cairo, 11 June 2002)

Some of those who came from Gaza under this provision also took advantage of new regulations concerning the ownership of businesses that had been passed in 1954, when Palestinians with sufficient capital were granted commercial licences and franchises to start their own businesses. Palestinians came to have a major presence in the tertiary sector, opening barbershops, restaurants, and sweet shops. The easing of ownership restrictions is reflected in a number of the interviews:

> I arrived in Cairo in the 1960s to work as a teacher of science. I also had shares in an auto repair shop with two Egyptian friends. At that time there was no regulation preventing Palestinians from owning businesses. Soon after, I put my wife's name on the ownership shares of the shop. After I left my job with the government, I was able to open another branch. (P21, Giza, 11 June 2002)

Most important, the laws that were amended during that period did not apply the word "foreign" to Palestinians in administrative matters. Not only were they able to move far more easily (albeit with the requisite entry permits) between Gaza and Egypt, thereby bolstering Gaza's economy, but, treated as nationals, they also had better access to state services. The following interview reflects both the impact of the new policies on employment and the free medical services from which Palestinians could now benefit:

> My husband came from Gaza to Hurgada via the Red Sea in 1962, when President Abd al-Nasser permitted Palestinians to work in the [Egyptian] government. He worked in the legal affairs section of the Ministry of Education. He met my [Egyptian] family while he was living there and we got married in 1968. While we were living together, he came down with epilepsy and was hospitalized for two months at

no charge in Khanka public hospital in Greater Cairo. (P12, 'Izbit al-Nakhal, 29 May 2002)

Many Palestinians were hired by the government, especially after the mass deportations in the wake of the 1967 war. They were permitted to work in administrative jobs and were posted throughout Egypt in rural and urban areas such as Samalut, Minya, and Matruh. Other Palestinians, too, were able to take advantage of new employment options in Egypt's public sector.

I worked in 1971 after I finished nursing college in the [Egyptian] Ministry of Health. I had a very comfortable situation since I had all the advantages given to government employees, including medical insurance and pensions. This is added to the incentives and allowances. (7/43, Hehya, 15 July 2002)

Even before the legal changes were enacted, the Free Officers had made education, health, and other services available to Palestinians. Almost from the beginning, Nasser opened government schools to Palestinians on the same basis as Egyptians. Public education for them became free of charge from primary school onwards, including university for qualifying students. While no figures were found concerning university enrollment for Palestinian residents of Egypt, from the mid-1950s to the mid-1960s, 5,642 Palestinian university students from Gaza were educated in Egyptian universities.[26] Even with regard to such issues as land ownership, where restrictions had always applied to foreigners, an exception was made for Palestinians. Thus, while Nasser's Law 15 of 1963 tightened traditional land ownership restrictions by preventing foreigners[27] from owning any kind of land in Egypt, its very first article exempted Palestinians "until the Palestinian territories are liberated from the occupiers and Palestinians return to their homeland."

Sadat and the Aftermath of the al-Siba'i Assassination

The Golden Era, however, was not to last. On 28 September 1970, Nasser died suddenly of a heart attack immediately after mediating between PLO President Yasir Arafat and King Hussein of Jordan, who had been locked in the bloody "Black September" civil war in Jordan. Nasser was succeeded by Vice President Anwar Sadat, who had been one of the Free Officers. As had been the case when the Free Officers took power in 1952, policies toward the Palestinians initially remained unchanged under Sadat, who indeed seemed to follow the political course set by Nasser.

Meanwhile, popular sentiment against Israel ran high. With growing dissatisfaction with the "no war, no peace" situation, including strong anti-regime student demonstrations in January 1972, Sadat repeatedly vowed to fight "when the time was ripe." In October 1973, Egypt and Syria launched a surprise attack against Israel aimed at recapturing the territories it seized during the June 1967 war. Although the initial successes, especially the Egyptian army's crossing of the Suez Canal, were soon reversed by Israel (with the help of a U.S. airlift of military supplies), the war proved to be a watershed, providing the psychological boost that enabled Sadat to pursue diplomacy to recover the Sinai Peninsula. Central to Sadat's approach was rapprochement with the United States, under whose auspices Egypt signed two disengagement agreements with Israel in 1974 and 1975.

It was not until November 1977, when Sadat traveled to Jerusalem to address the Israeli Knesset (he had announced his impending visit at a special session of Egyptian parliament to which he had specially invited Yasir Arafat), that Egyptian-PLO relations began seriously to sour. After the visit, Sadat launched his "Egypt First" slogan. It was around this time that references in the press to Egyptian sacrifices and Arab (especially Palestinian) ingratitude were stepped up, thus laying the ground for the vicious anti-Palestinian campaign that was soon to follow.[28]

For the Palestinian population in Egypt, the turning point—repeatedly cited in our interviews—was the 18 February 1978 assassination in Nicosia, Cyprus, of Egyptian culture minister Yusif al-Siba'i[29] by the notorious Palestinian Abu Nidal faction.[30] Though Abu Nidal had been expelled from Fatah and the PLO with much fanfare in the early 1970s and was widely known to be their sworn enemy, the Egyptian government and media did not hesitate to stigmatize the Palestinians in general for the assassination. At al-Siba'i's funeral, Egyptian prime minister Mustafa Riyad declared, "No more Palestine after today."[31] The fallout of the assassination was immediately felt within Egypt's Palestinian community, with a flurry of arrests, surveillance, and detentions. Although the research for this book did not yield specific information on the number of Palestinians arrested after al-Siba'i's death, some interviewees reported that Palestinian houses were regularly searched for young men to bring in for questioning.

> The police made intensive arrest campaigns against Palestinians after the death of al-Siba'i. That day, the police came to the building where I live and asked about a Palestinian officer in the army, which was my rank then. My Egyptian neighbors spoke highly of me and I was lucky that they did not come again. (P1, Giza, Cairo, 10 May 2002)

By the time of the al-Siba'i assassination, almost five years had passed since the October 1973 war, and prospects for a brighter economic future were as distant as ever, disappointing the hopes raised by the disengagement agreements. The Egyptian public had thus had time to begin measuring the costs of long conflict, making them vulnerable to the propaganda already underway about Egyptian sacrifices and Palestinian ingratitude. A number of interviewees alluded to the backlash against them in the wake of the assassination:

> After the killing of al-Siba'i, Egyptians considered Palestinians as Jews [an allusion to Palestinian perceived economic power], although we are Arabs like them. One day the front window of my shop was broken. Of course, it was an Egyptian who did it. Why? What have I done to them? Is it only because I am Palestinian, like those who killed al-Siba'i? (P9, Wailey, 24 June 2002)

The al-Siba'i assassination triggered a spate of anti-Palestinian editorializing, which further inflamed popular opinion. "Disloyalty" became a trait frequently attributed to Palestinians.[32] Another endlessly repeated charge—mentioned by a great number of our interviewees as a standard and deeply ingrained idea about Palestinians—is that they "sold their land to the Zionists" of their own accord and therefore got what they deserved. Not atypical is the following passage from the popular Egyptian daily *al-Akhbar*:

> Each one of the thousands of people who participated in the funeral asked himself: Is this what we get for having waged four wars for those who killed him? For having deprived ourselves of bread in order to recover their lost land? . . . for having deprived our children of the places in the university

that were their due so they [Palestinians] could have them?
. . . for having tasted death so they could live? Are those
the words we sacrificed ourselves for so that Gaza and the
West Bank would be liberated before Sinai? Our people do
not deserve such ingratitude. (Mustafa Amin, *al-Akhbar*, 20
February 1978)

It was also during the period following the assassination
that reports of Palestinian wealth increased, which sharpened
resentments among poor Egyptians and fueled the Palestinians'
reputation for having "taken over" the Egyptian economy. As an
example of the kind of journalistic writing that encouraged such
notions, a 13 May 1979 article headlined "All These Fortunes for
Palestinians Living in Egypt!!!" appeared in *Egyptian Weekly
Magazine*. Among the article's claims were that 60 percent of the
shops in Central Cairo and Port Said were Palestinian-owned and
that 12,000 private import-export offices and 40 farms were run
by Palestinians. Exaggerating Palestinian economic power in this
way suggested to the local population that the Palestinians in their
midst were vampires sucking the blood of the Egyptian people.[33]

Of far more lasting practical consequence, however, were the
legal changes that followed al-Siba'i's killing. On 28 February 1978,
a mere ten days after the assassination, the authoritative *al-Ahram*
reported the prime minister's announcement that the government
would "reconsider all procedures that treated Palestinians as
nationals. The purpose [was] to rank Palestinians with other Arab
nationals and to safeguard national rights for Egyptians." Indeed,
the threat was soon carried out, with President Sadat issuing
administrative regulations 47 and 48 of 1978 decreeing that all
regulations treating Palestinians as nationals were to be annulled.
Ministries hastened to apply the regulations: "The Ministry of Labor
warned against issuing foreigners, including Palestinians, permits
for business or for creating offices for export/import. Exceptions
[were] made for those who had been married to Egyptian women
for the past five years" (*al-Ahram*, 7 August 1978). More specifically,
Law 48 concerned work in the public sector. Section 1 of Article 16
of the law stipulated that employment of Arab nationals should be
on a "reciprocal basis." This meant that the government of Egypt
would hire citizens only of countries that hired Egyptian nationals.
Needless to say, the stateless Palestinians were excluded under
this law.

The dismantling of Nasser's legislation favoring the Palestinians continued for the remainder of Sadat's regime, further tightening restrictions on employment and extending the restrictions to other spheres, especially education, where Palestinians saw themselves progressively deprived of their access to free education and to university study. Details of this legislation are discussed in chapters 4 and 5.

An often overlooked aspect of the cancellation of the regulations treating Palestinians as nationals is that it did not concern solely the Palestinians in Egypt. The measures had far-reaching consequences for Palestinians across the Arab world, at least with regard to education. For more than twenty years, Palestinians could be educated in Egyptian universities free of charge, and tens of thousands took advantage of the offer: From the mid-1960s until 1978, an average of 20,000 Palestinian students per year were enrolled in Egyptian universities.[34] In this sense, then, what ended with the legislation following the al-Siba'i assassination was the lingering legacy of Nasser's "sponsorship" of the Palestinian people. By enacting these measures, Sadat was signalling that Egypt was no longer the patron of the Palestinians nor the primary Arab defender of their cause.

Even as the local Palestinian community was stripped of its privileges, however, the formal break with the PLO did not occur for another two years, though the relationship became increasingly strained as Israel and Egypt moved closer to concluding a peace agreement. In September 1978, the Camp David accords were signed, followed by the signing of the final Egyptian-Israeli peace treaty in March 1979, when PLO-Egyptian relations were frozen. They were still "frozen" two and a half years later, when Sadat was assassinated on 6 October 1981, the eighth anniversary of the start of the October war, by members of the Egyptian fundamentalist organization al-Gamiat al-Islamiyyah. One of their major grievances was Sadat's separate peace with Israel.

The Mubarak Era

Sadat was succeeded by Husni Mubarak, who has been president of Egypt ever since. The first few years of the Mubarak's government witnessed a continuation of the policies of Sadat's last years, with employment restrictions confirmed and tightened, and new prohibitions further limiting Palestinian access to education,

albeit at a slower pace. Meanwhile, relations with the PLO began
to improve gradually in the aftermath of Israel's 1982 invasion of
Lebanon, and diplomatic ties were restored in 1983.

But as a weak and vulnerable community, the Palestinians
remained at the mercy of shifts in government policy and public
opinion triggered by external events in which they had no role.
In general, sympathy for the Palestinians coincided with Israeli
actions against them in an inverse relationship: the more brutal
the action, the greater the sympathy. Thus the 1982 invasion
of Lebanon and the siege of Beirut triggered an outpouring of
solidarity, reaching a peak at the time of the Sabra and Shatila
massacres. Support for the Palestinians also increased during the
first intifada that broke out in 1987, when Israel's "iron fist" policies
sparked widespread indignation. Political parties, unions, actors,
and ordinary Egyptians participated in demonstrations expressing
their solidarity with the Palestinian people under occupation.

On the other hand, Iraq's invasion of Kuwait in August 1990
and the February 1991 Gulf war, in which Egypt participated as a
member of the U.S.-led coalition against Iraq, provided the occasion
for a strong backlash against the Palestinians. Though many poor
Egyptians, resentful of Kuwait's great wealth, had shown support
for Iraqi leader Saddam Hussein following his occupation of Kuwait,
the Egyptian media (with the clear assent of the government, if
not at its prompting) seized upon the PLO's statements in support
of Saddam and the pro-Saddam demonstrations by Palestinians
in the occupied territories and elsewhere to launch another full-
blown propaganda assault on the Palestinians. One of the most
vicious attacks appeared on 22 September 1990, about six weeks
after the Iraqi invasion, in the popular daily *Akhbar al-Yawm*.
In a long open letter to President Mubarak, Egyptian journalist
Ibrahim Saada referred to the Palestinians as "opportunistic
cowards," "thieves," and "killers." He also harped on the well-worn
theme of Palestinian ingratitude toward those who had done so
much for them. Although many of the Palestinians who went to
the Gulf states were highly educated, he wrote that Kuwait had
given "everything" to "hundreds of thousands of Palestinians who
came to it destitute and illiterate." Specifically with regard to the
Palestinian community in Egypt, Saada replayed the myths about
Palestinian privilege and wealth, affirming that they "live in much
better and more refined conditions" than Egyptians. He also vastly
exaggerated their numbers, claiming them to be in the "hundreds
of thousands" at a time when their numbers in all likelihood did

not reach 100,000. As to what should be done about the resident Palestinians, Saada advised President Mubarak as follows:

> I do not ask for Palestinians in Egypt to be deported, but I ask you to prevent any more Palestinians from coming in. We already have hundreds of thousands of them in a country that suffers from overpopulation. I ask you to stop this Palestinian penetration of businesses in our economy and to end their declared and hidden monopoly on trade of consumer goods in our country.

He had five specific recommendations:

1. Prevent Palestinians from being active in the commercial, agricultural and industrial sectors of this country . . .
2. Give an ultimatum to Palestinians to liquidate their assets in agricultural, industrial, commercial, and vocational domains. They should be required to deposit their money in Egyptian banks and when the money runs out, the PLO should fund them.
3. Let no Palestinian student study in our schools, colleges or universities . . .
4. Allow no Palestinian graduate to work in Egypt.
5. Prevent political asylum seekers from being politically active. (Ibrahim Saada, *Akhbar al-Yawm*, 22 September 1990)

Well over a quarter of a million Palestinians were expelled from Kuwait and the other Gulf states during and after the war, including tens of thousands of Palestinians with Egyptian travel documents. Many of those who attempted to enter Egypt were turned back. Stories appeared in the Egyptian press about Palestinians detained at the airport and then deported, especially to the Sudan[35]; this included long-time Palestinian residents of Egypt.[36] Egyptian newspapers also published reports about Palestinian students registered at Egyptian universities being prevented from entering Egypt from abroad (*al-Sha'b*, 9 October 1990). Some students returning to Egypt from studying abroad suffered the same fate:

> My son, who was studying in Poland, graduated in 1991 and tried to come back to Egypt. In the airport, he was prevented from entering. That was a result of the Palestinian position on the Gulf war. He was forced to go to Sudan and then to Yemen, where he is now. (P16, 'Ayn Shams, 8 June 2002)

Harassment was not limited to Palestinian travellers trying to return to Egypt. Reports of petty measures taken in retaliation for the PLO position included actions against students inside the country. For example, as PLO-Egyptian tensions mounted during the Gulf war, Palestinian students in Mansura University were surprised to find themselves shut out of the examination halls with their seat numbers deleted. They were unable to persuade the president of the university, who claimed he was acting on order from the Ministry of Higher Education, to allow them to sit for the final exams.

On the "up" side of the opinion swings, the al-Aqsa intifada that erupted in September 2000 triggered enormous support for the Palestinians, with almost daily street demonstrations at particularly crucial junctures and the collection of funds to be sent to Palestine. Committees against Zionism and in support of the Palestinians were formed.[37] Newspaper headlines reflected the support of the Egyptian government and people for the Palestinians, and daily media programs reported on those injured and killed by Israeli forces. The outpouring of public sympathy, however, was directed primarily at Palestinians in the occupied territories; for the most part, it did not have a noticeable impact on Egyptian attitudes toward the Palestinians living in their midst.

As for government policy, in September 2003, hopes were raised within the Palestinian community when President Mubarak, responding to pressures from the Egyptian women's movement (supported by the National Council for Women), appointed a high-level committee to study a redrafting of the Egyptian Nationality Law of 1975. Under the old law, Egyptian men married to foreign women could pass their nationality on to their children and, after a certain period of time, to their wives, but the reverse was not true. One of the major reforms expected of the new law was that it would end this gender discrimination and grant Egyptian women married to foreigners the same right to transmit citizenship as Egyptian men. Given that an estimated third of all Egyptian women married to nonnationals are married to Palestinians,[38] the passage of such a law promised to be the most significant development for Palestinians in Egypt since the Nasser era, if not since their arrival.

In July of the following year, the Egyptian National Assembly did in fact pass "Law No. 154/2004 Amending Certain Provisions of Law No. 26/1975 Concerning Egyptian Nationality," which granted Egyptian women the same rights as Egyptian men with regard to conferring nationality on their children. Thus, Article 2 of the law states that an Egyptian national is a person born either to an Egyptian father *or* an Egyptian mother; in accordance with this law, any person born after the passage of the law automatically becomes an Egyptian national. As for persons born to an Egyptian father or mother *before* the activation of the new law, Article 3 states that those who wish to obtain Egyptian nationality must apply to the Interior Ministry; citizenship will be granted either by decision of the minister or one year after receipt from the ministry of the application stamped with the words "no objection." The law further stipulates a one-year grace period during which to apply.[39] According to a high official in the Justice Ministry quoted by *al-Ahram Weekly*, those who do not apply within this one-year period will "forever lose their right to be Egyptians."[40]

Implementation of the law with regard to Palestinians has been, to say the least, mixed. Children born to Egyptian mothers and Palestinian fathers *since* the law was passed have indeed received Egyptian citizenship automatically, without difficulty. But the situation is more complicated for the children of such marriages born *before* the law's passage. Although no exception is spelled out in the law, widespread inquiries confirm that Egyptian women attempting to file applications on behalf of their children—or indeed older Palestinians born of mixed marriages attempting to file for themselves—have consistently been turned away. The explanation given (orally) is that granting Egyptian nationality to Palestinians contradicts state policy, which advocates their return to their homes as mandated by UN General Assembly Resolution 194 (III) and which therefore opposes permanent resettlement (*tawtin*) in the host countries. A 1959 Arab League recommendation that prohibits granting Palestinians citizenship of other countries so as to preserve their Palestinian identity is sometimes specifically cited.[41]

A number of disappointed applicants have challenged this unwritten policy by filing suits at the Egyptian Council of State on the grounds of equality before the law; because no specific exception is made for Palestinians, challengers demand the same right enjoyed by Sudanese, Syrians, and all other nationalities who have been granted Egyptian citizenship under Article 3. According to our informants, applications on behalf of small children under the age of 10 are generally approved, whereas applications for older persons, especially those over 16, are most often rejected. Our inquiries have found no cases at all of qualifying mature adult

Palestinians winning such a suit. One of our informants, though his young child won his suit with the Council of State and was granted citizenship, has received no response to his own suit filed four years ago, at the same time as that of his child.[42]

Administrative Overview

A word of clarification may be useful for what follows concerning the administrative or bureaucratic bodies with responsibility for the Palestinian community. As mentioned earlier in this chapter, the Cairo-based "Government of All Palestine" had an almost entirely paper existence, but it did have one real function: It issued travel documents to Palestinians both in Egypt and in the Gaza Strip from 1949 until 1960. In 1960, Law 28 ruled that the GAP passports for Palestinians residing in Egypt proper be withdrawn and replaced by Egyptian travel documents issued by the Department of Immigration, Passports, and Nationality.[43] Travel documents for the Palestinian residents of Gaza were henceforth issued by the Egyptian administration in the Strip (the AOGG), which since the Egyptian-Israeli armistice had already been in charge of all other bureaucratic matters pertaining to Gaza residents.

The duality between the two bodies continues to this day. After the Gaza Strip was seized by Israel in the 1967 war and the Egyptian administration in Gaza was dismantled, a much-reduced AOGG was relocated to Cairo. This office, located in Madinat Nasr, continues to handle the passports and residency permits of those who entered Egypt from Gaza and their descendants, as well as all those who entered the country after 1967. Meanwhile, the Department of Immigration, Passports, and Nationality continues to handle these matters for all the pre-1967 arrivals and their descendants.

Notes

1. Brand, *Palestinians in the Arab World*, p. 45.

2. Ibid., p. 51.

3. Sarraj et al., *Arab Palestinians in Egypt*.

4. Brand, *Palestinians in the Arab World*, pp. 24–25.

5. An official of the British Middle East Office wrote the following in 1952: "In fact I cannot see that there is any hope of finding a suitable home for the unfortunate Gaza refugees and they are likely to be left there [Gaza] as derelicts living on the charity of UNO [United Nations Organization] for the indefinite time." Public Records Office, Foreign Office, Correspondence No 119/3/9, from T. C. Rapp of the British Middle East Office to J. Creswell, British Embassy—Cairo, 1952.

6. Peteet, "The AFSC Refugee Archives on Palestine, 1948–1950," pp. 109–110.

7. Summarized from PRO correspondence No 182/15 of 7 November 1950, from the British Middle East Office, Cairo to Middle East Secretariat, Foreign Office.

8. Roy, *Gaza Strip*, pp. 68, 80.

9. Letter from Sir Henri Knight, 5 June 1950. Filing number missing, Public Records Office.

10. Public Records Office, EE/1821/1 24 May 1950, from Sir Henri Knight.

11. Alex Pollock, citing the PRO Foreign Office minutes of Sir Henri Knight on 5 June 1950, wrote: "The scheme [suggested by Aly Shafie] involved the construction of a dam in the Wadi Arish (which has a catchment area of 10,000 sq. miles) at a place called Daqiqa, the site of an old Roman dam, and would have resulted in the development of some 200,000 acres of good land." See Alex Pollock, "The Potential of Microfinance and Microcredit in UNRWA: Developing Outreach and Self-sufficiency," paper presented at an International Symposium on The Palestinian Refugees and UNRWA in Jordan, the West Bank and Gaza, 1949–1999, CERMOC, Dead Sea, Jordan, 1999.

12. Roy, *Gaza Strip*, p. 66. In a series of articles not long after the signing of the UNRWA agreement on Egyptian efforts to assist the refugees, the semi-official daily *al-Ahram* reported Egyptian government involvement in projects aimed at providing employment, housing, schools, and hospitals in the Gaza Strip, though without financial responsibility for the projects, which would be funded by the UN, which allocated to Egypt $54 million for projects serving Palestinian refugees living [in Gaza] under Egyptian rule. These refugees numbered 270,000, of whom 75,000 were originally residents of Gaza (*al-Ahram*, 1 November, 2 November, and 11 November 1950). *Al-Ahram* also reported (5 June 1952) an Egyptian Health Department campaign to vaccinate 70,000 refugees in Gaza against contagious diseases.

13. In his *Philosophy of Revolution*, Nasser wrote that "Palestine was a significant, not just a peripheral factor, in galvanizing the Free Officers to act . . ." Quoted by Dajani, *Institutionalisation of Palestinian Identity in Egypt*, p. 18.

14. The Union was short-lived (1958–61), but Egypt retained the name UAR during Nasser's presidency.

15. Public Records Office, correspondence from British embassy in Beirut to the Foreign Office MES/ Richmond, 14 November 1952.

16. Report on an invitation by Colonel Nasser to Colonel Banks to study the problem of refugees in Gaza Strip, Public Records Office, VE 1826/28, 5 May 1954.

17. Aaron D. Miller, *The Arab States and the Palestine Question: Between Ideology and Self-Interest* (Washington, DC: The Center for Strategic and International Studies—Georgetown University, 1986), p. 61.

18. Dajani, *Institutionalisation of Palestinian Identity in Egypt*, p. 19.

19. The founders of Fatah, whose guerrilla strategy was entirely at odds with Nasser's approach to the Palestine problem, and who took control of the PLO following the 1967 defeat, had studied in Cairo and occupied leadership role in the Union. See chapter 6.

20. *Al-Ahram*, 3 September 1958.

21. Brand, "Nasir's Egypt and the Re-emergence of the Palestinian National Movement," p. 52. A later law affecting professionals (in this case lawyers) was Law 61 of 1968, Article 51 of which stated that those practicing law in Egypt should be Egyptian, with an exception made for Palestinians by "permitting the Council of Lawyers Syndicate to dismiss this condition for nationalist considerations with the approval of three-quarters of its members."

22. Brand, "Nasir's Egypt and the Re-emergence of the Palestinian National Movement." p. 32.

23. *Al-Ahram*, 1 May 1959.

24. Yassin, "Palestinians in Egypt," *Samed al-Iqtisadi*, p. 15.

25. Ibid.

26. Ibid.

27. A foreigner is defined as anyone who does not have Egyptian nationality. At the time, an Egyptian national was a person whose father was Egyptian; the children of an Egyptian woman married to a foreigner were foreigners.

28. Dajani, *Institutionalisation of Palestinian Identity in Egypt*, p. 31.

29. Al-Siba'i, a novelist and the editor of al-Ahram newspaper who had expressed sympathy and support for the Palestinian cause, was a confidant of President Sadat and had accompanied him to Jerusalem.

30. Sabri al-Banna (Abu Nidal) was sentenced to death in absentia by the PLO in 1974 for his operations against fellow Palestinians; the faction's terrorist attacks were aimed at Palestinian, Western, and Israeli targets alike. Patrick Seale, author of *Abu Nidal: A Gun for Hire* (New York: Random House, 1992), wrote of the al-Siba'i killing that "[t]he aim was to punish Sadat and give him a taste of what he, too, might expect" (p. 164).

31. Miller, *Arab States and the Palestine Question*, p. 64.

32. Karem Yehia, "The Image of the Palestinians in Egypt, 1982–1985," *Journal of Palestine Studies* 16, no. 2 (Winter 1987), pp. 45–63.

33. Dajani, *Institutionalisation of Palestinian Identity in Egypt*, p. 95. One of the very clear findings of our research was the extent to which this popular myth is without basis.

34. Sarraj et al., *Arab Palestinians in Egypt*; Yassin, "Palestinians in Egypt," *Samed al-Iqtisadi*.

35. See for example *al-Ahali*, Tharwat Shalabi, 11 September 1991; *an-Nahar*, 25 September 1991; *al-Fajr*, 25 September 1991.

36. See Takkenberg, *The Status of Palestinian Refugees in International Law*, p. 154, citing *an-Nahar* and *al-Fajr* dailies, both dated 25 September 1991.

37. See Hani Shukrallah, "Egypt: Rediscovering Palestine," *Journal of Palestine Studies* 31, no. 4 (Summer 2002), pp. 44–49.

38. Reem Leila, "The Long-Awaited Revised Egyptian Nationality Law Has Become a Reality," *al-Ahram Weekly*, 1–7 July, 2004.

39. Applications are to include the applicant's birth certificate and "foreign passport" and the birth certificates of both parents, as well as the mother's identity card and marriage contract. Also required are proof of the applicant's educational qualifications, four recent photos, and proof of a "clean" criminal record for those over 16 years of age. Applicants over 16 must also present documents proving that they have resided in Egypt for at least the past ten years. Ibid.

40. Ibid.

41. These clarifications were provided by the Cairo-based lawyers Ashraf Milad and Hala Abdul Qadar. Milad heads a law firm specializing in asylum issues, while Abdul Qadar is the head of the Egyptian Foundation for Family Development, an NGO addressing legal issues and acquisition of basic rights.

42. Milad and Abdul Qadar, as well as telephone interviews with various contacts familiar with/well-placed within the Palestinian community.

43 Khaled Azar, *Hukamat Umum Falastin fi Thikraha al-Khamin* [Government of All Palestine on its Fiftieth Anniversary] (Dar al-Horouq, 1998), p. 174.

Chapter 3

Settling and Surviving in Egypt

In the first two chapters, we provided a general context for the Palestinian community of Egypt, examining the successive waves of refugees into the country and the broad government policies and public attitudes that affected them. This chapter addresses another part of the overall context: Where did the refugees settle in the absence of permanent refugee camps, and what determined their choices? And, once settled, given the constraints facing them and deprived of the safety net provided by a dedicated aid agency, what strategies did they use to survive? How did the characteristics of their community affect their situation compared to that of their compatriots who went to Jordan, Syria, or Lebanon? In other words, what are some of the factors—beyond state policies and legislation outlined in the previous chapter—that shaped the construction of the community and set it apart from those in other host states? And finally, how did the Palestinians, mainly Muslim Arabs, integrate into Egyptian society, especially given the longstanding ties between Egyptians and Palestinians?

The first section of this chapter will explore settlement patterns, with special attention given to how they were shaped by the differing circumstances of the two principal waves of refugees. The second section will focus on the social networks that constituted their most valuable coping tool (indeed, social capital, or social networks, is an underlying theme of this chapter and those that follow). The pressures of the uncertainties of life in Egypt, and the community's overall lack of protection, inevitably affect individuals in different ways, pushing some to ever-greater efforts to assimilate, others to withdraw. These differing responses, partly generational, are dealt with in the last section on the impact of life in the *ghurba*, a place of exile.

Settlement Patterns

Broadly speaking, with regard to the two main "waves" of Palestinian influx into Egypt, those arriving in 1948 came independently, mainly as individuals or in small groups, while many of those arriving in 1967 had been deported en masse by the IDF from the newly conquered Gaza Strip and already had some connection with the Egyptian government, either as fighters or as employees of the Gaza administration. These differences strongly affected how and where they settled.[1]

Self-Settlement in 1948

By 1949, the Egyptian government had already closed down the emergency camps established in 'Abbasiyyah in Cairo and Azarita near Port Said, dismantled the last camp at Qantara Sharq, and transferred its residents to newly created camps in the Gaza Strip. From then on, except for the *temporary* camp of Mudiriyyat al-Tahrir set up in 1967 to process the incoming refugees from Gaza, no Palestinian refugee camps remained on Egyptian soil.

The absence of refugee camps profoundly shaped the Palestinian community in Egypt. Traditionally, refugee camps have permitted people to group together and relate to each other based on their common experience of dispossession and exile. Camps or exclusively Palestinian neighborhoods make it possible for refugees in the host country to replicate the settlement patterns of their home village and clan. In the Baqa'a refugee camp in Jordan, for example, sections or neighborhoods have been named after the parts of Palestine where residents lived before the exodus, such as *Hayy* Nablus (the district of Nablus) or *Hayy* Hebron.[2] In some cases, individuals coming to the host country were able to locate family members simply by looking for sections of the camps where others from their village were known to be concentrated.

In Egypt, where areas of dense Palestinian concentration are extremely rare, reconstruction of this kind was the exception and occurred exclusively in rural areas. The village of Jazirat Abu Fadil, 4 kilometers from Abu Kabir in the Sharqiyyah Governorate, is a good example. There, the research team found a marginalized, largely agricultural village of some 150 Palestinian families from Beersheba living much as they had lived in Palestine, with little infrastructure and without electricity, telephone, or water services. The village *'umdah* (the Egyptian term for *mukhtar*, or

village head) was the son of the previous *mukhtar* in Beersheba
and had been nominated by the villagers to take over when his
father died. Seen very much as the father of the community,
the *'umdah* regulates internal matters, represents the village in
government meetings to lobby for services for the village, and
reports any problems to the Palestinian Labor Union,[3] which has
a presence in many such rural areas and which coordinates with
the government to make sure things run smoothly.[4] A number of
villages around al-'Arish in northeastern Sinai, also populated by
refugees from Beersheba, likewise have replicated social patterns
from Palestine, with traditional *mukhtars* retaining their positions
and serving as mediators with the Egyptian authorities. In the
case of these villages, it is important to mention that the refugees
arrived together and often belonged to extended families or clans,
as in the following testimony from Qanayyat, a small town in the
Sharqiyyah Governorate.

> All of the Palestinians who live here are from one family—
> the al-Nawasrah. Some are from the Abu Nusayr family
> or descend from the Husayniyyah family. They came from
> Beersheba in the aftermath of the 1948 war. They first lived in
> mud houses and then built homes in *Hayy* al-Arab. Today we
> have more than 20 families with at least eight members each.
> (7/40, Qanayyat, 15 July 2002)

In some cases, the choice of where to settle was influenced by
Egyptian land ownership laws, such as Law 874 of 1949, which
stipulated that agricultural land without established owners
belonged to the state but could be used with state permission. It
was under this law that some of the refugees entering in 1948 were
able to settle:

> This land is for the government. When the al-Nawasrah first
> arrived from Bir al-Sab' (Beersheba), they stayed on this land
> in Qanayyat and they divided the land among themselves
> and each paid £E 25 yearly as rent to the government. (7/41,
> Qanayyat, 15 July 2002)

The refugees' social networks in Palestine, their socioeconomic
and geographical background, and the nature and direction of their
flight all influenced decisions about where and how they settled.
As indicated above, proximity to Palestine as well as the landscape
itself played an obvious role in many settlement decisions: Some

of our interviewees expressly said they had wanted to find areas that ressembled the land they had been forced to leave. Al-'Arish, the closest region to Palestine, is a good example of the proximity factor: It has been estimated that at least 15 percent of Egypt's Palestinian community is concentrated there.[5]

Others settled near the temporary camps where they first took refuge:

> We chose to remain in 'Abbasiyyah, not far from the camp where we first stayed near al-Muhammadi mosque in an empty space. The Palestinian men went to talk to the *shaykh al-hara* [the representative of the families in that area] to get permission to settle on the land near the mosque and the cemetery. Men started collecting bricks from roads and built the *ishash* (simple houses made of hay) in which we lived. Ever since then we were called 'Arab a-Muhammadi.' (Um Ahmad, PP1, Madinat al-Salam, Cairo, 17 January 2002)[6]

Not surprisingly, people tended to go to areas where other Palestinians had already settled or where they had contacts. A large number of Palestinians settled in the Sharqiyyah Governorate, where many reported having a grandparent of Egyptian origin. One of our interviewees spoke of longstanding pre-1948 contacts with Egyptians from Sharqiyyah:

> We are originally from Isdud. My uncle was the *mukhtar* there. The Egyptian Free Officers used to stay at his house whenever they were in Isdud.[7] After the war, my family went to Sharqiyyah. Before the war, many of the Egyptians from Sharqiyyah were working in Palestinian cities, so Palestinians had built their contacts with Egyptians while they were there. (Husayniyyah, 24 July 2002)

Decisions about settlement were often based on social and professional ties from the homeland:

> My father left in 1948. He went from Majdal to Gaza and then on to Abu Kabir. He chose this region because he knew many people through his business relations there. (7/28, Abu Kabir, 13 July 2002)

Many Palestinians from Majdal now live in Faqus, where the predominant profession is that of blacksmith:

> We left Yibna for Majdal when the war started. We went to Khan
> Yunis and to Faqus, where we knew there were Palestinians,
> particularly blacksmiths from Palestine. In addition, my
> brother was married in 1944 to a Palestinian woman who had
> lived in Faqus since 1936. (7/36, Faqus, 14 July 2002)

Palestinians who arrived as individuals mainly settled in larger
Egyptian cities. There, too, they tended to congregate whenever
possible in the same neighborhoods, though urban living and the
inevitability of extensive mixing made it impossible to recreate the
life patterns that were sometimes possible in the countryside. The
same held true for the Palestinians, mainly from Gaza, who entered
the country as "socioeconomic" migrants for work or study during
the 1950s and 1960s.

Government Assistance in 1967

The situation for those entering Egypt from Gaza in 1967 was
quite different from that faced by the refugees in 1948, and was
affected both by their mode of arrival and the composition of the
group. The fact that large numbers were deported, brought by the
IDF in trucks and buses and dumped at the Egyptian border, of
necessity involved the Egyptian military. Moreover, large numbers
of those who entered were already employed by or on the payroll
of the Egyptian government, primarily as military personnel (e.g.,
members of the 'Ayn Jalut Brigade or the Mustafa Hafiz fedayeen),
as policemen, or as employees of the AOGG.

Consequently, unlike the 1948 refugees, many of the 1967
entrants received some government assistance in settling and
in other ways as well. Employees of the AOGG who could not
be absorbed into the scaled-down Gaza administration that was
reconstituted in Cairo were provided with jobs elsewhere (but
paid by the AOGG).[8] As mentioned in chapter 1, many of the
1967 arrivals were hired for government civilian jobs during the
screening process at the Mudiriyyat al-Tahrir temporary camp.
The 3,000–4,000 PLA fighters who were kept as a "reserve" and
not deployed on active duty under Egyptian command at the Bitter
Lakes on the Suez Canal[140] were helped to find housing with their
families near military barracks. In Cairo, many settled in Wailey
in the Kubri al-Quba area, where a military base was sited; others
settled near bases in the 'Ayn Shams or Dar al-Salam areas.

The same held true for those who had been with the Mustafa
Hafiz forces. One of the young men who had been taken "hostage"

by the Israelis in the IDF sweeps of the Gaza Strip in 1967, for example, recounts the following:

> Because I had been shot in the leg, I did not pass the test [for the Egyptian army]. I joined my father [who had been with the Mustafa Hafiz 141 fighters] later in a flat in Wailey, where many of the people in the Mustafa Hafiz forces were living. (P9, Wailey, 24 June 2002)

Though there is no longer a base at Wailey and the barracks are long gone, to this day the area—along with 'Ayn Shams or Dar al-Salam—continues to be associated with the presence of large numbers of former PLA or Mustafa Hafiz personnel.

As we saw in chapter 1, some of the 1967 "hostages" were inducted into the Egyptian army and dispatched to various military bases outside Cairo. Their families, however, generally settled in the above-mentioned neighborhoods of Cairo, and that is where the soldiers returned when on leave.

> My father was expelled along with many other people from Khan Yunis. He was taken with other young men to Qantara to join the Egyptian army. The families of the newly recruited soldiers lived in 'Ayn Shams. (P11, 'Ayn Shams, 28 May 2002)

The civilians who entered Egypt individually in 1967—and who were not family members of the military men, employees of the Egyptian administration in Gaza, or given employment in other government departments—had to self-settle like the earlier refugee waves, generally in towns and cities. A number of these, however, were businesspeople, sometimes with connections to the regime, and relatively well-off.

Coping Strategies and Mechanisms

Adapting to a new environment inevitably poses great difficulties for an uprooted and dislocated refugee community, but the Palestinians in Egypt face unique constraints. In addition to the legal and attitudinal obstacles described in the previous chapter, they lack many of the assets that have helped Palestinian refugees in other host countries. This point is brought home indirectly by a 1994 study by the Norwegian research institute

Fafo entitled *Finding Ways: Palestinian Coping Strategies in Changing Environments*, which focuses on Palestinian refugee families living mainly in camps in the West Bank, Jordan, and Lebanon.[10] While some of its key findings resonate with ours—for example, the crucial role of social networks in determining where Palestinian refugees settled and in constructing the community— the Fafo study takes for granted conditions that not only make survival per se far easier but also facilitate the development and effectiveness of the social networks essential to coping in a new environment. These conditions include dense concentrations of Palestinians (both in camps and in almost exclusively Palestinian neighborhoods), significant numbers overall, the unfettered ability to form social clubs or associations, and the safety net provided by UNRWA. Before going into the livelihood strategies deployed by the Palestinians in Egypt, it is useful to address briefly some of the characteristics that set this community apart from their compatriots in the neighboring host countries and that affected their ability to adapt economically, socially, and culturally.

Special Characteristics of the Palestinian Community in Egypt

Perhaps the most important characteristics of the Palestinian community in Egypt are its extremely scattered nature and its minuscule size relative to Egypt's huge population. Egypt is a large country geographically as well, and Palestinians are dispersed throughout the northern governorates. Almost invariably they live in mixed communities or neighborhoods. Most Palestinians have little idea where their compatriots beyond their immediate circles are located; even PLO bodies have only approximate notions of Palestinian population distribution. The impact of such conditions on the formation of social networks is obvious.

The absence of refugee camps affects more than just settlement patterns. Refugee camps constitute a focal point for a displaced community, or what amounts to a "home base." In host states such as Jordan, Syria, and Lebanon, the camps constitute what have been called "cultural and national islands,"[11] a kind of focus of identity even for Palestinians who are well integrated into the host society. By grouping Palestinians in a relatively small area, camps ensure an umbrella for the refugee community and are an important factor in strengthening the cement that binds the community and the social networks. They also provide a measure of protection, however limited.

In the Palestinian context, the absence of camps means the absence of UNRWA, established in 1949 to provide immediate relief for the refugees pouring into the areas surrounding the newly created State of Israel. UNRWA fulfills many functions, but most importantly it provides a safety net. In the host countries where it operates, it continues to this day to provide basic foodstuffs, education in its schools, health care in its clinics, and a variety of social and welfare services to all registered refugees who need them, whether or not they reside in camps.[12]

Such services are not readily available to Palestinians in Egypt. The Egyptian government's aid efforts through the Higher Committee of Palestinian Immigrant Affairs were limited after the first years, and were restricted to those who possessed not-always-easy-to-obtain refugee cards.[13] The assistance provided by the PLO and its affiliated bodies has shrunk considerably over the years, especially since the financial crisis that followed the 1990–91 Gulf war and the shift in the PLO's focus to state-building after Oslo.[14] Moreover, as we discovered in our field research, many Palestinians who live outside Cairo were not even aware of the PLO unions and the services they offer.[15]

In a country where restrictions on Palestinian employment are severe and where Palestinian children no longer have free access to public education, the absence of such services can have dire consequences. A particularly dramatic example, which illustrates the lengths to which some Palestinians will go to obtain services taken for granted elsewhere, was recounted in *al-Ahram Hebdo* (22 October 1997):

> Seraj, a father of four children, two of whom attend private schools, receives a salary of £E 300 per month. He sold one of his kidneys to pay his children's school fees.

Unusual as this case may be, there is no doubt that lack of basic services combined with tight restrictions on the right to work have greatly increased the vulnerability of the community in an environment that was often not simply neutral but actively hostile. Against such a background, the role of social networks and social capital becomes all the more vital.

Social Networks and the Construction of Community

Central to all strategies of adaptation and survival is "social capital," the ability to secure resources through membership in social networks or larger social structures. Originally developed as a concept in economics to identify the social resources which, like physical capital and human capital, facilitate the achievement of goals,[16] social capital is a useful way of looking at how networks of mutual support, reciprocity, trust, and obligation can improve an individual's situation and wellbeing.[17] In contrast to human capital, which relates to skills and knowledge, social capital is embodied in relations among persons as they interact in families, workplaces, neighborhoods, local associations, and a range of informal and formal meeting places. Quite simply, it is the "the glue that binds."[18] The resulting networks provide support, fulfill immediate subsistence needs, and allow for medium and long-term investments to guard against vulnerability. The embedded nature of social institutions and kinship is critical for improving the individual's welfare and for providing a coping mechanism in exile.[19]

Despite daunting political and social constraints, the Palestinians in Egypt are managing to get by. At the heart of their coping strategies is social capital, and more specifically what Ben-Porath has called the "F-connections"—families, friends, and firms (or business relations).[20] In the case of the Palestinians in Egypt, these essential connections are underpinned by an additional form of "social capital": good relations with the host community. This is always important to refugee communities in exile, but it is particularly vital for Palestinians in Egypt for the reasons discussed above. Indeed, this form of social capital is so intertwined with the other forms of social capital—the networks made up of family, friends, and business acquaintances—that it is impossible to treat it separately. Paradoxically, while the attitudes of the Egyptian population in general have been notably volatile with regard to the Palestinians, perhaps nowhere in the Arab world has the degree of interaction and intermingling been as high as in Egypt, and Palestinians there probably rely on these relations more than anywhere else.

The Family

In all societies, the family represents the nucleus community, the basic unit of social organization and the primary source of shelter and protection against the uncertainties of the world. This is even more so in situations of exile: The family is central to the Palestinian community in the diaspora, and family support is a principal means of survival. In the homeland, the family provides security for its members and functions on economic, social, cultural, and political levels. In exile, it helps its members to adapt to new social and economic conditions.

The family plays an important role in taking on the burdens of social institutions destroyed through displacement, becoming a focal point for a support network of other Palestinian families and Egyptian friends and acquaintances mobilized to address daily livelihood concerns. Within the family and kinship network, helping and supporting other members to attain their objectives is ultimately seen as increasing the opportunities of and benefiting the family as a whole.

Many of our interviewees mentioned in passing the help provided not only by immediate family members but more distant relatives in such matters as obtaining residence permits, finding employment, underwriting travel for work abroad, investing in education, and so on. The following examples are typical:

> My uncle wanted to help my father pay university fees. He brought me to Gaza to study at al-Azhar University and he took care of all my expenses. (7/37, Faqus, 14 July 2002)

> When my uncles found out that I was unable to find work here in Egypt, they tried to help me find work in Gaza. They sent me a visitor's permit, and I worked with them in construction a few years back. (8/13, Shubra al-Khayma, 11 June 2002)

It goes without saying that the basis of family continuity and renewal is marriage. In Palestine, the typical marriage was traditionally between cousins (especially first cousins), a reflection of the importance of clan. The high rate of such marriages in Palestine undoubtedly contributed to the reproduction of particular Palestinian communities as distinct and bounded units, whether villages, refugee camps, or urban neighborhoods.[21]

Inevitably, however, traditional family patterns have become more extended and heterogeneous in exile, with marriages to individuals outside the clan or family becoming common, even the norm. Such marriages increasingly have been with Egyptians, although many Palestinians continue to favor marriage with fellow Palestinians, if not with kinsmen. For these last, ties to the homeland and identity are maintained and nourished through such marriages. The following interviewees typify this attitude:

> I preferred having my two daughters marry Palestinians so that they would always feel part of one family. (7/ 35, Faqus, 14 July 2002)

> Palestinian women are more understanding of the conditions of Palestinian men here. They have more respect and appreciation for the head of the family, plus they understand our traditions better. (7/31, Bilbays, 11 July 2002)

Among our interviewees who attached great importance to marriage within the community, several saw Palestinian weddings as a way of introducing their children to old village networks and where potential spouses could be assessed for their children of marriageable age. Some tried to replicate the culture back home at these events:

> My children's weddings were held the Palestinian way, with five to seven days of *taalile* (festivities for the bridegroom) before the wedding night. We usually do it in clubs and we bring Palestinian singers and dabkah dancers. (P17, 'Ayn Shams, 8 June 2002)

Many interviewees, however, related how difficult it was to maintain traditional Palestinian marriage patterns along family or clan lines. For these individuals, what counts is "actual social ties, obligations, attachments, and loyalties, and the networks built up out of these."[22] Exposure over time to Egyptian culture has made many Palestinians more open to "mixed" marriages; indeed, as has been mentioned, there is a longstanding tradition of intermarriage between Egyptians and Palestinians that predates the 1948 events. Many of our interviewees casually referred to Egyptian grandparents in passing, while for others a grandparent's marriage to an Egyptian formed part of their story:

> My grandfather used to buy armaments from Egypt and sell them in Palestine. During one of his visits to Egypt, he married my grandmother, who is Egyptian from Dyarb Nijim. As the situation deteriorated [in Palestine], he was unable to return with his goods [and settled in her village]. (7/38, Dyarb Nijim, July 2002)

Not surprisingly, intermarriage has vastly increased in the last decades. No data exist on the extent to which it is practiced, but anecdotal evidence and the findings of our study suggest that it is extremely widespread:

> We are all married to Egyptians. My father's marriage to an Egyptian helped him acquire his tax card for the television repair workshop that we have and for a work permit. It also helped us [the children] in our school and university education since we had reduced fees. My two sisters, after two years of marriage to Egyptians, have been granted nationality. I prefer marriage with an Egyptian since it facilitates the processing of paperwork during our residence here and creates one big integrated family within Egyptian society. (7/45, Minya al-Qamah, 11 July 2002)

> If a Palestinian woman has a choice, she would not marry a Palestinian man, in order to avoid administrative problems [for her future children]. (7/37, Faqus, 14 July 2002)

These interviews suggest the very practical benefits for Palestinians of having an Egyptian spouse, particularly an Egyptian husband who has traditionally had the legal right to pass his nationality on to his children automatically. Even though Egyptian women married to foreigners did not have this right prior to the amendment of the Nationality Law in 2004, such marriages did confer the right of residency on the spouse and their children—itself an important benefit. Thus, bluntly speaking, marriage with members of the host community has been a strategy for upward mobility and enhancing one's legal rights. Given the enormous difficulties of being stateless in Egypt, the passage of the new Nationality Law, which appears to allow Egyptian women married to Palestinians to pass Egyptian citizenship on to their children born *after* 2004, the attractiveness of this option, at least for some, can only increase.

Friends and Business Relations

Much like the case of intermarriage, Palestinian attitudes toward extensive mixing with Egyptians have varied. For many in the first generation, the bitterness of exile heightened their sense of longing for the close social ties of Palestinian village life, and such feelings often colored their reactions to the "other."

> Relationships today are very different from those in the past. Today, each family is enclosed in their house. No one likes even to see good things happening for others. In the past, neighbors supported each other. The neighbors helped each other by lending money or lending anything needed, like onions or garlic. Today, none of this happens. My neighbor's daughter got married and did not even invite us. (P4, Dar al-Salam, 18 May 2002)

In our interviews, we found many of the older generation whose nostalgia for the homeland was reflected in their preference to remain within their own group.

> All my friends and contacts are Palestinians who migrated with me in 1967. We live in the same area; we work together and we support each other . . . we rarely have social contacts with Egyptians. (AP3, Alexandria, August 2002)

Such attitudes, however, are increasingly rare, particularly among the second and third generations. Indeed, many young Palestinians reported feeling more "Egyptian" than Palestinian and considered themselves part of Egyptian society. Those who were brought up in Egypt often said that they did not feel culturally different from Egyptians and did not feel the need to seek out other Palestinians.

> I do not know any Palestinians. All my friends are Egyptian. My dad knows some Palestinians who I do not know. We have no Palestinian relatives [here]. I only know my [Egyptian] relatives from my mother's side. (P15, Dar al-Salam, 2 June 2002)

Speaking the same language (dialectical differences aside) and sharing the same basic culture, traditions, and (for the most part) religion, it is not surprising that close relationships have developed between many Palestinians and Egyptians. In addition to marriage, these relations include long-time friendships and commercial partnerships. Their importance is reflected in the following quote:

> We are on very good terms with our Egyptian neighbors. They are better than our family, especially because we live in a densely populated area. We support each other during illness. We have similar traditions. We visit each other. We lend each other money whenever any one of us is in need. Last year we

helped our young neighbor with wedding expenses. I can ask my neighbors for money whenever I am in need. I have done that once. It is even better than asking family members who are abroad. I avoid asking them for any favors. I have some relatives in Saudi Arabia that I do not like to ask for help because they are arrogant. They would do the favor and feel that they own you by doing it. (P1, Giza, 10 May 2002)

The genuineness of the personal affinities is not in doubt, but in a situation of stringent regulations and legal constraints—not to mention an environment that can quickly turn hostile under the impact of political developments—the utility of these relations is inestimable. The benefits run the full range, from an anonymous official's spontaneous overlooking of expired permits (the fact that unknown but large numbers of Palestinians have been living illegally in Egypt for years is itself an indication of such complicities) to conscious acts of support and solidarity. These last, in turn, range from small neighborly favors to acting as employment sponsor, putting oneself on the line, or offering gratuitous financial help. Many of the interviews throughout this study illustrate the range; a few examples suffice:

When my brother left for Austria, he had overstayed his re-entry visa. With the contacts that we have in the security services, we were able to sort out the re-entry and renewed his residency to enable him to come back to Egypt. (7/28, Abu Kabir, 13 July 2002)

I repair the cars of two Egyptian clients. They both work at the Ministry of Foreign Affairs. We always talked about the situation in Palestine and they always showed sympathy. We became good friends. Once I had a debt and I was asked to pay it, and I sought the help of one of these friends. He paid the debt and offered to bring me to Saudi Arabia, as he was supposed to be posted in the Egyptian embassy there. (8/13, Shubra al-Khayma, 11 June 2002)

Business relationships and partnerships are also common and a major source of "social capital" as a way of getting around Egyptian regulations limiting ownership rights for Palestinians.

Added to my father's work at the railway station, he used to work with Egyptian friends by investing in land or shops and then selling the property when prices went up . . . Today, we have made use of the back garden of our house, which is owned by the railway station, to build four shops. We invested in this in partnership with our Egyptian brother-in-law. The business is promising. We had to count on the family's good contacts with Security to sort out the problem with the railway station when they wanted to sue us because we used the back garden. We have very strong relations with the Egyptians on the social and the professional levels. (7/21, Salhiyyah, 8 July 2002)

Our field research has demonstrated the extent to which many Palestinians in Egypt have succeeded, through good luck, hard work, and the skillful use of social capital, to survive and in some cases to thrive. The relatively high integration attested to by some of our interviewees, however, is only part of the picture. The good relations—in some cases true friendships—that bind some Palestinians and Egyptians should not obscure the reality of the precariousness of Palestinian lives in Egypt. Thus, in spite of the fellowship and positive experiences enjoyed by some, for many and perhaps most Palestinians Egypt remains, though in varying degrees, essentially the *ghurba,* a place where in the last analysis they are *ghuraba* (strangers), where they are made to feel like strangers.

Fear and Mistrust in the *Ghurba*

The most essential ingredient—indeed the indispensable basis—of any social network is trust. While trust undoubtedly characterizes many Palestinian personal relationships in Egypt, the overall atmosphere in the country is frequently seen by Palestinians as one of mistrust, extreme uncertainty, and even fear. This perception profoundly affects the construction of the community, rendering volatile any social integration and community participation through civic and political involvement and empowerment. Tolerance of social diversity in the host state has varied over the years, the lack thereof often shaped by state policies toward the Palestinian "foreigners" and fueled by media campaigns. Many of our field interviews illustrated the distorting effect on community of such imposed external factors and the resulting insecurities.

Egypt has been living under emergency law intermittently since 1958 and continuously since 1981, when Sadat was assassinated.[23] Emergency Law 162 of 1958 gives the authorities extensive powers to suspend basic liberties, including banning demonstrations and public meetings, arresting and detaining suspects without trial for prolonged periods, and turning to state security courts whose procedures fall far short of international standards. It is in accordance with the Emergency Law that the activities of groups such as the Palestinians are strictly regulated, arrest sweeps are made, and surveillance is sanctioned.

Without doubt, the vigor of the law's application has varied considerably over the years, increasing in times of tension. As discussed in chapter 2, the singling out of Palestinians for surveillance intensified with the deterioration of PLO-Egyptian government relations, especially after Sadat's 1977 Jerusalem visit, and reached new heights with the al-Siba'i assassination in February 1978. Meanwhile, the Egyptian public, traditionally known for its good humor and tolerance, was heavily influenced at the time by media reports projecting negative images of Palestinians. As a weak, dispersed minority, the Palestinians had always been aware of their vulnerability, but the relative abruptness of their change of status in 1978 drove home as never before the precariousness of their situation. In the perception of many Palestinians, life in Egypt since that time has been characterized a constant and unbroken sense of insecurity. Thus, a Palestinian shopkeeper, recounting how his shop window had been shattered by Egyptian assailants in the wake of the al-Siba'i assassination, continued without pause to describe the anti-Palestinian hostility during the Gulf war more than ten years later, as if no time had elapsed between the two events:

> These were hard moments for us [after al-Siba'i was killed], when our treatment by Egyptians and the Egyptian administration changed. During the Gulf war, Egyptians were happy that Iraq was under attack by Egyptian and American forces. We, Palestinians, were afraid. We used to sit in our closed shops to watch news and avoid harassment from the Egyptians. (P9, Wailey, 24 June 2002)

In such a volatile atmosphere, Palestinians often see themselves as being at the mercy of events beyond their control, subject to harassment and security searches even following events in which there had been no Palestinian involvement.

> The attack against the Israeli tourist bus in Isma'iliyyah in 1989 or 1990[24] affected us . . . As Palestinians, our houses were searched frequently. (7/37, Faqus, 14 July 2002)

In times of uncertainty, the ties within a community take on special importance. For many Palestinians in other host countries, social clubs, sometimes organized around towns or regions of origin, reinforce bonds of solidarity and identity and help reduce the sting of exile by creating a sense of belonging and fellowship. In Jordan, for example, numerous societies organized along these lines have sprung up among Palestinians since the 1970s. Largely apolitical, these groups arrange cultural meetings, picnics, and weddings, help their poorer members, and mediate disputes among members.[25] Such clubs or associations would be particularly welcome in a dispersed refugee community in a country like Egypt, where they would help reduce the effects of scatteredness, strengthen a sense of solidarity and belonging, and help build confidence and a sense of security in difficult times. In Egypt, however, such social or cultural clubs are banned, and under the Emergency Law any meeting of more than five persons must receive prior security clearance. Even the unions connected to the PLO, which were created with the express approval of the state, are required to obtain permits whenever they host events. When such events are held, state security personnel are posted at the door and often can be seen taking notes throughout the gathering.

Attempts even to form mixed Palestinian-Egyptian clubs have been discouraged if not prevented:

> I tried to create a joint Egyptian-Palestinian social club. I went to the Ministry of Social Affairs and everything began falling apart from then on. I was asked to get security clearance and to go through many procedures and paperwork. I finally had to give up on it. (7/37, Faqus, 14 July 2002)

We also heard reports of loss of membership in Egyptian social clubs or of being barred from mixed sporting activities:

> We were members of the Nasser Club, where we used to pay £E 15–20 per family to renew our membership. During the

rule of Sadat, a decision was made to prevent Palestinians from joining clubs. So we lost our membership. My son played with the junior football players at al-Ahli club. Later, he was transferred to the Zamalek club. Then he was stopped altogether from playing with these clubs because he is Palestinian. (P17, 'Ayn Shams, 8 June 2002)

Though arrest sweeps have not been common in recent years, close surveillance of minorities, particularly Palestinians, continues. Some interviewees said Palestinian "agents" are used to report any actions or statements seen to run counter to the status quo to the Egyptian security forces. In an environment where suspicion reigns, it is not surprising that Palestinians tend to be cautious not only when dealing with Egyptians but also with fellow Palestinians. These sentiments were reflected by a number of our interviewees, such as the following:

It is better for me not to know Palestinians because this can cause trouble. We are not living in our homeland, and every move we make should be calculated. One should avoid people who may cause suspicion on the part of the government. (P2, Port Said, 17 May 2002)

Thus, despite common historical experiences and a shared identity, we found a number of Palestinian families in both rural and urban areas who reported keeping to themselves.

Many Palestinians live near us. We know that we are Palestinians, but we never visit each other. There is nothing special between us, just like our relationship with our Egyptian neighbors. Our Palestinian identity is not a reason for us to interact. (P11, 'Ayn Shams, 28 May 2002)

Similarly, a woman whose husband's family was brought from Gaza by the Red Cross after 1967 to join her father-in-law, who had entered Egypt separately, had this to say:

Ever since they settled, [my husband's family] did not contact any of those who came with them. We have limited contacts with Palestinian and Egyptian neighbors. My husband keeps telling me, 'Let us care about our own business' (*khalina bi halna*). (8/3, Abu Za'bal, 30 June 2002)

In a security-oriented state, it is perhaps not surprising if people become suspicious of one another and limit social interaction and responsibilities toward the community. Still, the response of such extreme withdrawal was relatively rare in our interviews—almost as rare as its polar opposite: Palestinians who, despite the uncertainties and anxieties inevitable in such an environment, have managed to create their own "imagined" Palestinian communities in the *ghurba*. Shibin al-Qanatir in the Qalyubiyyah Governorate, for example, is a close rural community whose members are from the same region of Palestine and mostly in the same profession. There, not only does everyone know each other, but, as one member of the community told us, "Though we are not all relatives, we all call each other cousin!" (8/12, Shibin al-Qanatir, 3 July 2002).

The experience of living in the *ghurba* elicits many responses. In looking at the livelihood strategies deployed by Palestinians in Egypt, we found a wide range of attitudes, from a high degree of assimilation to total isolation and withdrawal into the family. But the largest number of those we interviewed fell between these two poles, showing a sense of solidarity and a greater comfort level among fellow Palestinians, yet acceptance of and easy mixing with Egyptians in daily contexts. Without doubt, however, anxieties remain, ready to bubble up to the surface when a political crisis arises to remind Palestinians of how fast things can change in the *ghurba*.

Notes

1. As already mentioned, several thousand Palestinians entered Egypt from the Gaza Strip for socioeconomic reasons in the 1950s and 1960s, many in response to Nasser's efforts to alleviate the pressures in the Gaza Strip by encouraging qualified individuals to apply for public sector jobs. These would have settled through social or family networks.

2. Randa Farah, "Crossing Boundaries: Reconstruction of Palestinian Identities in Al-Baqa' Refugee Camp, Jordan," in *Palestine, Palestiniens, Territoire National, Espaces Communitaires* (Amman, Jordan: CERMOC, 1997).

3. The official name of the PLO-affiliated body is the General Union of Palestinian Workers (GUPW), but it was invariably referred to as the "Labor Union" in the many interviews where it was mentioned. The same holds true for the "Women's Union," actually the General Union of Palestinian Women (GUPWom). The popular designations will be used throughout this study. See chapter 6.

4. Field visit report, 14 July 2002.

5. According to the countrywide lists of Palestinians registered with the PLO Labor Union. Interview with Adel Attiyah, head of the Labor Union, 24 September 2001.

6. In 1984, the *ishash* were demolished and refugees were moved to Madinat al-Salam or 'Ayn Shams.

7. Isdud was on the Egyptian front line during the 1948 war, from May to mid-October, when the Egyptian forces were dislodged, and is frequently mentioned, for example, in the war memoir of Nasser, "Memoirs of the First Palestine War."

8. Brand, *Palestinians in the Arab World*, p. 59.

9. Sayigh, *Armed Struggle and the Search for State*, p. 170.

10. Signe Gilen et al., *Finding Ways: Palestinian Coping Strategies in Changing Environments* (Fafo, Oslo: Institute of Applied Social Science, 1994).

11. Gilen et al., *Finding Ways*.

12. As noted earlier, many of those entering Egypt in 1967 had been registered with UNWRA, but they lost their access to its services upon arrival.

13. In 1955, the Higher Committee designated the World Council of Churches to administer the assistance program, funded through the UN and later the U.S. Agency for International Development. Brand, *Palestinians in the Arab World*, p. 45.

14. See chapter 6.

15. Such lack of awareness is not accidental. Some union representatives reported that outreach using the media to announce activities for such groups is not allowed. Interview with Ali Jawhar, head of the Palestinian Charitable Association and the Palestinian Businessmen's Association, 22 October 2001.

16. James Coleman, *Foundations of Social Theory*, (Cambridge, MA: Harvard University Press, 1990), p. 304.

17. "Measuring Social Capital: Current Collections and Future Directions," 2000, Discussion Paper, November, Australian Bureau of Statistics, available at http://www.abs.gov.au/ 852563C30080E02A/0/6CD8B1F3F270566ACA25699F0015 A02A?Open.

18. Ibid.

19. Betty Morrow, "Identifying and Mapping Community Vulnerability," *Disasters* 23, no. 1 (1999), p. 7.

20. Ben-Porath in Coleman, *Foundations of Social Theory*, p. 304. The term was originally coined as referring factors influencing economic exchange, but it is equally applicable to the social exchanges of everyday living that drive/affect the broader context of survival in the host country.

21. Gilen et al., *Finding Ways*.

22. Ghabra, *Palestinians in Kuwait*.

23. The Emergency Law must be renewed every three years.

24. The February 1990 grenade attack on the tourist bus, in which eight Israelis were killed, was carried out by an Egyptian group to protest torture in Egyptian prisons.

25. Gilen et al., *Finding Ways*, chapter 4. The study mentions the existence of such associations both in Jordan and Lebanon.

Chapter 4

Residency and Employment

In a country like Egypt, beset by overpopulation and poverty, procuring a livelihood can be an intense struggle for the great majority of the population, whether Egyptian or Palestinian. What makes the Palestinian situation more difficult, as already noted, are the legal barriers to rights normally taken for granted: the right to secure residency, the right to enter and leave the country of residence at will, the right to work, to be educated, to own property. This chapter and the next discuss each of these areas and the regulations that govern them, highlighting in many cases the elaborate stratagems people use to circumvent the obstacles in order to survive. This chapter deals first with residence permits and travel documents and then with formal and informal employment.

Residence Permits and Travel Documents

Residency Categories and Renewals

Residence permits are the most important documents for living in Egypt: Without them, one must live virtually underground, in constant fear of being discovered and deported. Residence permits come in various categories and are issued by two separate bodies. For Palestinians who arrived in Egypt before 1967 (and their offspring and descendants), permits are issued by the Department of Immigration, Passports, and Nationality at the *Mugamma'*, the government complex on Tahrir Square in central Cairo where various government bureaucracies are located. For those who arrived during or after the 1967 war (mainly from Gaza) and their offspring and descendants, the permits are issued by the AOGG, the former Egyptian administration in Gaza relocated to Madinat Nasr in northeastern Cairo. The residence permits fall into five categories, according to the date of arrival of the head of household (or the original entrant on whom the residency depends): A, B, and C category permits, for pre-1967 arrivals, are issued at the *Mugamma'*; D and H category permits for post-1967 arrivals are issued by the AOGG. Residence permits are valid for variable durations, again depending on the arrival date. The residency renewal periods can be summarized as follows:

A: Arrival before 1948; renewable every five years, or ten years if proof of ten-year continuous residency in Egypt can be provided.
B: Arrival in 1948; renewable every five years.[1]
C: Arrival in 1956; renewable every three years.
D: Arrival in 1967; renewable every three years.
H: Arrival after 1967; renewable every three years (can vary according to the conditions of entry into Egypt).

Although residency requirements in Egypt have always been strict (see chapter 2), during the Nasser years their application was somewhat relaxed. Today, they are rigidly enforced: Residency is contingent upon providing a reason for remaining in Egypt. Possible reasons include education, licensed work, marriage to an Egyptian, or business partnership with an Egyptian. Bureaucratically, these various reasons take the form of a guarantor, which can be an institution (e.g., place of employment, school or university, the PLO Labor Union) or an individual (e.g., parent, spouse, employer, business partner). In all cases, an official document proving that the applicant lives in Egypt for one of these reasons, as well as the guarantor's relationship to the applicant, must be provided.

The payment of fees for renewing residency is also required. Given the widespread poverty in the Palestinian community, where many families are without regular income, this can be a major concern.

I usually run out of money when I need to renew the residencies for the six children and myself. I may need to borrow money or sell some of our belongings, such as a television or the double bed, which I had to do twice in recent years. (7/30, Bilbays, July 2002)

The renewal of the residencies cost us £E 500 for seven persons—my husband and my six children. I sometimes run out of money and borrow from my family to help pay the fees. (P22, Faysal, 15 June 2002)

Late payment can result in fines:

> I was once late in renewing permits for me and the children because I did not have enough money. They wanted to fine me £E 315. I submitted an appeal and was exempted from the fine. They renewed the residencies as usual. (7/30, Bilbays, July 2002)

In some cases where the residency has not been renewed for some years for various reasons, only payment of a substantial fine averts deportation:

> We had not renewed our residence permits for more than 14 years. Our father, who used to travel with the PLO army, looked after these issues. It was only when he was put in prison that we realized that we needed to renew them and we had to pay a penalty of £E 2,000. (7/25, Abu Hammad, 10 July 2002)

In both rural and urban areas, it is the women of the household who are frequently put in charge of handling bureaucratic and administrative matters such as renewing residence and travel documents or processing the children's paperwork for school. This is especially true in cases where Palestinian men have married Egyptian women:

> My wife usually takes care of renewing residence permits for me and the children, especially because we all depend on her as a guarantor for our stay. In addition, people in the administration are more sympathetic to her than they would be to me, a Palestinian. We usually pay £E 158 to renew each residency—every three years for me and every five years for my children, since their mother is Egyptian. I rely on the help of my brothers in Saudi Arabia and in Libya to pay such expenses. (P10, 'Ayn Shams, 23 May 2002)

> I sometimes rush around for days to finish paperwork to renew my children's and husband's residence permits. I am in charge of all the paperwork for travel documents and schools. All have three-year residence permits. The children get their residence permits based on the fact that I am Egyptian. (P22, Faysal, 15 June 2002)

One of the most common justifications for obtaining residency, besides marriage to an Egyptian, is proof of employment, generally in the form of a letter from the employer:

> I renew my residence each year based on my permit to work
> as an electrician using the licence of my workplace. (8/13,
> Shubra al-Khayma, 11 June 2002)

Employees of the AOGG, which is part of the Egyptian government, or of the PLO have the fewest problems with residence permits, because they are considered public sector employees. Even when they are retired, they can renew their residencies on the basis of proof of their pensions. This is reflected in a number of interviews.

The majority of Palestinians in Egypt, however, work in the informal sector, without work permits or stable jobs, and thus face the greatest obstacles in obtaining or renewing their residencies. Many have found creative ways of overcoming the problem. Some business owners are willing to provide the needed documentation as a favor:

> My husband gets his [residence permit] on the basis of a letter
> from a factory claiming that he works there. Although he does
> not work in the factory, the owner was kind enough to give
> him such a letter on yearly basis. (P22, Faysal, 15 June 2002)

Among the easiest work permits to obtain are taxi drivers' licenses, which can be used to renew residence permits. Our interviews revealed that numerous small shopkeepers or trades-men get their residence permits on this basis so as to avoid bureaucratic problems arising from having a small business or performing "unlicensed work." Imad, for example, is a licensed electrician and runs a repair shop out of his house, making relatively good money (almost £E 300 a month), but gets his residency permit thanks to a taxi license (P20, Dar al-Salam, 11 June 2002). Another owner of a workshop elaborates on this strategy:

> Getting a work permit as a taxi driver is much easier than
> getting it as an owner of an electrical repair workshop. That
> would require providing proof of commercial registration,
> insurance, and licences for the shop. All this requires money
> and permits that I can't provide. If an inspector comes to the
> workshop, I would need to give him five to ten pounds so that

he wouldn't report that the workshop is not registered. (8/11, Shubra al-Khayma, 12 June 2002)

Another relatively easy route to a residency permit is through an agricultural labor licence, which can be obtained with a letter from the PLO-affiliated Labor Union.

An agricultural labor permit usually costs one or two pounds. For a permit as a shop owner, I may need to pay £E 16 a month as insurance. In the past, I was able to get an agricultural labor permit easily, but now it is not so easy. The administration at the *Mugamma'* may ask to look at my hands and see that I don't have the hands of a farmer. (7/37, Faqus, 14 July 2002)

Residency permits for children are renewed automatically with those of their parents. However, children can be deported at age 18 if they are not still in school or at age 21 if they have not found licensed work upon completion of their university education. (Remaining in school itself represents a considerable financial burden, because Palestinians can no longer attend public schools for free and university fees are prohibitive for many if not most.[2]) Many in this position are forced to live illegally until they can provide the authorities with an official reason for their stay:

My son became an illegal resident when he turned 21. The officer at the *Mugamma'* told me that he would soon be deported. My son had never gone to school because he had a fever when he was a baby that affected his brain. (P24, Wailey, 24 June 2002)

If no other justification for remaining in the country can be provided, as a last resort a bank statement showing a balance of at least £E 20,000 *may* be accepted by the *Mugamma'*:

My second daughter is married to a Gazan who runs a business for a Saudi. He has neither a residence permit nor a work permit. He put £E 20,000 in the bank to get a residence permit but it has not yet been issued. (P22, Faysal, 15 June 2002)

Parents with some means often resort to this route in order to secure residence for unemployed children when they pass the legal age limit:

> We had to deposit £E 20,000 to get a residence permit for
> my eldest son when he turned 21. Now we have to deposit
> another £E 20,000 for our younger son. (AP2, Hilmiyyat al-
> Zaytun, 5 August 2002)

For many young Palestinian men and women, marriage to an
Egyptian is a means of legalizing their stay in Egypt. The legal
benefits of such marriages until recently were not equal, however.
As already mentioned, a Palestinian man marrying an Egyptian
woman traditionally gained a guarantee of residency only, but
not eligibility for citizenship for himself and their children. A
Palestinian woman marrying an Egyptian man, by contrast, could
look forward to receiving these benefits from her husband. The
impact of this legal gender divide on marriage decisions in the past
is evident in the following interview:

> My son will soon turn 21. His father and I are thinking of
> getting him married soon. We have asked for the hand of
> my niece, an Egyptian, but her parents refused because my
> son is Palestinian. We have ensured the situation of our two
> daughters, who are both engaged to Egyptians. Eventually
> they will get Egyptian nationality. (8/3, Abu Za'bal, 30 June
> 2002)

Although, in keeping with an unwritten policy, the 2004 Nationality Law is not being implemented with regard to Palestinians
born of Egyptian mothers prior to 2004,[3] the significance of the
law with regard to Palestinian-Egyptian intermarriage in the future
cannot be overstated. The fact that the law is automatically applied
to children born after 2004 to mixed couples where the mother is
Egyptian removes an important barrier to such marriages. More
than once in the course of our interviews, we heard of Egyptian
parents opposing the prospect of their daughters marrying
Palestinians. Their opposition, we were told, was motivated by
their concern for the future of their grandchildren, who at the time
of our field research would have been subject to a life without
protection or rights.

The Perils of Egyptian Travel Documents

The "Egyptian Travel Document for Palestinian Refugees"
comes in two very distinct types: one for Palestinians residing
in Egypt, and another for Palestinians who never had this right

(this latter is for travel only). The first type is issued on the basis of a valid residence permit, and, like residence permits, comes in categories A, B, and C for pre-1967 arrivals and their descendants and categories D and H for post-1967 arrivals. These permits are issued, respectively, at the *Mugamma*' and by the AOGG, but in contrast to the residency permit, they are valid for an unvarying five years.

Regulations governing the travel documents are strict. To ensure re-entry into Egypt, the Egyptian travel document holder with a valid residency permit who is traveling or residing abroad must either return to Egypt every six months or provide the Egyptian authorities in advance with proof of employment or of current enrollment in an educational institution abroad. In such cases, a one-year return visa may be granted. No extension or renewal can be granted through Egyptian embassies abroad. Any delay beyond the stipulated deadline can result in denial of entry or deportation.

The second type of Egyptian travel document, valid for travel only and carrying no rights of residency in Egypt whatsoever, is held by tens of thousands of Palestinians from Gaza and their descendants. During the decades when Gaza was under Egyptian administration, these documents were issued upon request to any Gaza resident. These were the documents used by the many thousands of Gazans who migrated, with the encouragement of the Egyptians, to Gulf oil states and elsewhere for employment from the late 1950s onward.[4] After Israel occupied the Gaza Strip in 1967, Gazans abroad who did not attempt to return to their occupied homeland continued to use these travel documents, which were renewed by the Egyptian embassy in the countries where they were employed. An estimate of the number of such documents can be gleaned from a 1994 document issued by the Egyptian Department of Passports, Immigration, and Nationality detailing the number of Egyptian travel documents issued according to residency category: For category E, "arrivals after the June 1967 war," the number given is 236,307.[5] Needless to say, the overwhelming majority of travel document holders in this category were not residing in Egypt.

The Palestinian holders of this type of Egyptian travel document were tragically vulnerable to the winds of fate and politics. The most terrible example was their situation arising from the 1990–91 Gulf crisis, already alluded to, when thousands either left on their own or were expelled from the Gulf states following the allied victory over Iraq. Most of some 30,000 Palestinians stranded in Kuwait, accepted by no state, were Gazans with Egyptian travel documents.[6] As for those who somehow managed to get to the Cairo airport, they were summarily deported along with their fellow Palestinians whose Egyptian residence permits had expired. Gazans fortunate enough to have Israeli re-entry permits for the Strip, and who reached the Cairo airport, were issued 72-hour transit visas by the Egyptian authorities; transit between the airport and the Rafah border crossing to the Strip took place under a "strict and humiliating police escort" (the costs of which were borne by the transitees) to prevent them from staying illegally in Egypt.[7]

The Gulf war of 1990–91 was not the only politically motivated mass expulsion from which Palestinian holders of Egyptian travel documents suffered. A second such instance, though on a far smaller scale, took place in September 1995, when Libyan leader Muammar al-Qadhafi, making the point that Palestinians should return to Palestine, called upon Arab states to expel their Palestinian residents to the West Bank and Gaza Strip. He himself set the example by expelling more than 1,000 Palestinian holders of Egyptian travel documents to the no-man's land on the Egyptian-Libyan border. Some managed to reach Gaza, where the PA was already in place, but Egypt granted transit visas only to those with Israeli re-entry permits; most were denied entry into or passage through Egypt. It is not known how many were legally permitted to enter Egypt or how many managed to sneak in. What is known is that several hundred remained stranded at Sallum camp at the border until January 1997, when Qadhafi finally consented to allow them back into Libya; even then, it was not until 18 April that they were transported in four buses from the Sallum border point to Tobruk in Libya. Others were allowed to join their families in Egypt.[8] The following interviewee refers to this episode:

> My brother used to live in Libya. He was among those stranded at the border. For nine months he remained in the camp, but he managed to get smuggled back into Libya. He worked illegally as a teacher in a private school and his salary was given to him as an allowance [per hour worked] but not as a salary. Fearing prison, he then managed to find a network of people to smuggle him into Egypt. Today, he has a bakery registered in his wife's name and lives illegally in Egypt with no papers at all. (7/27, 10 July 2002)

The fate of victims of such large-scale political events receives some public attention thanks to press coverage and human rights reports, but the hundreds if not thousands of cases of Palestinian residents or former residents of Egypt with Egyptian travel documents who are denied re-entry for transgressing—by carelessness or by force of circumstance—the rules of the travel document, or even due to bureaucratic red tape or error, go undocumented. For the Palestinian who has overstayed his visa, denial of re-entry, detention at the border, imprisonment upon arrival, or deportation are common occurrences. Such situations figured in a number of our interviews and ranged from the matter of fact or humdrum to the Kafkaesque.

Several of our interviewees referred to children whom they hadn't seen for years:

> Two of my children have been denied re-entry to Egypt. I have not seen them since they left [seven years ago]. One is a lawyer in Libya and the other has a photocopy center there. Neither has a work contract in Libya. (7/36, Faqus, 14 July 2002)

In some cases, even when papers are in order, the uncertainty about whether or not re-entry will be permitted is enough to make an individual discontinue work abroad:

> I used to go to Libya when the borders were open and travel was easy. The problem is that I had to come back to Egypt every six months to keep my Egyptian residence permit. I was unable to apply for a return visa [valid for one year] because I never had official work contracts in Libya and was working in various places. But in 1995, when I saw what happened to my brother when he returned from Yemen, I decided to come back. He was detained at the airport for several days and then deported back to Yemen despite the fact that he had an Egyptian travel document and had regularly renewed his residence. (7/37, Faqus, 14 July 2002)

The following stories give some sense of the situations that can arise from the combination of the rigid regulations governing the travel documents, the desperate need for work, and the precariousness of statelessness. They also shed some light on the refugee condition and the network of family spread across the Palestinian diaspora:

When Basel finished his preparatory school, he went to work for a car dealer in Libya. Five years later, his sister, who is married to an Egyptian living in Sudan, invited him to Sudan. He went there to work. Later, his mother managed to get him a permit to come to Egypt for 15 days, as his residence permit for Egypt had expired. He arrived in Egypt, and after his [temporary visitor's] visa expired, he was imprisoned. His psychological situation was very bad when he arrived, and the prison only made it worse. While he was in prison, his family tried to get him a permit for Sudan or Gaza so that he would have a place to go when the authorities deported him upon his release. His cousin in Gaza finally managed to buy him a visitor's permit on the black market for $1,500, but by the time he got out of prison the intifada had broken out, and even though he had the visitor's permit the authorities refused to deport him there. Eventually, his sister in Sudan was able to invite him again so that's where they deported him. (P23, Giza, 18 June 2002)

While many accept their fate of yet another exile, some choose a different solution:

In 1994, I went to Saudi Arabia for two years to work as a painter. I overstayed my residence there and in the meantime I had lost my re-entry to Egypt. As a result of overstaying my [Saudi] visa, I was put in prison for 45 days in Saudi Arabia and was then asked to leave. My aunt, who lives in Libya, helped me. She invited me to Libya, where I stayed a year and a half, working as a painter. Later, my aunt was able to get me a permit to go to Palestine [after the PA was established]. So I went to Gaza via Egypt and stayed there [Gaza] for a year and a half. I then applied for a tourist visa to Egypt and I got one for two weeks. As it expired and I wanted to remain in Egypt, I found a member of parliament and asked him to raise my case with the minister of the interior. He offered me three choices: be deported; pay £E 15,000 and apply for a tourist visa; or remain in the country illegally. I chose the third option. (7/39, Dyarb Nijim, 15 July 2002)

Although it is impossible to estimate how many Palestinians are living in Egypt illegally, our interviews (which represent only a very partial sample) suggest that the number is considerable.

Detaining stateless Palestinians with only an Egyptian travel document at the border is a common occurrence. One example is Abu Saqer, born in Cairo in 1976, a holder of an Egyptian travel document who had been living in Moscow. When his Russian residence permit expired, Abu Saqer decided to go to Egypt to see his family and to reapply from there to return to Moscow. Upon arrival at Cairo airport in August 2001, he was denied entry and sent on a plane back to Moscow. In turn, the authorities in Moscow prevented him from entering Russia because of his expired residence permit. He was stranded at the Moscow airport for some fourteen months.[9] He was eventually granted asylum in Sweden.[10]

Article 3 of the Arab League Casablanca Protocol on the treatment of Palestinians residing in Arab countries states that "When their interests so require, Palestinians presently residing in the territory of [name of signatory state] shall have the right to leave the territory of this state and return to it." Although Egypt signed the protocol in 1965, its provisions concerning travel have not been honored since the late 1970s. In effect, Egyptian travel documents are essentially *laissez-passer*, which offer no protection.

> My son has a category H travel document. He is able to renew his residence with his Egyptian wife as guarantor. Last year, he was with his friends at a summer camp, and they were calling him "Pasha" [a colloquial term for a military officer]. A security officer overheard and asked to see my son's ID. As he did not have his travel document with him, he was charged with impersonating an officer and put in prison for 11 months. Meanwhile, I was responsible for his expenses in prison and for the expenses of his wife and little daughter. I used to take him £E 200 every month. (7/29, Abu Kabir, July 2002)

When arrested, Palestinians may be sentenced or deported, regardless of the grounds for arrest. In some cases, state security officials require the families of the detained individuals to apply for visas to countries likely to accept them to facilitate deportation procedures. Sometimes, as in the case of Basel cited above, the family takes the initiative on its own.

Employment

In the absence of reliable statistics, it is difficult to profile a diverse and scattered population such as the Palestinian community in Egypt. An attempt at providing an overall picture of their economic status was made in *al-Ahram Hebdo* in October 1997. Though ten years old and impossible to verify, the (unofficial) estimates advanced in the article, which put the Palestinian community at 70,000, could serve as a rough indictor: 78 percent of the community was estimated to be living under the poverty line, 18 percent as having average salaries, and 4 percent as being wealthy.[11]

Similarly, no comprehensive data are available concerning Palestinian employment according to location and occupational category. Nonetheless, by piecing together information obtained from interviews with Palestinian officials in Egypt with access to countrywide Palestinian Labor Union registration lists,[12] we found certain occupations concentrated in particular areas. For example, al-'Arish (including Bir al-Abid, Shaykh Zayud, and Rumanah), which was believed to represent up to 15 percent of the Palestinians in Egypt, was found to have a preponderance of laborers, fishermen, skilled craftsmen, and farmers. In the Sharqiyyah Governorate (including Zaqaziq, Abu Hammad, Abu Kabir, Faqus, and Minya al-Qamah), merchants and farmers predominated. Port Said had a large number of teachers. In Cairo, the largest concentration of Palestinians in Egypt, the leading occupations reported included merchants, businessmen, PLO employees (PLA members and employees at the various offices, unions, affiliates, and so on), employees of the AOGG, teachers, wage laborers, and drivers.

During a September 2001 interview, the late Adel Attiyah, then the head of the PLO Labor Union, described the very broad employment categories of some 12,000 workers and employees then registered with the Union. Of the 12,000 total, approximately 1,000 were seasonal workers, 2,000 were drivers (with commercial licenses), and 8,000 were skilled (trained) workers. Registered employees in the public sector (mainly with the AOGG) numbered under 1,000, of whom almost 60 percent were retired. An additional 30 percent of public sector employees were reported to have joined the PA in Gaza or the West Bank.[13]

The Palestinian Business Community

Much has been made of the supposedly wealthy Palestinian businessman. Although a small segment of the community is wealthy, the deeply entrenched perception of Palestinian riches in Egypt, fueled by the media (as described in chapter 2), is highly exaggerated. A not-implausible 1993 article in *Rose al-Yusuf* entitled

"Palestinians in Egypt: Refugees and Millionaires" stated that 2,500 Palestinians have £E 15–20 million invested primarily in services and transportation.[14] A 1994–96 study by Sari Hanafi of Palestinian businesspeople in the diaspora found that over a quarter of the 62 he interviewed in Egypt owned industrial factories, while the largest number (less than half) were engaged in import/export. The remainder (a little less than a third) were involved in agriculture, tourism, construction, and services.[15]

Palestinians arriving in Egypt after 1948[16] who had enough capital to start their own businesses and who were granted commercial licences and franchises in the early Nasser years began to prosper, especially after the departure of much of Egypt's Jewish population in the wake of the 1956 Suez war and the nationalization of their businesses. Moving into sectors where Jewish businessmen had been strong, such as the wholesale and retail trade, manufacturing, small hotels, and restaurants,[17] Palestinians also developed an important presence in the tertiary sector, including barbershops, restaurants, and sweet shops.

Much of today's Palestinian business community in Egypt is from Gaza. Trade relations between Egypt and Gaza, established in the early 20th century, flourished during the Nasser period, as luxury goods produced in Gaza found a ready market in socialist Egypt. Following the 1967 war, many Gazans transferred their businesses and capital to Egypt, a move made easier by the fact that they shared a common currency. The large size of Gazan families and the tendency for multiple branches of businesses to be set up by various family members contributed to the Egyptian perception of inordinate Palestinian wealth. The more successful of the Gaza families, including the al-Ashi and al-Surafa, rapidly expanded into diverse economic activities. The community also proved adaptable: During Sadat's economic opening (*infitah*) starting in 1974, when Palestinian businessmen were perceived as an economic threat, many took Egyptian partners. Still, wealthy Palestinians in Egypt to this day do not exceed a few thousand persons.[18]

Bureaucracy and Regulations

The employment situation of Palestinians has not changed significantly since the Sadat regime abruptly canceled Nasser's liberal measures in 1978, starting with Law 48 that made the employment of foreigners in the public sector subject to reciprocity with other countries. This law effectively barred Palestinians from public sector employment without special dispensation—which applied almost exclusively to those working for the AOGG and the PLO and its affiliated bodies. In 1981, Article 26 of Law 137 applied the same reciprocity restrictions to the private sector, while Article 27 stipulated that foreigners could not practice their professions without a permit from the Ministry of Labor and a valid residence permit. Adding to the difficulties, a quota for foreigners in the private sector was introduced. Article 4 (Law 25 of 1982) stipulated that foreigners could not exceed 10 percent of the total workforce in any enterprise so as not to compete with the national labor force,[19] although certain exceptions were permitted if they served national interests. This law is still in effect today.

The most recent Egyptian legislation concerning employment does not alter this picture. Article 3 of Law 43 of 1988 establishes the following conditions for obtaining work permits:

A. The foreign employee can not compete with the national labor force.
B. The foreign employee must have certain qualifications that are needed by the employer.
C. The qualifications and expertise of the alien must match the job for which the permit is requested.

It is unlikely that Palestinians would have expertise or special qualifications that native Egyptians would not have, as suggested in point B, because Palestinians able to complete university would have obtained the same kinds of degrees as their Egyptian classmates. Beyond the specified requirements, there are other considerations that make employers reluctant to hire Palestinians, which are aptly summarized in the following interview:

> Finding a job is extremely difficult for young men here. In the private sector, it is stated that for every one foreigner there should be ten Egyptians. This is in addition to the requirement to insure the employee. Most companies do not want to provide insurance. Recruiting a Palestinian will also cause the company to be questioned by Security. So companies prefer not to have Palestinians working for them. (P16, 'Ayn Shams, 8 June 2002)

In such a situation, qualifications do not count for much:

> I applied to work in a restaurant that has several branches in Cairo. After I submitted my papers and provided proof of prior employment at a five-star hotel, I was refused because I am Palestinian. I had to look for another job and so I became a taxi driver. (P12, 'Izbit al-Nakhal, 29 May 2002)

Given the bureaucratic obstacles and drawbacks, small-scale enterprises that do hire skilled and unskilled Palestinian workers tend do so "off the books," without contracts, insurance, or other benefits. The fact that many Palestinians employed in the private sector are working illegally makes them vulnerable to exploitation in terms of working hours, working conditions, and pay. The employer, for his part, runs no risk, because with no legal recourse and with jobs so scarce, people are happy to accept employment whatever the conditions.

Informal Sector Employment

With entry into the labor market blocked or stymied by legislation, it is not surprising that most Palestinians in Egypt turn to the informal sector, creating their own employment options or working in small-scale, individually run enterprises. Palestinians with limited resources and basic education represent a dynamic class engaged in myriad activities that, if not highly remunerative, at least allow them to provide for themselves and their families. In general, with the increasingly apparent failure of rural and urban formal sectors to absorb new entrants to the labor force, more attention is being paid to the informal sector as a hedge against growing unemployment.[20] The informal sector, with its diversity of income opportunities both legal and illegal, has enabled many Palestinians to become economically active and more independent through their own enterprise.

In al-'Arish and Rafah, for example, many Palestinians have been successful in the informal sector as carpenters, tailors, mechanics, builders, and professional repairmen. They have penetrated these professions by competing with locals, even while gaining the trust of local consumers and potential clients. Many have set up workshops in their own homes. It is true that the location of these two towns near the border of Palestine, with Egyptian Rafah overlooking Palestinian Rafah on the Israeli-occupied side, has contributed to the local economy. Underground tunnels dug between the Egyptian and Israeli-occupied sides long enabled inhabitants to earn money smuggling high-quality but relatively inexpensive gold from Egypt to Gaza and Marlboro cigarettes, cheeses, pharmaceuticals, and other goods from the Israeli market to Egypt. Starting from the first intifada in 1987, Palestinians wanted by Israel were smuggled out to Egypt, and weapons were smuggled in.[21]

A survey conducted by the Ministry of Labor on the distribution of Palestinian laborers with work permits indicated that the largest portion of Palestinians in Egypt work as drivers.[22] We have already mentioned the ease of obtaining taxi permits and their importance as a fallback for obtaining residency based on employment. But many of the Palestinians in this category are engaged in transport and hauling. Compared with other fields of employment, transport has been less affected by political events and administrative decisions, and policies concerning the issuance of the various categories of driver's licences have not changed significantly.

> If the truck is there, you need £E 300 to apply for a licence and £E 150 for the insurance. Then you need to sit for the exams. (8/12, Shibin al-Qanatir, 3 July 2002)

Indeed, trucking and long-haul transport are among the most common professions in the Qalyubiyyah and Sharqiyyah governorates north and northeast of Cairo. Many Palestinian men followed their fathers in these professions, while others became involved through social networks. In time, many have come to own their own trucks. Political events—most dramatically the 1967 war—have affected the routes, but the trucking business has thrived.

> I started working on trucks and articulated transport trucks when I was 18; I used to help my father in his work and in taking care of his truck. I never changed businesses. Today I own five trucks. I bought them all during the 1980s and the 1990s. I have six Egyptian employees. (7/28, Abu Kabir, 13 July 2002)

The role of family networks in the trucking business is especially evident in the small town of Shibin al-Qanatir, which has a large Palestinian population and where truck driving is the most common profession. The following interview is a good example:

> My husband is an assistant to a truck driver. He makes £E 140
> a week, or sometimes £E 200, while a driver of a truck like my
> father's makes £E 600 a week and requires a category 1 driving
> licence. The income differs for my two brothers-in-law, who
> own transport trucks and each make at least £E 5,000 a month.
> My other brother-in-law repairs trucks. He charges £E 5 to £E
> 20 for a day's work. (8/12, Shibin al-Qanatir, June 2002)

Strategies for making a living adopted by lower-income earners
with little education are usually diverse and complex and include
an array of activities, with family members pooling their resources
earned in a variety of ways. While work in the informal sector can
be an avenue to success, more often, in both rural and urban areas,
it entails long hours for little pay. Often, the work is only seasonal.
The rewards are especially meager for those without skills or
education:

> My husband works in *saksonia* [collecting old clothing] and
> he then sells the clothes in the market. He works in cities
> around us as well, not only in Qanayyat. He works from 8 ا. .
> until 5 ا.. every day and makes £E 15 a day. My son, who
> did not go to school either, is a carpenter. He makes £E 10 a
> day. This barely covers his own expenses. I work in seasonal
> harvesting. I usually get 5 kilograms of rice or corn or the
> product that I am harvesting. I am never paid money. Our
> daily expenses may vary between £E 3 and £E 5 a day, added
> to the fact that we have five sheep that we butcher to eat.
> (7/41, Qanayyat, 15 July 2002)

Many families combine self-employment at various jobs and
salaried labor to meet their needs:

> I work as a tailor three days a week for 12 hours and make £E
> 150 a month. My daughter works as a secretary for 12 evening
> hours and makes £E 150. My son, who is a painter, makes
> more than £E 150 a month but has very irregular working
> hours. (P22, Faysal, 15 June 2002)

Very few interviewees in rural areas reported that they still
work in agriculture. As will be discussed in chapter 5, Palestinians
have not had the right to own agricultural land in Egypt since
1985. However, some of those we interviewed were engaged in

activities related to farm work. Faqus, for example, is known for its concentration of blacksmiths:

> My husband was trained as a blacksmith in Yibna [near Ramla, in Palestine]. I used to help him by knocking on the iron and blowing the *kur* [bellows]. The best season for our work is the harvest season, since the *manjal* [sickle] and other harvesting tools are in demand. My children all learned these skills from their father. (7/35, Faqus, 14 July 2002)

Another blacksmith from the same town relates the following:

> I have worked as a blacksmith ever since I was in the fourth elementary class back in Yibna, Palestine. I depend on God for my income. I have been working here for a long time now. I do not have a shop. I have worked on the streets since 1948 when we arrived. At night I keep all the equipment behind the wall of the cultural center. They are kind people. They let me do this. (7/ 36, Faqus, 14 July 2002)

The few agricultural workers the team interviewed appeared to be the most vulnerable we encountered. Income from agricultural work is low and seasonal fluctuations make it difficult to earn a steady income. These issues are reflected in the case of 55-year-old Murad of Salhiyyah, who has been in farming all his life. His wife also works in seasonal agriculture. During harvest seasons, they have money and food, but work is not available at other times, meaning that they are often unable to pay for electricity, water, and other basic services. His three sons, unskilled laborers, have tried to fill the gap. Ahmad, the second son, for example, is employed in a workshop for ten hours a day and then works repairing refrigerators and electronic equipment (7/22, Salhiyyah, 8 July 2002).

Some families that perhaps start with more assets manage to move ahead through ambition, hard work, and cooperative effort, despite the difficulties faced:

> I go to university three days a week. When not at university, I deliver produce from the land we own and from the lands around it. I drive the pickup truck and deliver the produce to the central vegetable distributorship [*wakaleh*] in the city. In the evening, I work in the coffee shop we established. My brother also works in a coffee shop with my brother-in-law.

The coffee shop pulls in a profit of £E 60 to £E 130 a day. (7/21, Salhiyyah, 8 July 2002)

The following interview gives another example of how informal work can be used to support an education and move up the scale:

My son Atif, who is now an adjunct professor at al-Azhar University, got his position on his own. His father died when he was young. He had to make the money for his education and to help with household expenses. Atif worked in the evenings at a blacksmith's shop when he was at preparatory school. In secondary school, he became a bus driver's assistant. When he finished school and started his college education at the Social Welfare College, he worked at a Laundromat. He then applied for higher education at the Institute for Arab Research and got a job at the Red Crescent hospital. He made £E 200 a month for four years. (P12, 'Izbit al-Nakhal, 29 May 2002)

Working Women

When asked about women who work, many males interviewed said that they think women are better off at home taking care of their children and the household. Women are often seen in their traditional role as mothers, while men see themselves as being responsible for protecting the home and earning an income. A woman from a rural area recounts the following:

My husband is an *arzuki* [wage laborer]. Some days he works and others he doesn't. I am expected to run the house and manage its expenses with only £E 5 a day. I wanted to help, especially since I am an Egyptian *fallaha* myself. I asked my husband if I could buy ducks and chickens and breed and sell them. He refused and said, "You will bring us shame." As you know, these are the attitudes of Palestinians! (8/3, Abu Za'bal, 30 June 2002)

Such attitudes are rare among those who have had the opportunity to receive an education. In such cases, the husband may encourage his wife to work not only out of economic need but for a more satisfying lifestyle:

I got married when I was still at university. When I graduated from the faculty of arts, I traveled with my husband to the

Emirates. We both worked there. He taught in the army [as
a technician] and I taught in a government school. Since we
came back, I have managed a day care center that I established
with the help of my husband. (8/8, Abu Za'bal, 2 July 2002)

In general, our interviews supported the notion that traditional
attitudes about the "shame" of women working have become
less common over time. Women have assumed increasingly vital
roles in income generation and making household decisions.
Unemployment among males and economic stresses have increased
pressures on women to earn a living. Many women in both urban
and rural areas reported being engaged in various kinds of informal
commerce, including micro-trading—for example, buying small
items like lipstick from a supermarket and selling them on the
street.

I had a big wooden board made for me. I started buying large
amounts of goods and selling them from a street cart [*basta*
or *farsha* in the Egyptian dialect] in the market in 'Ayn Shams.
My eldest son used to help me after school. (P13, 'Ayn Shams,
23 May 2002)

Far more common, however, was the trading of modest quantities
of goods between Gaza and Egypt. This kind of trading is more
easily carried out by women, who are generally better at dealing
with the authorities (police, customs officials, tax agents) at the
borders and who are traditionally subjected to less scrutiny than
men. The requirements for such commerce are modest: a limited
initial investment to buy the goods and a base in Palestine, usually
with relatives or in-laws, through which to sell. The family also
provides a social network of customers. The reported profit from
an average trip, interviewees told us, ranges from £E 1,000–2,000.

To improve our financial situation, my wife traded goods
between Gaza and Cairo. She went to Gaza with an Israeli
visa and sold the goods that she took from here and bought
goods there. When she arrived in Gaza, she stayed with my
family in our family house. At first, she used to pass without
being noticed. When she increased the amount of goods, she
started paying duties every time she traveled. This was not a
problem; on many occasions, she would pay some money to
the tax collector [customs officer] and he would let her pass

without paying any duties. This all stopped when the intifada began. (P10, 'Ayn Shams, 23 May 2002)

Women commonly work to supplement the family income. Mustafa's wife "works in seasonal agriculture, at harvest time. She makes usually seven to ten pounds a day" (7/39, Dyarb Nijim, 15 July 2002). Mustafa owns a juice shop, which does not provide a regular income. Two of the family's four children are still in school, and two daughters are engaged and expected to furnish their marital homes,[23] making the extra income, however small, necessary.

A growing number of women are taking over as heads of households. Many interviewees reported having been abandoned when their husbands secured positions with the PA in Gaza in 1995. Even before the move to Gaza, many wives of PLO fighters were left on their own for long periods of time. An Egyptian woman, now divorced, is an example:

> I worked in the morning as a cleaner when I was 20 and went to sewing classes in the evening. When I finished the classes, I worked as a seamstress for an actress, Madame Zuzu. This was when I met my husband. After we got married, he made me quit. However, after he left us to go to Lebanon, I had to go back to work. I had my family's sewing machine, so I started working in an underwear factory. I also sew clothes for my daughters' friends. (P1, Dar al-Salam, 9 June 2002)

In such cases, women's responsibilities double—they are left in charge of both running the house and earning an income outside the home. Some of our interviewees expressed frustration or anger at the number of husbands who neglect their responsibilities while pursuing their own pleasures and interests, but felt they had no choice but to forge ahead. Many amply demonstrated the proposition that women are better than men at "gritting their teeth and getting on with the work."[24]

Work Abroad

Even in the heyday of Nasser's liberal policies toward Palestinians, employment opportunities in Egypt were scarce. From the late 1950s onward, large numbers of Palestinians—especially from Gaza—sought work abroad. Later, PLO institutions helped publicize job opportunities in the Gulf and other Arab countries such as Libya and Yemen:

Yemen used to advertise employment vacancies at the PLO office. I applied soon after I finished my master's degree. I was accepted to teach and I lived there for ten years. However, I came back to Egypt regularly to renew my residency. (7/40, Qanayyat, 15 July 2002)

Expertise and education were the principal qualifications needed to apply abroad, and those who had benefited from Egypt's free schooling and university education were strong candidates.[25] Social networks also played a major role, with early arrivals having jobs in a foreign country helping family members find work there. On the Palestinian side, work abroad not only provided a job—in many cases with higher salaries than could be dreamed of in Egypt—but sometimes also good education and better opportunities for their children:

In the late 1960s, my husband, who had a diploma from the Institute of Teaching in Egypt, had a job opportunity in the Emirates. He applied and relied on the help of his cousins who lived there. He resigned from the Egyptian Ministry of Education and settled in the Emirates. His salary was more than 1,600 Emirati dirhams. Our four sons and I soon followed and we stayed for twenty years. Today, Muhammad studies medicine, Abdallah is in architecture school, Ahmad attends engineering school, and Mahmud is at a medical engineering school. (8/8, Abu Za'bal, 2 July 2002)

However, as we have seen, what were once promising (if often risky) options ended in the early 1990s with the expulsion of most Palestinians from the Gulf states following Iraq's invasion of Kuwait and other regional events. Most of the accounts we heard of working abroad referred to the past. Interviewees also spoke about how they spent or invested the money they were able to set aside, with many drifting into the informal sector:

I went to Saudi Arabia for the first time in 1977. I used to work for two to four months at a time as a professional painter or mason on construction sites and then would return to Egypt. At that time the fare to Saudi Arabia was £E 100. Later, I started going for a year at a time, making at least £E 1,000 to £E 2,000 a month. I would then come back to Egypt, stay for a month and then go to Palestine and work for a few months. I would then return to Egypt and go back to Saudi Arabia. In

Saudi Arabia, ten of us lived in one house. When I returned
to Egypt for good, I started selling vegetables with a street
cart [*basta*] and then rented this shop to sell sugar cane juice.
(7/39, Dyarb Nijim, 15 July 2002)

Both skilled and unskilled Palestinians sought work in the Gulf,
often relying on relatives or friends already there to procure visas
for them.

I was in the Liberation Army of the PLO. After I began receiving
a pension, I asked my sister, who lives in Saudi Arabia, to help
me get a visa, and she did. I worked at the Saudi Ministry
of Water for eight years. When the Gulf war started, I had a
problem renewing my residency there, so I had to come back.
I now have a shop for ready-to-wear clothing. I pay rent and
taxes for the shop. But the work is seasonal, with income
increasing and decreasing accordingly. (P5, Dar al-Salam, 18
May 2002)

As already noted, the Gulf was not the only destination for
Palestinians from Egypt seeking work. Libya was also very
popular, especially as it was right next door to Egypt; employment
opportunities closer to family were preferred. Moreover, until
Qadhafi's expulsion of Palestinians to the border in 1995,
Palestinians in the country had enjoyed virtually the same rights
and privileges as Libyans.

In 1969, my father came to Cairo to continue his education.
He studied for four years to be a technical assistant in the
field of electronics. He worked in Egypt for a year and
then left for Libya, where he worked in a TV repair shop.
Meanwhile, he created a family by marrying my mother and
having two children. Ten years later, he returned to Minya
al-Qamah, where my mother's family lived, and opened his
own workshop. While we were growing up, he expanded his
workshop to Zaqaziq. Today, I am in charge here and he is in
charge of the other branch. (7/45, Minya al-Qamah, 11 July
2002)

Few Palestinians remain in Libya today. Even after the crisis was
resolved, those who returned saw their salaries cut in half and
many new obstacles to employment put in their way.

The number of Palestinians from Egypt currently working abroad is not known, but it is likely to be small. Certainly, work abroad is no longer an outlet for Palestinians in Egypt that can be sought with much hope of success.

Notes

1. Anecdotal evidence suggests that after the age of 50, the applicant can renew his or her residence permit free of charge every five years.

2. See chapter 5.

3. Unless they won a suit filed with the Egyptian Council of State; see chapter 2.

4. According to Sara Roy, some 20,000 Gazans left for jobs in the Gulf states under state-sponsored emigration in the three years from 1959 to 1962 alone, with the big emigration yet to come. Roy, *Gaza Strip*, p. 85.

5. Yassin, "Palestinians in Egypt," p. 6, citing a document at the Egyptian Foreign Ministry.

6. Abbas Shiblak, "Living in Limbo: Preliminary Observations on Canada Refugee Camp," paper for Refugee Studies Program, 1997.

7. Takkenberg, *The Status of Palestinian Refugees in International Law*, p. 154.

8. Amnesty International, "Annual Report for Libya," 1998, http://www. amnestyusa.org/annualreport.php?id=DE295B7AC32AF3BB80256A0F005C02D5& c=LBY.

9. Raed Jaber, *al-Hayat*, 9 November 2002.

10. UNHCR Representative, Egypt, personal communication 29 May 2003.

11. *Al-Ahram Hebdo*, 22 October 1997.

12. Palestinian ambassador Zuhdi al-Qudwah on 23 September 2001; Karim al-Iraqi , the head of social affairs section of the PLO Labor Union, 17 July 2002; Ali Jawhar, 22 October 2001.

13. Interview with Adel Attiyah, 24 September 2001.

14. *Rose al-Yusef*, 13 September 1993, in Lamia Raei, "Forgotten Population: A Case Study of Palestinians in Cairo" (master's thesis, Department of Sociology and Anthropology, American University in Cairo, 1993).

15. Sari Hanafi and Olivier Saint-Martin, "Problematic of Borders' Dwellers: The Condition of Palestinians in North Sinai" [in Arabic], *Palestinians in Egypt* (Ramallah, West Bank: Shaml, 1996).

16. The Palestinians who had established themselves earlier, some of whom were undoubtedly wealthy, and who had acquired Egyptian nationality, are not discussed in this study.

17. Dajani, *Institutionalisation of Palestinian Identity in Egypt*, p. 89.

18. The premature interruption of our study prevented us from interviewing members of this group.

19. Ratified by Law 83 of 1982.

20. Michael Todaro, *Economic Development*, 6th ed. (London: Longman, 1997), p. 269.

21. S. Farrell, *The Times*, 20 May 2002.

22. UNICEF, "Analysis of the Conditions of Palestinian Women and Children in Egypt" [in Arabic] (unpublished draft, 1996).

23. This is the tradition in Egypt; in Palestine, it is the man who usually assumes that responsibility.

24. Deepa Narayan et al., *Crying out for Change (Voices of the Poor)* (Washington, DC: Oxford University Press, 2000).

25. Zureik, *Palestinian Refugees and the Peace Process.*

Chapter 5

Education, Health,
and Financial Assets

Livelihoods are sustained through tangible assets (physical, economic, and financial) and intangible assets, including the rights (and access) to employment, education, and health care. This chapter continues the discussion of both kinds of assets Palestinians in Egypt use to earn their livelihoods.

The first section addresses education, the main route to securing decent employment and a stable future. Since the cancellation of the Nasser-era privileges accorded to Palestinians in this domain, access to education has been complicated. Most of the section on education deals with evolving restrictions and exemptions and how Palestinians have adapted to them. Access to health services has been the least problematic and is the area where our interviewees expressed the greatest satisfaction. The section dealing with health is therefore the briefest, mainly consisting of an outline of the services available to the community. The third section looks into tangible assets commanded by the community in the form of real estate and at the laws and changing policies limiting land ownership. It also touches upon financial capital and how Palestinians use the financial resources at their disposal—mainly pensions and remittances—to improve their prospects. As mentioned in the introduction, our field research was interrupted before we were able to begin interviewing members of the business community, so our sample consists of less affluent members of the Palestinian community.

Education

Overview

The Egyptian educational system is composed of elementary, preparatory, and secondary levels. The secondary level has both academic and vocational streams. All levels are offered by public, private, and religious (*azhari*) schools in both urban and rural areas. Public schools are free for Egyptians. Private school fees vary from £E 700 to £E 3,000 a year. *Azhari* schools provide free education to students of all nationalities provided they have Egyptian residence permits.

In addition to the regular educational institutions, the *manazil* system makes it possible for students to obtain a diploma through home study; in Egypt, *manazil* is used almost exclusively by families unable to pay the school fees. Students under the system study the state-approved curriculum at home and sit for the government's final exams without having attended formal classes:

> My six children attended private schools. When my husband left for Gaza, where he works as a cleaner in the Gaza Airport, and stopped sending money, I took them out of school. I had them study at home [*manazil*]. This was much cheaper, especially since we used to borrow the books assigned from the neighbors because I did not have money to pay even for that. I will make sure they get their certificates even if I need to beg. I should arm my children with education. (7/30, Bilbays, July 2002)

Another alternative is literacy classes, which are provided by mosques throughout Egypt for a nominal yearly fee. For some members of the community, however, even a very modest sum is too much to afford. The youngest daughter of one of our interviewees, forced to leave school to help her mother when her father had a major illness, recounts:

> I tried to attend literacy classes. I finished the first level, but I could not sit for the exams because they wanted me to pay the fees, £E 15, and I could not. (P22, Faysal, 15 June 2002)

At the level of higher education, private universities in Egypt require fees from all students, whereas public universities are free for Egyptians. To attend public universities, Palestinians must pay fees in foreign currency. Al-Azhar University offers free university education in the faculties of Arabic language and *Shari'a* (the science of Islamic religious law), but the other faculties require payment in foreign currency.

Fluctuating Access

Beginning in the mid-1950s and continuing for some two decades, Palestinians enjoyed free public education at all levels on the same basis as Egyptian nationals. This situation changed abruptly in early 1978, when the Sadat government canceled the Nasser-era privileges for Palestinians, and a ministerial decision (from the Ministry of Education) decreed that Palestinian children be transferred from public to private (i.e., paying) schools. The suddenness of the change is reflected in the following interview:

> All my children received their education for free because Palestinians were treated like Egyptians. Only my daughter was unlucky, because the change in treatment of Palestinians happened when she was at school. I made her study at home [*manazil*] until she finished. (7/44, Hehya, 15 July 2002)

The ministerial decision specified that if there were no private schools in the district, Palestinian children could go to government schools. For this, a paper from the head of the municipality had to be submitted to the *Maktab al-Wafidin* (General Administration for Foreign Students) along with other papers pertaining to the student's educational level.

Some people were able to "slip through the cracks" and escape bureaucratic scrutiny:

> Today my children are at government schools. At first no one knew that they were Palestinian and I never brought up the issue. Several years later, their Palestinian identity was discovered and I was asked to pay for the three previous years. Now, every year I get a letter from the governor of educational affairs asking me to prove that there is no private school in this area so my children can go to the public school. (7/38, Dyarb Nijim, July 2002)

The ministerial decision exempted children of employees of the PLO, the AOGG, and other public sector employees, including retirees. These children were provided free education up to the university level, even after the formal break with the PLO following the signing of the Egyptian-Israeli peace treaty in 1979.

> I had been educated in Egyptian public schools. I then earned a technician's diploma from the college of nursing in Cairo,

and upon graduation in 1971 was hired by the Ministry of Health. So my children also had their school education free of charge in public schools. (7/43, Hehya, 15 July 2002)

The post-1978 restrictions on primary and secondary education were soon extended to the university level, governed by the Ministry of Higher Education, and Palestinians accepted by Egyptian universities were required for the first time since the Nasser years to pay university fees, in pounds sterling (GBP). Some were able to receive help from the PLO to fund their university education.

> The foreign fees for Palestinians attending university were imposed in 1979. Abdallah was then at university. There were then 187 Palestinian students at Zaqaziq University. They held a sit-in in front of the Palestinian embassy and obliged the PLO to pay GBP 1,200 for each student. (7/40, Qanayyat, 15 July 2002)

Others were not so lucky:

> In my last year at the faculty of commerce at Zaqaziq University, the decision to require Palestinian students to pay fees in foreign currency was passed. In the early 1980s, I was asked to pay the pound sterling equivalent. My sister had to leave university because my family was not able to pay for her. (7/38, Dyarb Nijim, July 2002)

In addition to the fee requirement, the 1978 decision also restricted the access of foreigners to certain university faculties, notably medicine, pharmacology, engineering, economics, political science, and mass communications.

> My daughter could not study architecture because Palestinians were not allowed to attend certain schools at the university. With the help of some contacts, we managed to receive permission for her, but we needed to pay the foreign fees despite the fact that I had been a government employee. And in 1987 when my son came first in his class in Alexandria in the high school exams, he could not study engineering. Neither the ministry nor the university would admit him. He did not want to study a trade, so he did not continue with his higher education. (AP3, Alexandria, August 2002)

Education restrictions were confirmed periodically, and sometimes expanded. Thus, while decisions 87 (1983) and 75 (1984) of the Ministry of Higher Education merely reaffirmed the Palestinians' foreign status and reiterated the ban on their entering technical faculties such as medicine and engineering,[1] Article 2 of Ministerial Decision 394-A of 1992 added that foreign students could not exceed 10 percent of the total student body. While Article 3 of the same decision restated the ban on the study of certain disciplines, it specified that these subjects could not be studied "without the permission of the university director," thereby implying that exceptions were possible. Priority in accepting foreign students was given to recipients of government scholarships and students who finished their secondary education in *azhari* schools.

> My father was a government employee, but we all went to *azhari* schools. Today, at al-Azhar University, I have no problems. My father still works for the government and my mother is Egyptian. I even applied for a Mubarak Scholarship and I got it. They help students by giving them £E 200 to £E 300 a year. (7/21, Salhiyyah, 8 July 2002)

University tuition was far beyond the means of all but a small fraction of Palestinians, and fees continued to rise. By 1991, they had reached GBP 2,000 for the first year in the human sciences faculties and GBP 1,000 for the following years. The fees at the scientific faculties (for those students who had obtained the required special permission to enroll) went up to GBP 3,000 for the first year and GBP 1,500 thereafter.[2]

The result of the imposition of fees and other restrictions was a dramatic drop in the number of Palestinian students enrolled at Egyptian universities: From an average of 20,000 students a year from the mid-1960s up to 1978, the figure dropped to 4,500 a year in 1985[3] and to just over 3,000 a year by 2000.[4] Certainly, the overwhelming majority of Palestinian university students in Egypt had always come from other Arab countries (and, before 1967, from Gaza as well), but the falling numbers affected resident Palestinians at least as much.

Meanwhile, the PLO had been directly subsidizing university fees for the children of at least some of its employees, but these outlays were affected by the cutoff in funding from the Gulf in retaliation for the PLO's statements during Iraq's occupation of Kuwait in 1990–91.

> As my husband was working at the PLO, we used to provide papers [for the subsidies]. When the Gulf war started [1991], my daughter was at university and we submited the usual papers, but they were not recognized. The PLO later stopped funding students at all universities. My daughter had to leave the university. (P30, 'Izbit al-Nakhal, 13 June 2002)

In general, the prohibitive cost of higher education for Palestinians was a subject of great concern, especially for the resident community. In 1992, Ministerial Decision 24/722/92, Article 5, Section 10 facilitated access to higher education for certain categories of Palestinians, notably the children of PLO and public sector employees. The move, which involved reducing university fees to 10 percent of the full amount, appeared to be related to the Palestinian–Israeli peace negotiations that had begun following the October 1991 Madrid conference and that ultimately led, however indirectly, to the signing by Israel and the PLO of the September 1993 Oslo Accord setting the framework for a peace settlement. Just a month later, on 30 October 1993, the General Administration for Foreign Students (*Maktab al-Wafidin*) of the Egyptian Ministry of Higher Education sent an official letter to the cultural attaché of the Palestinian embassy clarifying the categories of Palestinians exempted from paying 90 percent of the university fees. The categories were as follows:

- Children of public sector employees,[5] including retirees; children of Egyptian widows and divorcees; and children of women who have passed Egyptian high school exams;
- Continuous residents of Egypt—those who were born in Egypt and have completed all levels of basic education in Egyptian schools;
- Students needing financial assistance who can submit papers verifying their economic circumstances.

The decision to exempt the children of public sector employees, especially of PLO personnel, from 90 percent of the foreign fees was formalized at a meeting between the Egyptian minister of higher education and his Palestinian counterpart in spring 1995. The PA had already been established in Gaza, with a foothold in the West

Bank, and the meeting had been arranged to institute ways aimed to facilitate the enrollment of Palestinians in all faculties of Egyptian universities as a way of supporting the Palestinian state-building project; at the same time, the ban on studying certain subjects (e.g., medicine, engineering) was also dropped. An announcement to this effect followed the meeting.[6]

Though a 90-percent exemption is certainly substantial, the reduced fee still amounted to GBP 100–150 a year, a considerable sum for most Palestinians in Egypt. The requirement of payment in a foreign currency made settling the fee all the more difficult, though in some cases (seemingly arbitrary) this was not applied.

> I study engineering at King Fuad University. My mother has problems paying the fees for me and my sister, who is graduating this semester. We both pay 10 percent of the fees in pounds sterling . . . sometimes the administration at the university asks us to pay in pounds sterling and at other times we are asked to pay the equivalent in Egyptian pounds. This makes us sometimes pay less or more, depending on the conversion rate. (PP9, Port Said, 18 June 2002)

For some families, the school fees were completely beyond their means. We were told of a number of cases where students or parents resorted to subterfuge to assure an education for their loved ones.

> When my sister was born, my Egyptian grandfather registered her as his daughter. This gave her an Egyptian identity document that enabled her to study at school with no problem of paying fees. It was only when we wanted to go to Palestine that we had to change her papers to show that she is Palestinian. (7/46, Minya al-Qamah, 11 July 2002)

We also heard of cases of forging documents to prove Egyptian nationality—a tactic that often failed:

> When Muhammad was at university and we were unable to pay his fees, we tried to forge a divorce paper for him to make use of the advantages given to the son of an Egyptian divorced woman. The university administration was not satisfied with the paper and asked to see the two people who testified to the divorce. That was impossible, since we hired just any two passing men when we did it. (7/22, Sharqiyyah, 8 July 2002)

The consequences of being caught at such forgeries were dire:

> My other son, Ahmad, forged an Egyptian ID to prove that he
> is Egyptian so he could go to school without paying fees. But
> my daughter's ex-husband told the police, who put Ahmad in
> prison and prevented him even from studying *manazil* when
> he got out unless the fees of all the previous years were paid.
> (7/22, Sharqiyyah, 8 July 2002)

A far more common tactic, reported to us by many, was simply to
attend university courses without paying fees. A number of students
we interviewed told us that they paid security guards to let them
into the university and then paid administrative staff members to
let them sit for the exams; in some cases, they paid the minimal
registration fees required of Egyptians and promised to pay the
foreign fees upon completion of the coursework. But lacking the
official foreign student registration and without university identity
cards, they were in a vulnerable position. In most cases they were
unable to pay the accumulated fees when the time came. As a
result, many students who attended the classes and even passed
their exams did not receive a degree.

> Even though I had to pay only 10 percent of my children's fees
> [because I work in government], it was expensive for me on
> my salary and I couldn't pay them. So my children, Abla and
> Mahmud, went to university and attended courses but did not
> receive their diplomas. (7/43, Hehya, 15 July 2002)

Often we were told that students who successfully completed
their course work and exams had hopes that the PLO would pay
the outstanding foreign fees, and in fact for some years—especially
up to the Gulf war—this was generally the case. Moreover, in the
early 1990s, UNRWA's Cairo Office and the Palestine Department
of the League of Arab States raised more than $600,000 for the
payment of university fees, mostly to allow Palestinian students
who had completed all the requirements for graduation to obtain
their diplomas and to permit those in their final year to graduate.[7]
In addition, generous donations are occasionally made by affluent
Palestinian businessmen or Egyptian actors and actresses. During
the second intifada, the Palestinian embassy in Cairo received
many donations to support Palestinian students in Egypt who
were unable to pay the foreign fees, but almost all of these were

for students whose families lived in areas of Palestine under siege by the IDF during spring 2002, particularly Jenin.

The case of Palestinians attending classes but not receiving diplomas was re-examined by the Egyptian government in 1997. Some Egyptian educators counseled against making exceptions to the rule. For example, the president of Cairo University, Dr. Faruq Isma'il, opposed the exemption on the grounds that the school would then have to exempt other Arab students as well.[8] Though the Egyptian government did not enact any blanket "amnesty," President Mubarak did agree to exempt some Palestinian students from paying the fees.[9] Short of such interventions, university certificates were not granted.

> My daughter Rabab studied at a Hotelerie and Tourism College but she was not given the diploma because I could not pay the 1,800 pounds. Now she cannot work since she cannot prove that she did all the course work and sat for the exams. (7/29, Abu Kabir, July 2002)

Some students take this philosophically. The son of one of our interviewees (8/8, Abu Za'bal, 2 July 2002) reported that he finished attending university but because he had not been able to pay the fees, he never got his diploma. However, he added that he didn't mind. "What is important," he told us, "is that I got my education."

At the pre-university level, some interviewees told us that Palestinians with economic difficulties could apply for state support, or *bahth ijtima'i*. Many reported that requests were usually accepted after a visit by a government social worker. The procedure was described as follows:

> By applying to the Ministry of Social Affairs, it was possible to demand an assessment of the economic condition of the family based on which a certificate of poverty would be issued and a reduction of fees granted . . . We in the diaspora have nothing but education to protect us. I say this knowing that I cannot get a job with a university certificate because I am Palestinian. (8/2, Shibin al-Qanatir, 4 July 2002)

The *bahth ijtima'i* process has reportedly accelerated since the outbreak of the second intifada, as Egyptian government officials have tried to take account of the fact that harsh economic conditions in the PA areas meant that many Palestinians in Egypt no longer receive remittances from their relatives in Gaza. The process is sometimes facilitated by the Palestinian embassy. According to Fathi Kuttab, of the embassy's education office, the Egyptian Ministry of Education informed him that Palestinian students in public schools who could demonstrate need would be referred to the Ministry of Social Affairs, which in turn would exempt qualifying students from paying the fees. Ninety such applications had been processed through the embassy during the previous school year.[10]

> I used to pay £E 200 a year for each son. Two years ago, Palestinians were exempted from fees and are to be treated as Egyptians. This was good for my children. (8/9, Abu Za'bal, 3 July 2002)

At the university level, the minister of higher education announced a 50-percent reduction in university tuition for Palestinian students at public universities for the three academic years from 2000 to 2003.[11] This reduction, however, applied to those Palestinians not already covered by the 90-percent exemption, mostly Palestinian students from other countries.

Given the pervasive poverty in the community, fee reductions, especially at the university level, affect a relatively small number of Palestinian families in Egypt. For many in the community who must struggle to get by, educating their children is simply not an option; in fact, they no longer even think of education as a basic right:

> I was never able to fund my children's education. The boys had to get vocational skills to work. One learned to work with gypsum and paints. Two went to a tailor's workshop, and the last one is in a carpentry workshop. (7/25, Abu Hammad, 10 July 2002)

Some of our interviewees argued that having an education is not all that important, especially when many people even with good university degrees cannot find jobs:

> Metal [the trucks] is a priority over education, since it secures a future for the children. (7/31, Bilbays, 11 July 2002)

Beyond the impact of pushing the poorer members of the community into insecure informal employment, another consequence of the cost and difficulties in accessing education is that girls are more likely to leave school early for marriage. Many of the families interviewed believed that marrying young girls off can be advantageous: It means having "one less mouth to feed," and if the husband is better-off than the family, the household's economic conditions may be improved:

> My oldest daughter went to school until age 16. Priority was given to her marriage, to alleviate some of the costs. The same is true for our second daughter; she was 15 when some of our relatives asked for her hand. (P22, Faysal, 15 June 2002)

The youngest daughter in this same family described how she had to drop out of school when her father became gravely ill:

> I went to school until third grade. My family couldn't pay the fees. I never even sat for the exams because they coincided with my father's illness. We did not have a choice. I am sad to have stopped school. I always wanted to be like other girls, who go to school and live their lives. (P22, Faysal, 15 June 2002)

Health

Health Services Available to Palestinians

No regulations limit Palestinian access to health care in Egypt. What follows are the main types of health facilities available to the community.

The Palestine Hospital, run by the PLO-affiliated Palestine Red Crescent Society,[12] is located in the northern Cairo suburb of Heliopolis. It serves mainly Palestinians insured by PLO institutions and their families as well as current and former employees of the AOGG. Some Palestinians employed in other sectors obtain medical insurance through the PLO-affiliated Labor Union. The hospital also serves any uninsured Palestinian or Egyptian at private sector hospital rates. In addition to its medical facilities, the hospital has a pharmacy.

Charitable clinics, usually linked to mosques, are found throughout Egypt. The Palestinians interviewed expressed satisfaction with the level of services provided in such centers, reporting them to be conveniently located, efficient, and moderately priced:

> I do not have medical insurance at the Red Crescent Hospital even though I could apply for it because money is already taken out of my membership [dues] at the [PLO] Labor Union. However, the hospital is quite far from my house. I prefer to go to the clinics attached to the mosques, where I pay £E 3 per visit. (P9, Wailey, 24 June 2002)

Egyptian public hospitals are also found throughout Egypt. Palestinians who are or were employed by the Egyptian government receive free medical treatment. Though their families are not covered, uninsured persons, Egyptian or Palestinian, pay only modest fees for treatment in public hospitals. However, Palestinians tend to avoid the public health services, reporting inadequate cleanliness, inefficiency, and overcrowding.

Health clinics for maternity and early childcare are located in many areas. Few women interviewed said that they used them. Those who did expressed relative satisfaction but reported overcrowding and poor hygiene.

Private clinics in rural and urban areas charge, on average, between £E 20 to £E 35 a visit. Many Palestinians resort to private clinics only in emergencies or for critical conditions, though others who are better-off use them more often:

> I am insured at the PRCS [Palestine Red Crescent Society]... When my wife needed an operation, the Palestine Hospital did not have the speciality we needed. We had it done in a private hospital and paid £E 12,000. For follow-ups, my wife goes to a nearby private clinic where she pays £E 25 per visit. (P16, 'Ayn Shams, 8 June 2002)

> We can go to private clinics and pay £E 20. The money I could save by being treated at the Palestine Hospital, where I have medical insurance, would be used for transportation to get me there, so I prefer not going. (P9, Wailey, 24 June 2002)

Health Concerns

In general, our interviewees expressed satisfaction with the quality of health services available in their neighborhoods or districts. For minor medical needs, the services are affordable and adequate. The most frequent complaint about health care was related to access to special medicines for chronic diseases. Medicines, especially if purchased from a private pharmacy, tend to be expensive and can have a major impact on the family's budget:

> My wife and I have diabetes. We need £E 102 worth of medicine per month. (P9, Wailey, 24 June 2002)

> We usually buy medicines from the Palestine Hospital, where they reduce the price by 70 percent. But often, the medicines we need are not available. (P16, 'Ayn Shams, 8 June 2002)

Other common complaints include the need to travel long distances to access health care, the difficulties and cost of reaching health care facilities, and the high cost of major operations.

But while Palestinians express relative satisfaction with health services in Egypt, the consequences of not having a safety net cannot be overemphasized. Any unexpected health crisis can require full mobilization of available resources. One of our interviewees told us about the financial crisis her family suffered when her husband had a heart attack, requiring her to sell the land she had inherited from her family to cover the hospital bills (8/3, Abu Za'bal, 30 June 2002). In addition to selling property, many reported selling gold and borrowing from family and friends to help pay for medicine and hospitalization.

The case of Ahmad, a tailor and family breadwinner, illustrates how a serious illness can disrupt the household's fragile situation, with lasting consequences. When he had a heart attack, donations and loans from relatives helped the family survive, but his youngest two children were forced to leave school permanently to help care for their father and because the family could no longer afford school fees. Ahmad was eventually able to return to work at a reduced level, but the family continued to suffer from the reduced wages and the impact of accumulated debts. (P22, Faisal, 15 June 2002)

Financial Assets

This section looks at how Palestinians use the financial assets at their disposal to achieve their goals or simply to survive, and how they deal with or circumvent the limits and legal obstacles confronting them. In particular, it looks at land ownership and property rights and the various forms of financial capital.

Palestinians and Property Rights in Egypt

Egypt traditionally has placed tight restrictions on land ownership by foreigners, for example, on property located near international borders and agricultural land (Law 62 of 1940; Law 124 of 1958). For a time, however, Palestinians were privileged compared to other foreigners concerning the right to own land. As noted in chapter 2, during the Nasser era Palestinians had been explicitly exempted from Law 15 of 1963 barring foreigners from owning land. Remarkably, this privilege long outlasted the loss of their exemption from "foreigner" status in 1978, because Article 2, chapter 3 of the 1963 law *specifically* stated that Palestinians could own land in Egypt "until the Palestinian territories are liberated from the occupiers."[13] Thus, it was only in 1985, when Land Law 104 superseded (and canceled) Law 15 of 1963, that Palestinians lost the right to own land.

In the meantime, in 1976, Law 81 had been passed preventing foreigners from owning real estate (buildings and plots of land, generally in more urbanized areas). Palestinians, however, were not affected, because at the time they were still exempted from foreigner status. In 1978, when their treatment on a par with Egyptian nationals ended, the 1976 law suddenly became relevant to them. Article 2B stipulated that foreigners could own real estate with permission from the Ministerial Council[14] under the following conditions:

- Only one property for the purpose of private residence or private business could be owned.
- The property could not exceed 1,000 square meters.
- Payment for the property must be made in foreign currency through a local bank.
- Ownership of the property could not be in partnership with an Egyptian.

The article further stated that the offspring of an Egyptian woman married to a foreigner had the right to inherit the property.

The law could also be applied retroactively. In one documented case, a Palestinian head of household arriving in Egypt in 1967 purchased a piece of land from a local Egyptian. When the Egyptian government began a sewage project on his property, it initially promised compensation for the land, the value of which he states was £E 135,000. No compensation was paid, and the failure to pay was later claimed to be legal on the grounds that Palestinians were not allowed to own land in Egypt.[15]

The requirement under Law 81 that foreigners needed the Ministerial Council's permission to own real estate was canceled by Law 106 of 1985, even though the new law also incorporated the conditions for foreign ownership spelled out in Article 2B of the 1976 law (see above). Several years later, these conditions for foreign ownership were amended by Law 56 of 1988, as follows:

- The surface area of the property must not exceed 3,000 square meters.
- Property subject to the law of archaeology protection cannot be owned by a foreigner.

While changes in the 1976 law governing real-estate ownership affected some Palestinians, the legislation with the greatest impact on the community was the above-mentioned Law 104 of 1985 barring foreign individuals and companies—without exception— from owning agricultural property or fertile lands in Egypt. Article 1 was especially relevant, because in principle Palestinians were the only foreigners who still owned agricultural land at the time the 1985 law was enacted. This article stipulated that foreign-owned agricultural land would revert to the state within five years of the law's taking effect. It is worth noting that much of the agricultural land held by Palestinians in Egypt was land they had reclaimed, and some Palestinians had relied on the land as a financial guarantee for renewing their residency every year. The PLO protested the 1985 law, but to no avail.[16]

In light of the new legislation, Palestinians had to get rid of their agricultural landholdings within the allotted time span to avoid uncompensated expropriation. Some sold their properties at below-market prices; others registered them in the name of Egyptian in-laws or Egyptian friends or partners. However, false registration makes for vulnerability by sharply limiting legal redress in the event of ownership disputes. Some of those we interviewed reported having been cheated out of their properties when Egyptian associates denied their ownership rights. Though contracts were often drawn up to try to protect the Palestinian owners, they weren't always successful. One of our interviewees, whose case turned out favorably for him, recounts the following:

> I owned a piece of agricultural land with two other Palestinians before 1982. I also bought a farm of 72 feddans [288 dunams] of rehabilitated land in Isma'iliyyah at a time when Palestinians had the right to own such land, so I had no problem registering it. Later, when the law was issued barring Palestinians from owning land, I decided to turn my share over to three Egyptian acquaintances. One of them told me that if I died, he could guarantee that my male offspring would know that the land really belonged to me, but he could not guarantee that his sons-in-law would not claim it [upon his death]. So he was honest and withdrew from the deal. One of the other Egyptians later tried to deny my ownership, but in the end we met and were able to solve the problem. (P17, 'Ayn Shams, 8 June 2002)

Government inefficiency sometimes worked in favor of Palestinian owners:

> My father came back from Saudi Arabia in 1966 and built this house [a three-story building], and bought a piece of agricultural land, which was then permitted. He also bought a shop to sell clothing. The 15 feddans of agricultural land that he bought were not registered at the Property Registration Department. When the decree preventing Palestinians from owning agricultural lands was issued, our land was not registered, so no one knew it was owned by Palestinians. After 1985, we had to sell some parts of it to create a new business for my brother. (7/37, Faqus, 14 July 2002)

Many people registered their land at the Property Registration Department without declaring ownership. The implementation of the decisions concerning property ownership was left to the discretion of the administration. Many of the people we interviewed, especially those with an Egyptian wife or mother, were not worried about the on-the-books restrictions on foreign land ownership.

> We own three buildings and some agricultural land. We bought land in 1975 and were planning to build a house on it, but my mother refused because it was on the main street and she did not think it was a convenient location for a building. The land was registered in her name because she has Egyptian

nationality. Today, poor farmers work the land. We do not take any rent from them. In 1980, we bought another piece of land on which we built the house. In 1995, we bought another piece of land and built a warehouse on it. In 1998, we bought a building where we keep our goods and where we have shops to rent. We also bought another piece of agricultural land, which is registered in my [Egyptian] wife's name. All the other buildings are registered in my own name. In case of any problems, I can transfer the registration to my mother or wife. (7/38, Dyarb Nijim, July 2002)

The vulnerability and risks associated with the earlier partnerships, which could not be legally registered, were eliminated in 1997 with the passage of the Guarantees and Investments Incentives Law (Law 8 of 1997). This law gives foreigners the right to own businesses on a larger scale within the context of business partnerships where 51 percent of the property is owned by an Egyptian.

Financial Resources

Financial capital here falls into two main categories: available stocks (e.g., cash, bank deposits, jewelry) and monetary inflows (e.g., wage income, pensions and remittances, transfers from the state). This section will focus in particular on how Palestinians used these various forms of financial capital to improve their economic status and extend their meagre resources.

Pensions

Employment in the public sector—by the AOGG, the PLO bodies, or (in earlier periods) directly by the Egyptian government—offers a number of advantages. Though public sector salaries tend to be lower than those in the private sector, the income is stable and a pension is guaranteed. Insurance is also provided after retirement for the employee and often for his family as well. Moreover, work days are generally shorter, allowing the employee to conduct other business after hours. Thus, for enterprising individuals, public sector employment can provide a base for other ventures:

My father was an employee at the railway station. He was also a partner with many Egyptians in commercial businesses that

> he ran in the afternoon . . . Today, we run four shops that we
> set up after my father died. We invest in the agricultural land
> my father had and we have his pension of £E 460 a month.
> The house where we live is owned by the railway station.
> (7/21, Salhiyyah, 8 July 2002)

Palestinians who worked in the AOGG or with one of the PLO entities receive a pension from the PLO after retiring. Living expenses in the Palestinian territories are much higher than in Egypt, and salaries, accordingly, are higher. Taking advantage of this, many retired PLO employees make use of social and family connections in Gaza to have their pensions diverted to Gaza, where the amount paid is higher and delivered in hard currency.

> I get my pension from Gaza. My son takes the check and
> cashes it on my behalf in Gaza. I get the equivalent of £E
> 1,200. (P17, 'Ayn Shams, 8 June 2002)

Some people we interviewed received small pensions from the government simply for having been registered as a worker with the Labor Union. One man who worked seasonally as a blacksmith reported:

> I also get £E 80 [a month] from the Egyptian government as
> a pension since I was registered as an agricultural laborer,
> despite the fact that I never worked as a farmer. This is
> the licence that I got fifteen years ago. I renew it yearly by
> providing a letter from the Labor Union and paying £E 50.
> (7/ 36, Faqus, 14 July 2002)

Remittances

Palestinians who went to work in the Gulf states often felt responsible for helping their immediate and extended families.[17] In many cases, the remittances were shrewdly invested to increase the family's resources:

> My brother left for the Emirates in the early 1960s to teach.
> He helped us greatly to expand out truck transport business.
> We had one truck when he left; today we have five. He used
> to send us money. Business was bringing business. And our
> work expanded. (7/28, Abu Kabir, 13 July 2002)

Many with jobs abroad contributed to—or entirely paid for—the education of siblings or other family members:

> My brother in Saudi Arabia sends 150 pounds to each of my four sons who are at university. (7/26, Abu Hammad, 10 July 2002)

> When I returned from my ten-year stay in Yemen, the regulations stated that Palestinians should pay for university education in foreign currency. My brother and sister were then at university. I paid for their university education until they finished. (P8, 'Ayn Shams, 23 May 2002)

Remittances from abroad were invested in the education and professional development of family members. In this way, the remittances constituted a base for long-term investments in Egypt.

> After my husband finished his studies at the teachers' institute in Egypt, he was hired by the government. Ten years later, he went to work in the Emirates. We used to send money to my brothers-in-law, who bought us a piece of land and even supervised the construction of a house for us. When we returned, we had a house. On the first floor, we established a publishing house that my husband runs and a children's nursery that I run. (8/8, Abu Za'bal, 2 July 2002)

Palestinians in Egypt were also dependant on remittances sent to them by relatives who joined the PA in Gaza. When they arrived in Gaza, some were able to send the equivalent of $100–$150 to their families back in Egypt. Many Palestinians reported that they depended totally on this money. However, the deteriorating conditions and soaring unemployment at of the outbreak of the second intifada interrupted the regular payment of PA employees and put an end to the flow of remittances from Palestine.

Savings and Investment

Very few people interviewed reported using banks for their savings. Those who are able to save usually invest whatever surplus they have into businesses. A good example is a man in Abu Kabir who owns three transport trucks and who told the research team that he does not have a bank account, even though he would have no trouble opening one. Instead, he invests whatever he has in various businesses (7/28, Abu Kabir, 13 July 2002).

Buying property (either directly or through a family or friend) is one of the most common means of saving in both rural and urban areas. A number of Palestinians from Gaza also still own inherited properties there. Whether used for agriculture or to develop a business, property can generate income for the family.

> I have an orange grove in Gaza that I recently decided to convert from fruit production to seed production, since I heard seeds can bring in more profit. I also receive rent from shops there, which is collected by my nephew who still lives in Gaza. (P1, Giza, 10 May 2002)

Gold is one of the most common ways of saving money, especially in rural areas; it is rare to find a Palestinian (or indeed an Egyptian) woman who does not possess gold jewelry and bracelets received as part of her dowry or subsequently purchased with savings. Gold obviously does not generate income, but at least it either holds or increases its value, an especially important consideration in inflationary times, and can be easily converted into cash. A number of our interviewees noted that when family belongings must be sold in times of need, the woman's belongings—notably her gold—are the first to go. This divestment strategy is "gendered in its impact and an indicator of women's particular vulnerability and lack of decision-making power within the household."[18] It is important to add, however, that gold and jewelry are generally not seen in sentimental terms, but as assets that can be sold during emergencies. Such saleable property often constitutes the family's only safety net.

> The gold I had was eventually sold to get us out of debt. My husband had no regular job since he left the PLO. I was helping with work and with my gold savings. (P6, 'Ayn Shams, 18 May 2002)

In a number of cases, it was also clear that the decision to sell was the woman's:

> I was able to help my son by selling the pieces of gold left to me so that he could start his own business, an Internet shop. After he graduated, he was unable to find a job. Every time

> he would apply, he would be told, "You are Palestinian." (8/2,
> Shibin al-Qanatar, 4 July 2002)

Land is another saleable asset, though selling it takes time. In all cases, however, selling personal belongings and property is generally a strategy of last resort.

> We had a piece of land in Gaza inherited from my grandfather.
> When we were having financial difficulties, we sold it. The
> money helped my oldest son to get married and my other son
> to buy a taxi, which was registered in my name as an Egyptian
> to avoid any problems. (P12, 'Izbit al-Nakhal, 29 May 2002)

Another common way to save money for unforeseen expenses or specific purposes is by joining with a group of relatives or neighbors in a cooperative (*gama'iyyah*). To be able to do so, however, requires at least a minimum of surplus income.

> Being part of a *gama'iyyah* forces its members to save, but
> you need a regular and stable income. My husband is a part-
> time tailor and does not earn enough to cover our expenses.
> So how can we save in a *gama'iyyah*? (P22, Faysal, 15 June
> 2002)

Each member of the cooperative regularly contributes a set amount. At the end of each month, members can take turns borrowing money. In all regions where we conducted interviews, we found that the main purpose of the cooperatives was to pay for school/university or residence renewal fees. Not all experiences with cooperatives were positive, however:

> Our money was embezzled in a *gama'iyyah* from which we
> expected to get £E 20,000. My brother in Saudi Arabia was
> sending me money and I needed to save for the children's
> school fees, so I became part of a *gama'iyyah*. I was paying
> £E 500 monthly. For ten months I paid to this cooperative. By
> chance, I discovered that the *gama'iyyah* had collapsed in
> the seventh month, but the woman in charge was still taking
> money from me. We had a big fight when I tried to claim my
> money. I threatened to call the police. She paid me some of
> the money but she still owes me £E 2,250. (P10, 'Ayn Shams,
> 23 May 2002)

Help from the State

Egyptian government subsidies for students in need were mentioned earlier in the chapter. In the 1970s, the government also included Palestinians in the distribution of food ration cards. This practice continued even after the dramatic change in policy toward the Palestinian community in the late 1970s. In 1980, for example, Article 3 of Resolution 22 stipulated that ration cards be issued to needy Palestinians and Sudanese who had been living continuously in Egypt. However, as many of our interviewees reported, this was discontinued, although we were unable to determine when.

> The government gave us a green ration card and then later it was a red card. It helped us buy staples, but this stopped some years ago. (7/36, Faqus, 14 July 2002)

> God helped us in those times because we used to get food through the food ration card that the government distributed. Now this has stopped. (8/3, Abu Za'bal, 30 June 2002)

An old man who sells candy and cigarettes from a pushcart near the Suez Canal in Qantara told the team that he was imprisoned from 1947 to 1970 for selling drugs. After serving his sentence, he was released to join his family in Qantara:

> I get a monthly subsidy from the Ministry of Social Affairs. It used to be £E 10; now it is £E 25. I used to get £E 30 from the governor of Gaza during the [holiday] feasts. However, to get this money, I have to travel to Cairo. Because of old age and illness, I stopped going, so I no longer get it. (P31, Qantara, 19 June 2002)

Despite their difficulties, none of the Palestinians interviewed wanted to ask for money rather than earning it themselves. Dignity and appearances are central concepts, and taking charity is seen as a last resort:

> I hear often that the Administrative Office of the Governor of Gaza gives subsidies in some seasons to Palestinians. I never go there. My dignity prevents me from accepting money from others. (7/ 36, Faqus, 14 July 2002)

Notes

1. Yassin, "Palestinians in Egypt," *Samed al-Iqtisadi*, pp. 15–16.

2. Ibid., quoting Qaddusi's article "The Ghost of Ignorance Haunts 24,000 Palestinians in Egypt," *al-Sha'b*, 4 February 1992.

3. Sarraj et al., *Arab Palestinians in Egypt*; Yassin, "Palestinians in Egypt," *Samed al-Iqtisadi*, p. 11.

4. Press release dated 20 December 2000 from the office of minister of higher education concerning a decision to reduce public university fees to 50 percent for Palestinians students.

5. The PLO is considered part of the public sector.

6. *Al-Hayat*, 9 April 1995.

7. Interview with Ron Wilkinson, an UNRWA official currently in Amman who was working in Cairo at the time, December 2003. UNRWA continued to maintain a one-person office in Cairo to handle administrative issues may arise relating to Gaza.

8. *Al-Ahram Hebdo*, 22 October 1997.

9. Safwat al-Sharif, Egypt's minister of information, stated that the amnesty would benefit the children of Egyptian mothers and the widowed or divorced wives of Palestinians in the public sector as well as the children of Palestinians living continuously in Egypt (*al-Ahram*, 18 September 1997).

10. Interview, 8 July 2003.

11. Letters from the Information Office of the Minister of Higher Education to the Palestinian Cultural Attaché. The letters, which were obtained from the Palestinian cultural attaché's office, had no official reference numbers.

12. The Palestine Hospital and the Palestine Red Crescent Society are discussed at greater length in the next chapter.

13. Palestinians' privileged access to employment and education denied foreigners was linked to provisions mandating that they be treated like Egyptian nationals, meaning that the resulting privileges automatically ended when those provisions were canceled.

14. The Ministerial Council, which comprises the ministers of the interior and justice, among others, is in charge of permits for foreigners; the Council's decisions are published in the Official Gazette.

15. AP7, Notes from field, Dar al-Salam, 4 May 2003. This case was documented by a student as part of an assignment to meet with and learn from Palestinians in the Cairo area in an AUC course taught by the author on Palestinian refugee issues.

16. See Brand, *Palestinians in the Arab World*, p. 63.

17. Ghabra, *Palestinians in Kuwait*.

18. Narayan et al., *Crying out for Change (Voices of the Poor)*.

Chapter 6

Egypt and the PLO:
Politics and Privileges

Although officially established in East Jerusalem,[1] the PLO almost certainly would not have seen the light of day had it not been for the extraordinary Palestinian organizational ferment in Nasser's Egypt of the late 1950s and early 1960s—and the strong political backing of Nasser himself. Created in 1964 under the auspices of the Arab League, the body was not truly representative of the Palestinian people and lacked autonomy of decision. Nevertheless, in the five years before it was taken over by a new, more representative leadership, it had succeeded in establishing a solid institutional framework that remained fundamentally unchanged and, equally important, had been formally recognized as an independent entity by all the member states of the Arab League.[2] The movement that spearheaded the 1969 takeover of the PLO, and which has dominated it ever since, was Fatah. Although founded in Kuwait, Fatah, too, can be said to have its roots in Egypt, for it was in Egypt that its founders and leaders received their political formation and learned firsthand the art of organizing and mobilizing.[3]

Yet for all Egypt's importance in the emergence of the Palestinian national movement, its small and marginalized Palestinian community was for the most part too absorbed in the struggle for survival to participate in these larger events. Palestinian activism in Egypt in the 1950s and 1960s was largely led by Palestinians from Gaza and elsewhere in the diaspora who had come to Egypt to study.[4] Yet as Laurie Brand has shrewdly pointed out, it was, in a sense, the very "marginality" of the local Palestinian population that made Nasser's enthusiastic sponsorship and encouragement of Palestinian mobilization possible, because the community was too small to pose any kind of threat. In the Gaza Strip, by contrast, Palestinian organizing efforts had from the outset been closely monitored by Egyptian intelligence and sharply curtailed.[5]

This chapter will briefly look at the evolving relations between the PLO and the Egyptian government. It will then look at the PLO's institutional framework in Egypt, including the PLO mass unions and other affiliated bodies. A third section will focus on benefits and privileges enjoyed by members of the community affiliated with the PLO. A final section will look at one of the consequences of the establishment of the PA in the occupied territories under the Oslo accords: the return of thousands of Palestinians to Gaza as of the mid-1990s.

Egypt and the PLO: A Political Overview

In the years immediately following the Nakba, there was no Palestinian political movement as such.[6] This was not only because of the disarray following the catastrophe of 1948, but also because the dominant ideology of the time was Arab nationalism, which considered Arab unity a prerequisite to the liberation of Palestine. Most Palestinians subscribed to that ideology. As mentioned in earlier chapters, Nasser made Palestine the central plank of his emerging pan-Arabism, opening Egyptian universities to Palestinian students from any country and encouraging Cairo-based Palestinian organizing efforts that encompassed Palestinians from across the Arab world. Even before the creation of the PLO, diaspora-wide Palestinian student and workers' organizations[7] had been founded in Egypt, as well as an activist Palestinian women's league that was later instrumental in establishing the PLO-affiliated women's union.

It was in the early 1960s that Nasser, in an effort to burnish his pan-Arab credentials (which had suffered with the 1961 breakup of the UAR), began to emphasize the need for a separate Palestinian political entity[8] at meetings of the Arab League, which he dominated. At the January 1964 Arab Summit in Cairo, Ahmad Shuqayri, the Palestinian delegate to the Arab League, was asked to initiate contacts with the aim of establishing such an entity. When he went beyond the original concept by including military units and military training in the plan, Nasser supported him and persuaded the league to go along. Indeed, the addition served Nasser's purpose, for his sponsorship of the PLO was in large part aimed at countering the growth of Palestinian groups advocating armed struggle, and the military element strengthened the new organization's appeal.[9] In general, it should be emphasized that

Nasser's support of Palestinian institutional development was always subordinated to his larger political aims, both in terms of advancing his pan-Arab agenda and strengthening his hand vis-à-vis the other Arab states, and controlling and co-opting Palestinian mobilization by bringing it under his umbrella.

The Arab nationalist ideology[10] had begun to be challenged in the late 1950s, most prominently by Fatah, a movement founded in Kuwait in 1959 by a group of Palestinians led by Yasir Arafat, Salah Khalaf (Abu Iyad), Faruq Qaddumi, and Khalil Wazir (Abu Jihad), who had begun their activism in the Palestinian Student Union (PSU) in the early 1950s.[11] Fatah's central idea was that the Palestinians must not depend primarily on the Arab states for help but must liberate themselves through armed struggle. Though the idea was fully developed only after Arafat and his comrades left Egypt for the Gulf in 1957, it had begun to germinate during their student days in Cairo.[12]

Fatah and the other commando groups did not attract a wide following until after the June 1967 defeat ended the dreams of liberation through Arab unity.[13] Although Nasser had earlier bitterly opposed the guerrilla groups,[14] he quickly took stock of the new situation. Recognizing Fatah as the most important and most moderate of the guerrilla factions, he began to cultivate it, furnishing arms and training facilities within months of the war's end[15]; later, he continued to provide crucial diplomatic support.[16] The PLO's sharp criticism of Nasser for his acceptance of the second Rogers plan in August 1970 led to a serious falling out, with the PLO offices in Cairo and the Cairo-based PLO and Fatah radio stations closed down. Still, when the Resistance was under deadly assault by the Jordanian regime in September 1970 following fedayeen provocations, Nasser intervened. His last act before his death of a heart attack on 28 September was to broker a truce between King Hussein and Arafat, thereby ending the most acute phase (Black September) of the bloody fedayeen-Jordanian government showdown of 1970–71.

As was seen in chapter 2, relations between the PLO and the Egyptian government continued to be strong for some time after Nasser's death: Egypt, for example, co-sponsored the resolution at the 1974 Rabat Arab summit proclaiming the PLO the sole legitimate representative of the Palestinian people. But relations began to deteriorate with the 1975 Sinai II disengagement agreement, which basically signaled Egypt's withdrawal from the Arab-Israeli conflict. Tensions were further aggravated by Sadat's visit to Jerusalem in

November 1977 and the Arab Summit in Tripoli soon after, where the PLO joined Syria, Algeria, and South Yemen in an anti-Egyptian coalition. The formal break occurred when Egypt and Israel signed their peace treaty on 17 March 1979. Relations between Egypt and the PLO, "frozen" for more than three years, did not begin to thaw until the early 1980s, particularly following Israel's summer 1982 invasion of Lebanon and siege of Beirut, which outraged Egyptians.[17] More recently, especially since the 1993 Oslo accords, Egypt has endeavored to play an active role in the peace process. The restoration of relations with the PLO, however, had little impact on the status and situation of the Palestinians in Egypt.

The PLO in Egypt

Institutions

The PLO maintained a powerful presence in Egypt until the late 1970s. With money flowing in from the oil-rich Arab states, supplemented by a "liberation tax" on Palestinians working in the Egyptian public sector as of 1969,[18] the PLO had ample funds to disburse in Egypt despite its growing military and administrative apparatus in Lebanon after its expulsion from Jordan. Its presence in Egypt included five mass unions and the Palestine Red Crescent Society with its network of health clinics (see below). Through its own offices and departments, it ran various welfare programs, administered the Martyrs' Fund, and provided subsidies for Palestinian students both local and especially from elsewhere in the Arab world. The PLO also helped local Palestinians with bureaucratic problems and certain personal status issues, fulfilling many of the functions of an embassy. Although Fatah was the dominant faction of the PLO, it also had its own bureau in Cairo, the only PLO faction to do so.[19]

Cairo had long been the hub of Palestinian diaspora activities, but this role ended with Egypt's change in policy after the mid-1970s. When the PLO resumed activities in Egypt after the resumption of diplomatic ties in 1983, its orientation, by default, was more local. Also, during the more than three-year freeze, its presence had been reduced to the Labor Union and two offices handling everyday affairs for the community,[20] and it never again regained its earlier size and influence. Still, its presence remained significant until the early 1990s, when the abrupt end to donations from the Gulf states caused by PLO political positions during the 1990–91 Gulf crisis led to a cutback in its activities. This trend was accentuated by the establishment of the PA in the occupied territories in 1994 and the decision to shift priorities to state-building. Many PLO-related institutions and offices (including medical; see Palestine Red Crescent Society section below) were transferred to Gaza, and the budget for PLO activities in Egypt was slashed. Moreover, because the PLO in Egypt had always served first and foremost the members of the local community who were associated with it, its principal constituency was itself greatly reduced when many of these relocated to Gaza as of 1995.

Thus, since the mid-1990s the PLO presence in Egypt has been mainly the Palestinian embassy, the remaining four unions operating at a reduced scale, and the Palestine Hospital. Aside from issuing Palestinian passports, the embassy's main tasks seem to be facilitating the transfer of wounded from Gaza to Egypt for medical treatment (since the intifada); securing entry permits from Israel for travel to Gaza; and helping Palestinians re-enter Egypt by securing the proper permits from the Egyptian government—either for short visits or, for those wanting to return for good, residency.

Unions and Affiliated Bodies

It bears emphasis that the PLO unions in Egypt, like the PLO infrastructure in general, were not set up for the benefit of the local population. The unions, which operated in Arab countries where there was a significant Palestinian presence, had two principal functions: mobilizing Palestinians behind the Palestinian national project and serving the local communities. In places with large Palestinian populations, the two were more or less congruent; in Egypt, however, the second goal in practice took a back seat. Furthermore, in several of the unions—notably the GUPS, and to a lesser extent the Women's Union (even though not headquartered in Egypt)—the diaspora focus seemed to predominate until the reorientation of Egyptian foreign policy in the mid-1970s and especially the precipitous drop in Palestinian student enrollment in Egyptian universities after 1977. From then on, the PLO unions in Egypt became more Egypt-centered, albeit focused especially on the local population with PLO ties. This involved mainly those who entered Egypt in 1967 or after. As the unions in Egypt became more local in orientation, their "national project" aspect shrank to insignificance, and they became almost exclusively involved with dispensing aid.

Traditionally, there were five Palestinian unions in Egypt: GUPS, GUPW (hereinafter the Labor Union), GUPWom (hereinafter the Women's Union), the General Union of Palestinian Teachers (GUPT), and the General Union of Palestinian Writers and Journalists (GUPWJ). Of these, the GUPS, historically the most important, was permanently closed in 1977. In addition to the unions, there is also the Palestine Red Crescent Society, which has a slightly different status. Finally, the PLO has several affiliated bodies, including the Palestinian Charitable Association.

The mass mobilization function of the PLO-affiliated bodies in the early years is best exemplified in the GUPS. It was established in 1959, when the PSU in Cairo (which had been run by Arafat and his comrades from 1952 to 1957) joined with Palestinian student organizations in other Arab countries and beyond to form, with Nasser's support, a diaspora-wide Palestinian student movement. Its activities went far beyond ordinary student politics. Heads of state and political leaders met its delegations, and in 1965 it organized an international symposium on Palestine attended not only by students but by political leaders and intellectuals from fifty-eight countries, an enormous success that was seen at the time as a breakthrough not just for the GUPS but for Palestine.[21] It did not become part of the PLO until after its 1969 takeover by Fatah and the commando organizations.

GUPS activism ultimately got it into trouble. In January 1972, it joined with Egyptian students in massive riots protesting Sadat's "no-war-no-peace" stalemate, and in a foretaste of what was to come, Sadat singled out the Palestinians as being the fomenters of the disturbances and arrested large numbers of them.[22] Their demonstrations against the Sinai II agreement in September 1975 led to the deportation of many Palestinian students, the sharp curtailment of GUPS activities, and various punitive measures that dramatically reduced the number of Palestinian university students in Egypt.[23] The union was closed down in November 1977 at the time of Sadat's visit to Jerusalem, the event that marked his true break with the Palestinians.

After the GUPS was banned, four unions remained in Egypt, although only the labor and women's unions had any real importance. Contributing to their longevity was their avoidance of any political activity whatsoever and the care they took to cultivate the support of Egyptian allies (the Egyptian Trade Union Federation, in the case of the Palestinian Labor Union; solidarity groups, in the case of the Women's Union).[24] Their survival in Egypt, according to some observers, has been to an extent contingent upon maintaining close contact with state security.

The Labor Union

The Palestinian Labor Union (modeled after the Palestinian Arab Workers Organization established in Haifa in 1925) was founded in Cairo in 1963 and became part of the PLO when it was established the next year. The Labor Union, like the other Palestinian mass unions, aimed at diaspora-wide Palestinian mobilization, but it never neglected the local community. Thus, even while traveling throughout the Arab world to establish contacts for a broad organization, it recruited Palestinian workers in Egypt itself; its first office was in the industrial area of Helwan.[25] The union reached out to Palestinians throughout Egypt by creating branches in agricultural and industrial areas such as Sharqiyyah, Fayyum, Qina, al-'Arish, and Qalyubiyyah, as well as Cairo. The top positions in the union were traditionally held by members of the PLO from the diaspora or fighters who had been with the PLO in Jordan and Lebanon.

The aim of the union has been to help its members find and maintain jobs and to improve employment conditions, securing shorter working hours, guaranteed sick leave and paid holidays, and protection against arbitrary dismissal. Thanks in part to its efforts, under Egyptian Law 58 of 1971, Palestinian workers with permanent residence status in Egypt were exempted from having to acquire work permits. This victory, however, was nullified after the al-Siba'i assassination, when the law was revoked.

The Labor Union was the only PLO union in Egypt allowed to remain open when Egyptian-PLO relations were frozen after the signing of the Israeli-Egyptian peace treaty in 1979. At that time, however, Palestinian union activity was limited to the following:

- Sending out letters to facilitate issuing/renewing of work and residence permits for applicants in Egypt.
- Providing financial assistance for families after a member's death and helping with funeral expenses if necessary.
- Networking among skilled job seekers and employers.
- Defending the rights of Palestinian laborers.
- Establishing Palestinian cemeteries in various locations. (Three were built by the PLO.)
- Distributing aid to needy union members.

Since the mid-1990s and the establishment of the PA, even these reduced functions have become largely beyond the means of the Labor Union, whose principal task is now issuing letters verifying employment to facilitate obtaining work and residence permits (alluded to in many of our field interviews) and other administrative functions. It also provides members with medical insurance taken out of membership dues. At the time we did our field research, the union listed a membership of about 11,000 wage laborers and about 1,000 public sector workers (mainly PLO and AOGG employees or retirees) through its seventeen branches and sub-branches.[26] Although even today the Labor Union remains the largest and most important Palestinian union in Egypt, and despite its potential for outreach through its many branches, our interviews in the field indicated that many Palestinians in dire need had never heard of it.

The Women's Union

The PLO's Women's Union was established in Jerusalem in 1965, but a Palestinian women's organization (the "League of Palestinian Women") had been founded in Cairo two years earlier, in 1963, by a group of Palestinian graduate students led by Samirah Abu Ghazalah.[27] Similar to the other PLO unions, its goal was to mobilize Palestinian women to serve the Palestinian cause and to provide services to the community. In 1968, the union established al-Wijdan, a mother and child care center in the 'Abbasiyyah district of Cairo, to provide poor families with free medicine and treatment using funding from Palestinian businessmen. The center was closed in 1974–75 by the authorities for what was deemed "political activity"—putting new roofs on the homes of Palestinians who lived in the area. This experience only strengthened the union's traditional avoidance of any discussion of Egyptian domestic matters or activities that could attract government scrutiny. The Women's Union has gone out of its way to reach out beyond the Palestinian community, regularly inviting the wives of various Arab and foreign ambassadors to their functions[28] and welcoming interested Egyptians as members. Such activities fall within its efforts to promote understanding of the Palestinian situation. The union recently published a calendar with brief descriptions of Palestinian life under Israel's reoccupation of the West Bank and Gaza as of 2002.

One of the most important activities of the Women's Union in the past was subsidizing students. During the PLO's "flush years," the sums disbursed were considerable. According to the head of the union interviewed in 1997, a total of £E 30 million had been spent over the years to fund 2,600 students in Egypt.[29] This figure is significant as an indicator of the Women's Union's former "diaspora orientation," because only a small fraction of these funds would have gone to local Palestinians, with the vast majority underwriting Palestinians from elsewhere in the Arab world. In any case, the union has tried to maintain the tradition to the extent possible with its very limited means.

> When my children attended school, I used to get £E 200 from the Women's Union to help pay the fees. (P31, Qantara, 19 June 2002)

Further reductions followed the shift of PLO priorities after 1995. The union continues to pay private school fees for a small number of poor families, but it does so at a reduced level. In some cases, it has ceased payments altogether:

> The PLO was in charge of university education for Palestinians serving with it. Moreover, the Women's Union paid school fees for the children of PLO employees. The family would give the bills to the union and the union would pay. That stopped four years ago. I do not know why! (P7, 'Ayn Shams, 23 May 2002)

Other traditional Women's Union programs such as literacy classes and loan support schemes have been discontinued because of insufficient funding and lack of full-time staff. With fewer resources, the union has continued to do what it can to provide material help and financial subsidies:

> I also receive new or used clothing from the Women's Union. In most cases, the sizes are wrong, but I take them and try to sell them and buy things for the house. (P18, Dar al-Salam, 9 June 2002)

> The Women's Union gives me £E 20 every time I visit them. I try to seek their help, but I am unable to get a regular subsidy from them. (7/25, Abu Hammad, 10 July 2002)

As part of its objective of preserving Palestinian traditions and identity while building women's assets through income-generating projects, the union engaged low-income women in traditional Palestinian embroidery and helped them market their products:

> I worked for the Women's Union making embroidered dresses. We sold them in hotels like the Sheraton and Hilton. I left because the money wasn't enough for the amount of work. (8/3, Abu Za'bal, 30 June 2002)

The Women's Union also continues to hold a yearly bazaar—part of a long-standing tradition—which sells, among other things, locally produced Palestinian embroidery and other items. The union has a folk group called Chorale Abbad al-Shams. A folk dance troupe has performed in the past with the Egyptian national dance troupe and throughout the Middle East, raising money and publicizing the Palestinian cause abroad. However, it has involved only a small number of Palestinians, mainly those whose parents are affiliated with the PLO.

Palestine Red Crescent Society

The Palestine Red Crescent Society was originally established as a national Palestinian medical organization in 1968 in Jordan, after the Battle of Karameh, and it soon came under the umbrella of the newly reconstituted PLO. In 1970 it opened a branch in Egypt, establishing clinics in areas with significant Palestinian populations. The Palestine Red Crescent Society also established medical centers in Maniyal, Alexandria, Zaqaziq, and Tahrir. When the PLO was forced to leave Lebanon in 1982, Cairo became the organization's headquarters and remained so until 1995, when it moved to Gaza. During those years, the multi-story Palestine Hospital, a major medical facility with some 20 specialties and a large pharmacy, was built in Heliopolis. A childcare center, called Jerusalem, was created in Madinat Nasr for hospital employees. Other new facilities were opened, including a socio-medical center and, at 'Ayn Shams, a rehabilitation institute that also served, according to the hospital director, as "a unique training center for therapists working with the handicapped."[30] In 1983, to satisfy the growing need for nurses and paramedical personnel, the Palestine Red Crescent Society opened the al-Falujah Nursing Institute, which offered a three-year program for registered nurses and a two-year program for technicians and paramedics. The school was a godsend for many Palestinians who were no longer permitted to study science or medicine in Egyptian public universities. The hospital also provided a recruitment center for qualified graduates who might otherwise have had difficulties finding work:

> I studied at the nursing college that was linked with the Red Crescent before it was moved to Gaza. I was even given a subsidy of £E 38 a month. (8/12, Shibin al-Qanatir, 3 July 2002)

With the establishment of the PA in 1994, many Palestine Red Crescent Society activities were transferred to Khan Yunis in Gaza, including the rehabilitation center, the training center, and the al-Falujah Nursing Institute. All Red Crescent medical centers throughout Egypt were closed except the Palestine Hospital, which now serves some 20,000 persons under the medical insurance program. The hospital provides medical care for those working at PLO institutions as well as for current and former employees of the AOGG. It also serves the families of the Association of Palestinian Martyrs and Injured and handles the cases referred to it by the PA because of inadequate facilities in Gaza.

Those with medical insurance pay 10 percent of the standard fees for consultations and operations and 20 percent for medicine. Although the Palestine Hospital provides care for anyone who needs treatment, it does so at private sector rates. In an interview, hospital director Dr. Muhammad Zaghlul expressed regret that it was not possible to treat uninsured Palestinian free of charge, explaining that the hospital has had a huge budget deficit as a result of severe cuts following the PLO's 1995 decision to give priority to the establishment of health centers in Gaza and the West Bank. He also noted that money deducted from the salaries of PLO employees for medical coverage is not being paid to the Red Crescent, nor is the hospital being reimbursed for the medical cases referred to it by the PA in Gaza. The director added that he sometimes asks the PA minister of health for financial assistance for critical cases.[31]

Many of the Palestinians interviewed said that Palestine Hospital's location in Heliopolis makes it difficult to reach. Transportation costs leave many reluctant to seek care at the hospital, even if they have insurance. In addition, medicine for chronic diseases is not always available, and traveling back and forth to obtain subsidized medicine is not always practical.

Despite the cutbacks, the Palestine Hospital is an important source of employment for Palestinians. While most private sector companies have a 10-percent ceiling on foreign workers, as mentioned in chapter 4, the Palestine Red Crescent Society is considered a foreign investment, where the ceiling for foreign labor is 41 percent. According to the director, the actual number of Palestinians employed at the hospital exceeds 40 percent, because many Palestinian women married to Egyptians work there as Egyptians, and most of the doctors with Jordanian nationality are Palestinians.[32] However, a number of interviewees reported that personal connections are necessary to be hired:

> I applied to work at the Red Crescent Hospital, but my application was completely ignored. The hospital gives priority to Fatah people. They are the ones who were recruited and the ones who were helped to go to Gaza. There is a double standard, and *wasta* [personal connections] plays a strong role in the hospital administration. (P8, 'Ayn Shams, 23 May 2002)

In addition to its medical function, the Palestine Red Crescent Society is a national humanitarian society that provides a wide range of services to Palestinians. It sponsors classes for women to learn sewing and traditional Palestinian embroidery patterns, and it has a permanent exhibit of Palestinian handicrafts to market their products, among others. It also has a social center, which is perhaps the most important meeting place for Palestinians in the region. It sponsors a dance troupe, called Falujah, whose mission is to preserve Palestinian culture and identity in exile and to spread awareness of the Palestinian cause.

Other PLO-affiliated Bodies

Another PLO-related organization that provides some services to needy Palestinians is the Palestinian Charitable Association, established in 1983 and funded by the Palestinian Businessmen's Council. Unlike most of the PLO-affiliated organizations, the Charitable Association does not limit its services to the PLO community. Its activities—which include subsidizing education and health services and channelling job opportunities to Palestinian job seekers and employers—prospered in the early 1990s, but its resources are now limited. It currently serves several hundred Palestinian families who live below the poverty line; several hundred more families are on the waiting list.[33] Many of those assisted by the association are women whose husbands abandoned them when they left to join the Palestinian Authority in Gaza in the mid-1990s:

> When the PA was set up in Gaza, my husband left me to go back without taking care of the family expenses here. I had to seek help from the Charitable Association. I get an irregular subsidy of £E 50 from the association. (7/29, Abu Kabir, July 2002)

> When Abu Alia left me, my mother and my sister helped me with the main household expenses . . . I also get a subsidy from the Charitable Association of £E 80 a month. I also get £E 50 monthly from the Ministry of Social Affairs since I am a divorced Egyptian. With the income I make from sewing underwear for a factory and trading of goods brought from al-'Arish, I am able to manage. In seasons like Ramadan, many people give charity through the Charitable Association, which can reach £E 400 to £E 500. (P18, Dar al-Salam, 9 June 2002)

The Businessmen's Council, which funds the Charitable Association, has an indirect link to the PLO. In the early 1980s, Palestinian businessmen had sought to create an organization of their own in order to play a role in the social, cultural, and economic affairs of the community. With the Egyptian government fearing that such an organization could be co-opted for political purposes, and the PLO worrying about a potential challenge to its own dominance in the community, the Palestine Red Crescent Society stepped in and formed the board of trustees of what was to become the Palestinian Businessmen's Council. The board involved Palestinian businessmen in financing PLO institutions and in its decision making. In this way, the business community was brought within the fold of the PLO. The Council, however, had little success. The first attempt to organize it failed, and a new council was formed in 1996. According to its current head, Ali Jawhar, the council is not very active because of personal differences among the members.[34] The Businessmen's Council and the Charitable Association remain linked, however, and Ali Jawhar is the head of both organizations.

One of the PLO-affiliated bodies that caters exclusively to the families of PLO personnel is the Association of Martyred and Injured Palestinians. The organization serves the families of some 500 PLO members killed or wounded, providing assistance through monthly subsidies.

> My son was a martyr in Gaza. He was killed after he returned to Palestine after the establishment of the PA. My husband, who is a PA officer now, left us ten years ago and stopped sending us money. He divorced me two years after my son was killed. To survive, I depend on a pension from the Association of Martyred and Injured Palestinians. They pay me the equivalent of 180 Israeli shekels.[35] (P4, Dar al-Salam, 18 May 2002)

Even an organization with so sacred a mission among Palestinians has suffered budget reductions, and services have been cut back: The association used to help pay school fees but no longer does so.[36] In addition to its financial subsidies, however, the organization does continue to cover medical treatment at the Palestine Hospital for the families it serves.

Working for the PLO

In addition to its primary role as the locus of Palestinian resistance and the Palestinian national movement, the PLO, through its military forces, administrative infrastructure, unions, and associated bodies, was the largest employer of the Palestinians in Egypt until the move to Gaza. The leadership cadres of almost all the PLO-affiliated bodies were PLO appointees brought in from the outside, though many of them had gone to university in Egypt. Needless to say, this was also true of all PLO officials in Egypt with diplomatic status, first and foremost those of ambassadorial rank: the head of the PLO office (since 1993 the Palestinian embassy), the PLO ambassador to the Arab League (based at the Palestinian embassy), and the PLO representative in charge of the Palestinian file at the Arab League (based at Arab League headquarters). Other PLO positions, including at the unions, medical clinics, and so on, would be occupied by "local" Palestinians. The largest number of "local" Palestinians employed by the PLO, however, was associated with or retired from the various military units, especially the PLA.

For those associated with it, the PLO offered stability through regular incomes, pensions, free education up to the university level, reduced university fees, and subsidized or free health care at the Palestine Hospital. Association with the PLO also meant relative ease in obtaining residency and travel documents from the government. These privileges were not affected by the ups and downs of PLO-Egyptian relations.[37] The decline in benefits later experienced by PLO employees and their families was a result of the PLO financial crisis in 1991.[38]

Almost without exception, those associated with the PLO were part of the influx entering Egypt in the wake of the 1967 war. Many were with the 'Ayn Jalut Brigade of the PLA, then under Egyptian command. Several thousand were retained on active duty (under Egyptian command) and deployed at the Bitter Lakes on the Suez (except for a year deployed in Syria in 1970–71) and fought in the 1973 war.[39] A larger number of 'Ayn Jalut veterans were settled in Cairo, officially as "reserves"[40] but actually free to pursue their own affairs following Egypt's reorganization and reduction of the brigade. Some of these, especially after the PLO's takeover by the commando organizations in 1969, joined in fighting under direct Palestinian (generally Fatah) command. Palestinians "based" in Egypt fought in Jordan in the civil war and its aftermath in 1970–71, the Lebanese civil war, in south Lebanon, and against the Israeli invasions in 1978 and 1982. In many cases, as noted in earlier chapters, families of the fighters had been brought from Gaza to Cairo after the 1967 war; in other cases, the fighters married while in Egypt. In both situations, their families remained behind as they went to fight elsewhere. The peripatetic movement of the fighters—and their long absences—were reflected in many of the interviews:

> My father was the first to arrive in Egypt, because he was working with the PLO. His grandfather was Egyptian, so he used to come to Sanhud [in Qalyubiyyah Governorate], where he married my mother. He was traveling most of the time to Jordan, Iraq, or Lebanon. He would then come back to Egypt to stay for some time before leaving . . . (7/46, Minya al-Qamah, 11 July 2002)

> Several years after the 1973 war, my husband left for Lebanon with the PLO and fought there. He then went to Libya after the PLO was expelled from Lebanon [in 1982]. The moment the PA went to Gaza, he joined them and was one of the first

to arrive. For more than ten years, my husband did not return
to Egypt. (P4, Dar al-Salam, 18 May 2002)

Beyond the absences, it is clear from many of the interviews
that very often the men did not take their responsibilities to their
families very seriously. Um Karim's husband, for example, fought
with the PLO army in Jordan [during the 1970–71 Palestinian-
Jordanian fighting], moving afterwards to Syria before being sent
to Lebanon:

> He used to come and check on me and the baby I had when he
> was in Jordan. He came to see us every three to eight months
> and would send us some money every now and then. I had to
> work as a maid to have a regular income, especially because
> my [Egyptian] family's condition is no better than mine, so I
> had to depend on myself. When he was in Lebanon, he stopped
> sending money. (P13, 'Ayn Sham, 23 May 2002)

After the PLO fighters and guerrilla organizations were expelled
from Lebanon following Israel's invasion in 1982, the fighters who
had previously been based in Egypt returned. Some remained in
the PLO ranks and others retired, often trying to find other work.
One of the privileges of having been a fighter with the PLA, or
employed by the PLO, was that they could more easily leave Egypt
without the anxiety of whether or not they would be allowed to
return, since the PLO would always issue them letters providing
reasons for their travel and assuring their re-entry.

> After my husband left the Liberation Army, he went to find
> employment in Libya. There he worked in a field that he had
> always wanted to be involved in—steel and iron polishing.
> When he returned to Egypt, he started his own business.
> Today he has a workshop where he spends most of his time.
> (P9, Wailey, 24 June 2002)

Many former PLO officers tried to set up their own businesses
after leaving the force, while still drawing pensions:

> My father worked for the Liberation Army until 1975. He then
> resigned. Having been in Lebanon with the PLO, he decided
> to export and import clothing with some Lebanese partners.
> Then he decided to import cars. Through some contacts, he
> decided to go to Iraq and start a construction business. In

1985, he returned to Egypt because of the Iraq-Iran war and started a construction company in Egypt. I worked with my father for four years before I went to Yemen to work in the same construction field. Soon afterward, I came back from Yemen to take over my father's ceramic tile business. (7/38, Dyarb Nijim, July 2002)

Through the Labor Union, the PLO often also acted as a clearing house for jobs abroad and even helped cover travel expenses.

Through the Labor Union, it was announced in all faculties at Egyptian universities that Yemen was looking for teachers. I applied and was accepted. The PLO office then helped in buying the [plane] tickets to Yemen. (P8, 'Ayn Shams, 23 May 2002)

In later years, as already indicated, PLO services and privileges were reduced as a result of the financial crisis following the 1990–91 Gulf war. This trend continued and deepened as the peace process shifted the PLO's priorities, climaxing with the establishment of the PA in 1994. From then on, PLO-related salaries in Egypt were cut, and aid programs, scholarships, and subsidies, already much reduced, for the most part ceased altogether. Many of our interviews reflected, either directly or in passing, how this change had affected their lives.

But while the new situation that grew out of the Oslo process caused hardship for many, for others it offered an unimagined opportunity: the fulfilment of the long-cherished dream of return to the homeland.

Relocating to Gaza

When the PA was established in the territories in 1994, the Palestinian embassy in Egypt called for those who wanted to relocate to Gaza to submit their applications for employment with the PA. Former PLO fighters were given priority, but Israel had the final say as to who was allowed to enter.[41] This being the case, the PLO was required to present a list of potential returnees to Israel for approval. Refugees who had been expelled from Palestine in 1948 were not part of this move, probably so as not to create a precedent with regard to the Palestinian right of return. Those permitted to enter the territories had almost invariably arrived during or after the 1967 war.

Israel's veto power was illustrated in several interviews, including the following:

> I applied to the Palestinian embassy for work in one of the ministries when the PA was established in Gaza. My uncle worked in Gaza and I was hoping that my application would be accepted. When my uncle invited me to go to Gaza, I was denied a visitors permit by the Israelis since it seems there is a blacklisted person with the same name. I want to live in Palestine and have Palestinian nationality. (7/21, Salhiyyah, 8 July 2002)

Palestinians granted permission to go to Gaza were given Palestinian identity cards upon arrival and issued Palestinian "passports" or travel documents (*laissez-passer*) renewable every three years. Reliable statistics on how many actually entered Gaza are not available, but according to the Palestinian ambassador to Egypt, Zuhdi al-Qudwah, some 45,000 Palestinians left Egypt for Gaza after 1995.[42] While this number may be high, certainly many thousands made the move. When the team was interviewing families in Dar al-Salam, Wailey, and other places where PLO people had lived, we were repeatedly struck by indications of the extent of the return: Time and again people would point out empty apartments—sometimes almost entire buildings—vacated by owners or occupants who had gone to Gaza. More than once we were told that we were "too late" for our survey, as most of the Palestinians in the neighborhood had already left.

Many present or former PLO employees pulled strings or used their influence to get their children jobs with the PA:

> I helped all my children to get work in the PA. I was a lieutenant myself in the PLO army. Today all my sons have Palestinian IDs and have good positions with the PA. (P1, Giza, 10 May 2002)

Without doubt, most of those who returned to Gaza from Egypt had been with the PLO, both active and retired, but they were not the only ones who wanted to go. Return to Gaza and the West Bank was seen by many as a way of escaping the humiliating status they had endured in the *ghurba*. An example of this kind of attitude is the following:

As far as I know, those who used to work for the PLO were the ones able to apply for a Palestinian ID. I would love to have any passport other than this [Egyptian] travel document. Even when I ask to marry a woman, I am refused because her parents don't want their grandchildren to suffer. (8/2, Shibin al-Qanatir, 4 July 2002)

In addition to the normal aspirations for return, a number of other reasons made finding work with the PA or in Palestine an attractive option. For PLO stalwarts, it was a chance to be part of the state-building enterprise. Especially for first-generation Palestinians, return meant the chance to rebuild ties with their families. For others, it was a way of seeking employment stability and a sense of belonging that had been lacking in Egypt. For still others, it offered a chance to regularize their legal status; we often heard that young Palestinians with problems renewing their residence permits at age 21 and who had problems finding employment were more likely to try to leave for Gaza.

Some young people who entered Gaza on the strength of their parents' PLO connections ended up living by their wits, blending into an informal economy or even working in Israel:

My father, who was then working at the PA, tried to get me a job with the PA but my mother wouldn't allow it. I worked during these two years as a laborer in Israel. I also worked in a gas station and sometimes as a painter. (7/46, Minya al-Qamah, 11 July 2002)

For those unable to find jobs with the PA but who still wanted to return to Gaza, a number of other possibilities were open. Palestinian women whose parents still lived there were able to apply for them (and their families) to join them through the family reunification program.[43]

Another means of entering Gaza was to apply for a visitor's permit (*tasrih ziyarah*) through family members living in Palestine. The permit, usually valid for three months, was issued by Israel, which tightly controls the borders of the PA areas. In many cases, however, Palestinians would overstay their permits.

I know many people who left here and now live there [Gaza] with no IDs or legal papers and who have exceeded their stay ... I wonder how they are living there. (P5, Dar al-Salam, 18 May 2002)

Some Palestinians who received permits to enter Gaza did not move there permanently but used them to lay the ground for an eventual return, establishing a base for themselves in Palestine and then returning to Egypt to wait for the economic and political situation to stabilize. Some bought property as a long-term investment; others rented houses and made seasonal visits between Gaza and Egypt. Similarly, a surprising number of interviewees saw the marriage of their children to Gazans as a first step to their own return to Palestine.

> All my children are married to Palestinians, so when the situation gets better in Gaza, we will be able to go back. It will then be very easy for both the husband and for the wife to return. (8/11, Shubra al-Khayma, 12 June 2002)

Many young women who were not able to finish their education in Egypt were sent to Gaza to marry Palestinian relatives in order to ensure that the coming generation would live in Palestine.

For many, the return proved difficult.[44] It is common for Palestinians, especially young people who have never been there, to imagine the homeland as "heaven on earth," with images passed down from parents and grandparents of citrus groves, green fields, warm family, and neighborly, helpful relations. Arriving in Gaza, they found dire economic conditions and a society scarred by long years of harsh occupation. They also found a more conservative society and different customs from what they were used to in Egypt, making adaptation difficult for some. The desire to reconnect with family sometimes also turned sour.

In a number of cases, men had not only started a new career in Gaza, but also a new family. A young man whose father was a PLO official who had joined the PA and whose mother was Egyptian recounts the following:

> We had always maintained a close relationship with my uncles, aunts, and cousins in Gaza. They often came to our house here in Egypt. After having settled in the West Bank, where he was living with his Palestinian wife in Tulkarm, my father wanted us all to join him. So, we left and stayed with them for six months. The situation was bad for us, so we went to Khan Yunis in the Gaza Strip. My father insisted on having my sister marry his nephew. They got married and she was living with her in-laws, who were treating her badly. After four months she wanted to return to Egypt. Because

we didn't have good relations with my uncle, we returned to Egypt. My mother got divorced from my father and my sister got divorced from our cousin. A few months afterwards, my sister delivered a baby girl in Sanhud. Our experience in the West Bank and Gaza was difficult and my mother doesn't have relations with Palestinians any more. (7/46, Minya al-Qamah, 11 July 2002)

Sometimes, return ended in tragedy:

My son wanted to go live with his father in Gaza, so he did. He finished his high school exams at an UNRWA school in Gaza. When he finished his education, he joined Hamas. On his nineteenth birthday, he was out with his friends and they harassed some Israeli soldiers standing on an observation tower. The soldiers could not take this and Muhammad was shot in the head. He died on the spot. We all went to Gaza on hearing the news. My son became a martyr. His father had married another woman and it was not suitable for us—my five children and me—to remain, so we decided to return to Egypt. My two daughters quit university there and came back a few years ago. (P4, Dar al-Salam, 18 May 2002)

Those who had relocated to Gaza and decided to come back to Egypt faced major problems. If they had stayed away for more than six months without obtaining the necessary permit, they were denied re-entry into Egypt, putting those who had overstayed their three-month Israeli visitors permits in a particular bind. Many Palestinians are currently living in Gaza illegally, as stateless persons. The research team was told of many cases of Palestinian women in this situation who had married in Gaza and subsequently lost their legal status in Egypt:

My son and daughter now live in Gaza. My daughter lost her Egyptian residence permit because she got married and did not come back within six months. (7/30, Bilbays, July 2002)

With the outbreak of the al-Aqsa intifada in September 2000, the situation in Gaza changed dramatically. PA salaries were reduced, and the economy slowed to a standstill as a result of increasingly frequent Israeli closures and curfews. Some who had attained legal status in Gaza tried to go back to Egypt until the situation in the Palestinian territories improved:

> My elder son returned here in March 2002. Work had become
> very slow for him ever since the intifada started. He is back
> now working in construction. My other son bought a taxi
> in Khan Yunis. He also complains of the stagnant economic
> situation. I told them to join the PLO, which could have
> ensured them regular salaries. They preferred informal work.
> (P5, Dar al-Salam, 18 May 2002)

Many of those who left for Gaza had kept their apartments in
Egypt, but others had liquidated everything before the move and
had no place to go back to. Others incurred debt in the process:

> When we decided to come back due to family problems,
> I had to start looking for work in Egypt. I first worked as a
> truck driver with my cousins but because we did not own the
> vehicle, we had enormous debt. I now earn a living by making
> furniture. (7/46, Minya al-Qamah, 11 July 2002)

Most frequent, however, were bureaucratic difficulties. For many
who returned, obtaining a residence permit became a problem for
the first time. Though the Palestinian passport (*laissez-passer*) is
recognized by more than eighty states,[45] those who acquired it and
renounced their Egyptian documents paid a heavy price if they
decided to go back to Egypt. Regardless of how short the duration
of their stay in Palestine and regardless of how many years they
had lived in Egypt, they became *de facto* and *de jure* foreigners and
had to apply for resident permits as foreigners. The "privileges"
they used to have in Egypt were lost.

> I hold the Palestinian travel document because I was given
> a Palestinian identification document. I thought it would be
> better to have a Palestinian travel document. It turned out to
> be more difficult. Life in Egypt became more expensive for
> us. With the Egyptian travel document, we had privileges,
> especially since I am a former 'Ayn Jalut officer. My children
> were able to go to public schools. But now we are considered
> foreigners. (P11 'Ayn Shams, 28 May 2002)

Even for those who retained their Egyptian travel documents,
residence permits, which in the past had been relatively certain for
the families of PLO employees, became problematic:

My father, who now works with the PA, issued us all Palestinian identification documents, but we kept our Egyptian travel documents. Since we came back from Palestine, the Office of the Gaza Governor has not agreed to renew our residence permits using the Egyptian travel document. They require us to get a Palestinian travel document on which basis the residence will be given since we now have Palestinian identification documents. (7/46, Minya al-Qamah, 11 July 2002)

Ever since I took a Palestinian identification document in Gaza, I must renew my residence permit every year, whereas I used to renew the Egyptian travel document every three years (since I came in 1967 as part of the PLO army). I renew my residence permit on time to save myself the hassle and to avoid the harassment I may get from some government office. (P5, Dar al-Salam, 18 May 2002)

Just as there are no reliable figures on the number of Palestinians in Egypt who left for Palestine, so are there none on how many returned to Egypt. Furthermore, from our interviews we were led to understand that a number of those who have come back still hope to return to settle in Gaza when calm is restored.

Perhaps surprisingly, the difficulties and harsh realities encountered in Gaza did not always dampen the romantic notions of return. Despite everything, a number of our interviewees have continued to see living in the homeland as an end to their struggles:

My son was living in Libya when the [Libyan] authorities confiscated his house and deported him and his family in 1997. While he was there he lost his Egyptian residence permit. Through his cousins, he was able to get a permit to visit Gaza, but that expired and he is now living there illegally with no papers. But at least he is living with his family in the homeland. (AP3, Alexandria, August 2002)

Notes

1. The PLO was launched by the first Palestine National Council held in Jerusalem, 28 May–2 June 1964.

2. Brand, *Palestinians in the Arab World*, p. 29, notes that the basic structures established in 1964 have remained, despite further development.

3. According to Alan Hart, whose biography of Fatah leader Yasir Arafat was written in collaboration with Arafat himself and other members of his top leadership, Arafat's plan up until March 1957 had been to make his headquarters Cairo and to organize his movement there. Hart, *Arafat: Terrorist or Peacemaker?* (London: Sidgwick & Jackson, 1984), pp. 119–20.

4. Arafat is probably the only major figure of the Palestinian movement to have spent most of his childhood and adolescence in Egypt, attending primary and secondary school as well as university in the country.

5. Brand, "Nasir's Egypt and the Re-emergence of the Palestinian National Movement," p. 43.

6. The closest thing to a developed "Palestinian" party or group until the late 1950s was George Habash's Arab Nationalist Movement (ANM), founded in Beirut in the early 1950s. Although it was a pan-Arab movement, its membership was dominated by Palestinians, and it put greater emphasis on the Palestine issue than the other Arab nationalist movements of the period such as the Baath. The ANM had close ties with Egypt into the 1960s, but relations cooled, especially after Nasser's sponsorship of the PLO.

7. The General Union of Palestinian Students (GUPS) and the General Union of Palestinian Workers (GUPW), respectively. See "Unions and Affiliated Bodies."

8. Nasser had not been the first to call for a Palestinian political entity. The GUPS, for example, had already called for a Palestinian entity, a liberation army, and a liberation organization, but Nasser was the first to have the power to implement it. Brand, *Palestinians in the Arab World*, p. 74.

9. Nasser was correct in this assumption; Abu Iyad writes of how the PLO's creation resulted in the defection of numerous fighters from Fatah's ranks. See Abu Iyad (Salah Khalaf) with Eric Rouleau, *My Home, My Land: A Narrative of the Palestinian Struggle* (New York: Times Books, 1981), chapter 3.

10. In addition to Nasserist pan-Arabism, the Baath party had been preaching Arab nationalism since the 1940s.

11. Arafat, running on a slate with Abu Iyad, was elected president of the PSU in September 1952 and remained president until he got his degree in 1956, at which point Khalaf became president. Abu Iyad, *My Home, My Land*, pp. 20–21. The importance of the PSU far exceeded what is usually thought of as a student union.

12. The platform on which Arafat and Khalaf ran in the PSU elections of 1952 (their nine-member slate included six of their own group, which became the nucleus of Fatah) already emphasized that the Palestinians could rely only on themselves—an idea that ran completely counter to the prevailing Arab nationalist thought. Abu Iyad, *My Home My Land*, p. 21. See also Hart, *Arafat: Terrorist or Peacemaker?*, pp. 117–19.

13. The ANM of George Habash, Nasser's former protégé, transformed itself into the radical Popular Front for the Liberation of Palestine.

14. Nasser had feared that guerrilla raids launched from the Arab states bordering on Israel would provide Israel with a pretext for massive retaliation. In fact, Fatah raids encouraged by Syria were a factor in Israel's launching the 1967 war.

15. The meeting at which this was decided took place in November 1967. Hart, *Arafat: Terrorist or Peacemaker?* pp. 268–70. See also Abu Iyad, *My Home, My Land*, pp. 262–63.

16. Among other things, he brokered the 1969 Cairo agreements between the Lebanese army and the PLO, giving the PLO a foothold in Lebanon.

17. Even after PLO-Egypt relations were restored, they remained volatile for some time; PLO offices were closed for six months in 1987 in anger over PLO statements at a Palestine National Council meeting in Algiers.

18. Brand, *Palestinians in the Arab World*, p. 60.

19. All other commando factions had been expelled from Egypt by Nasser in 1970 for their role in the anti-Nasser demonstrations in Amman and elsewhere during the crisis over Egypt's acceptance of the Rogers plan; they were never allowed back. See Dajani, *Institutionalisation of Palestinian Identity in Egypt*, pp. 18, 64.

20. Brand, *Palestinians in the Arab World*, p. 62.

21. Ibid., pp. 77–78.

22. Dajani, *Institutionalisation of Palestinian Identity in Egypt*, p. 45.

23. Ibid., p. 46.

24. Ibid., p. 49.

25. See Brand, "Nasir's Egypt and the Re-emergence of the Palestinian National Movement," p. 39.

26. Interview with Adel Attiyah, 24 September 2001.

27. Reflecting the fragmented nature of Egypt's Palestinian community, Brand cites Abu Ghazalah's comment that "the fact that in Egypt there were Palestinians so close to each other sharing the same problems and struggle yet not knowing about each other, was a problem that needed to be remedied." "Nasir's Egypt and the Re-emergence of the Palestinian National Movement," p. 94.

28. Dajani, *Institutionalisation of Palestinian Identity in Egypt*, p. 64.

29. *Al-Ahram Hebdo*, 22 October 1997.

30. Interview with Dr. Muhammad Zaghlul, director of the Palestine Red Crescent Society Hospital—Palestine, 29 April 2003.

31. Ibid.

32. Ibid.

33. Interview with Ali Jawhar, 22 October 2001.

34. Ali Jawhar, oral communication, 13 July 2003.

35. To increase the amount, the money is paid in Gaza and later exchanged for Egyptian currency.

36. Interview with Barakat al-Farra, representative of Fatah and the director of the Association of Martyred and Injured Palestinians in Egypt, 25 October 2001.

37. University education was an exception: It was not until 1992 that the children of PLO employees were exempted from 90 percent of the fees required of foreigners.

38. A contributing factor in the privileged status may have been that senior PLO officials for the most part maintained very close relations with Egyptian government officials, although this did not necessarily affect the conditions of ordinary PLO employees.

39. Sayigh, *Armed Struggle and the Search for State*, p. 331.

40. Ibid., p. 170; see chapter 1.

41. "Refugees in the Middle East Process," Palestinian Refugee ResearchNet, accessed at http://www.arts.mcgill.ca/MEPP/PRRN/prmepp.html.

42. Interview, 23 September 2001.

43. Israeli conditions for the right of residence are as follows: (a) the person was registered in the Israeli census in the newly occupied territories in 1967, (b) the person holds an Israeli identity card, and (c) he or she has been visiting the territories regularly, at least every six years, since the census was conducted (Hovdenak et al., *Constructing Order*, p. 67). The family reunification program was carried out through those who had Israeli identity cards which later became Palestinian identification cards (and were approved by the Israeli authorities).

44. Because all our interviews were conducted in Egypt, those who talked about their own experiences relocating to Gaza had returned.

45. Abbas Shiblak, *The League of Arab States and Palestinian Refugees' Residency Rights*. Shaml Monograph Series (Ramallah, Palestinian Authority: Shaml, 1998).

Chapter 7

Palestinian Protection
under International and Regional
Conventions

Everyone has the right to freedom of movement and residence within the borders of each State. . . . Everyone has the right to leave any country, including his own, and to return to his country.

—*Article 13, Universal Declaration of Human Rights*

Everyone has the right to a nationality. No one shall be arbitrarily deprived of his nationality nor denied the right to change his nationality.

—*Article 15, Universal Declaration of Human Rights*

In much if not most of the world, there is a disconnect between the rights and protections people are guaranteed under the law (both national and international) and the rights and protections they actually enjoy. This is undoubtedly more salient in the case of refugees and stateless persons. With particular regard to Palestinian refugees, there is in addition a controversy as to what protections they are entitled to under international conventions.

In order to understand the legal situation of the Palestinians in Egypt and what protections they do—or should—have under international and regional treaties, it is necessary first to review the evolution of the Palestinian refugee question in the organization most deeply involved with the issue (and, some would argue, having the legal and moral responsibility to resolve it): the United Nations. Thus, while earlier chapters have focused on Egyptian administrative policies and regulations affecting the Palestinians in Egypt, this chapter examines Palestinian legal rights—both as *refugees* (if they qualify as such under established definitions) or as *stateless persons* (if they fall within the "displaced" category assigned to those who lost their homes as a result of the 1967 war)—under international and regional treaties and other instruments of public international law.

When Palestinian refugees began flooding into the neighboring Arab states as of spring 1948, they received an immense outpouring of sympathy. Palestine was the "hottest" issue in the Arab (and indeed Muslim) world, where populations could not but be moved by the plight of Arabs or Muslims like themselves who been driven from their homes by what were seen as foreign usurpers backed by colonial powers. In many places, local inhabitants provided food and shelter or supplies to help refugees camping out in orchards or fields; volunteers were organized to provide medical services.[1] Governments provided shelters in schools and other public buildings, as well as food and supplies, all within the limits of poor and largely agrarian societies lacking infrastructure.

The unquestioned assumption at the time, however—not only in the Arab countries but worldwide—was that the situation was temporary and that as soon as the fighting ended, the refugees would be able to return to their homes. This assumption seemed authoritatively confirmed by UN General Assembly Resolution 194 (III) of December 1948, which stated that the refugees should be "permitted to return [to their homes] at the earliest practicable date." It was seen as inconceivable in the Arab world that a solution proposed by the United Nations and enjoyed the apparently unanimous support of the Western powers could not be imposed on the fledgling state of Israel, which owed its very existence to the United Nations. However, as the refugees' stay became prolonged, putting undue strain on already fragile economies, attitudes in the host countries began to shift.

For the Arab states, refugee "repatriation" became the cornerstone of their Palestine policy. In their view, the international community in the form of the United Nations had created the refugee problem by forcing the November 1947 partition resolution on Palestine against the clear wishes of over two-thirds of the population. This being the case, it was felt, the international community had the moral obligation to compel Israel to take back the refugees it had expelled or otherwise driven out. This position, while rooted in genuine convictions and a sense of justice, had clear pragmatic implications, particularly for the host countries. It also had obvious implications for the treatment of Palestinian refugees residing within these countries.

The first part of this chapter traces the history of UN involvement in the Palestinian refugee problem and the various UN conventions relating to refugees, and shows how some segments of the refugee population—including the Palestinians in Egypt—have "fallen through the cracks," left virtually unprotected. The second part of the chapter addresses the position of the Arab League and the gap between its official statements, especially the 1965 Casablanca Protocol, and the actual treatment of Palestinians by its member states, particularly (in the last two decades) Egypt.

International Protection

The United Nations and the Refugee Problem

The dramatic worsening of the situation on the ground in Palestine immediately after the passage of UN General Assembly Resolution 181 in November 1947 and the all-out Haganah offensive launched in early April 1948 made the impossibility of any "peaceful" implementation of the UN partition plan patently obvious to the world community. On 14 May 1948, the same day that Britain's Mandate over Palestine formally ended, the UN General Assembly created the position of UN Mediator for Palestine, whose tasks were to promote a truce between the parties and to work toward "a peaceful adjustment of the future situation in Palestine."[2] By the time of the mediator's appointment, more than 300,000 Palestinians had already fled or been driven from their homes, either to parts of Palestine not yet engulfed by war or across international borders into neighboring countries. With the entry of the Arab state armies on 15 May, the fighting intensified and refugee crisis worsened. In June, the United Nations created the Disaster Relief Project, with a 60-day mandate to coordinate emergency aid efforts among relief organizations and the governments of countries where the refugees had fled. In November 1948, the Disaster Relief Project was succeeded by the UN Relief for Palestine Refugees, which in turn was superseded over a year later by the UNRWA.

Meanwhile, the UN mediator, Count Folke Bernadotte, a diplomat who had gained international recognition for his work as the head of the Swedish Red Cross during World War II, had arrived in Palestine in late May. Despite his successful mediation of a 30-day cease-fire in June, he was having a difficult time "promoting peaceful adjustments," especially because once on the ground his views on the requirements of a lasting solution evolved rather quickly and soon included the need for substantial revisions in the UN partition boundaries, mostly to the benefit of the Arabs. With the refugee flight intensifying as Israel conquered more territory beyond the UN-allocated Jewish state, Bernadotte began firmly insisting that assuring the refugees' right to return was an essential precondition for a settlement. Never very popular on the Israeli side, Bernadotte became enemy number one among the "dissident" Zionist groups, Irgun and Lehi (the "Stern gang").[3]

On 16 September 1948, Bernadotte submitted his report to the UN General Assembly.[4] On the refugee issue, he emphasized that the "right of the refugees to return to their homes" must take place "at the earliest practical date."[5] In his view, it was

> undeniable that no settlement can be just and complete if recognition is not accorded to the right of the Arab refugee to return to the home from which he has been dislodged . . . It would be an offense against the principles of elemental justice if these innocent victims of the conflict were denied the right to return to their homes while Jewish immigrants flow into Palestine.[6]

Bernadotte also declared that "because of large-scale looting, pillaging and plundering and of instances of destruction of villages without military necessity," Israel had a "clear" liability "to restore private property to its Arab owners and to indemnify those owners of property wantonly destroyed."[7] Although he acknowledged that most of the refugees "may no longer have homes to return to" and that "resettlement" in Israel would present problems of "special complexity," he insisted that whether the refugees were repatriated or resettled elsewhere, their "unconditional right to make a free choice should be fully respected."[8] He also emphasized that it was "indispensable" for the General Assembly to "take a firm position on the political aspects of the problem" and that only with "firm decisions" would the two sides "acquiesce" in a settlement.[9] Word of the tenor of his report preceded his return to Jerusalem the next day, and upon arrival, on 17 September, he was assassinated by members of the Stern Gang, a terrorist group (also involved in the Dayr Yasin massacre) led by Yitzhak Shamir, who later became prime minister of Israel.

The UNCCP

In the "Specific Conclusions" of his report, Bernadotte summarized his recommendations concerning the refugees as follows:

> [T]he right of the Arab refugees to return to their homes in Jewish-controlled territory at the earliest possible date should be affirmed by the United Nations, and their repatriation, resettlement and economic and social rehabilitation, and payment of adequate compensation for the property of those choosing not to return, should be supervised and assisted by the United Nations conciliation commission.[10]

His recommendation was that the UN conciliation committee should be established to work with the UN to "ensure the continuation of the peaceful adjustment of the situation in Palestine," to make recommendations, and "to supervise the observance of" the arrangements decided by the United Nations, including with regard to refugees.[11]

These two recommendations—concerning the refugees and the conciliation committee—were at the heart of UN General Assembly Resolution 194 (III) of 11 December 1948.[12] Both are embodied in the resolution's now-famous paragraph 11, which

> *Resolves* that the refugees wishing to return to their homes and live at peace with their neighbors should be permitted to do so at the earliest practicable date, and that compensation should be paid for the property of those choosing not to return and for loss of or damage to property which, under principles of international law or in equity, should be made good by the Governments or authorities responsible;

> *Instructs* the Conciliation Commission to facilitate the repatriation, resettlement and economic and social rehabilitation of the refugees and the payment of compensation and to maintain close relations with the Director of the United Nations Relief for Palestine Refugees and, through him, with the appropriate organs and agencies of the United Nations.

But the UNCCP as created by the General Assembly, in contrast to Bernadotte's more limited concept of a facilitating body, not only charged the new body with the late mediator's mandate to "*promote*" peaceful adjustments, but decided to "*extend the scope*

of the negotiations" and to "[Instruct] the Conciliation Commission
to take steps to assist the Governments and authorities concerned
to *achieve a final settlement of all questions outstanding between
them.*"[13] BADIL co-founder Terry Rempel argues that the resulting
dual mandates assigned the UNCCP—the broad mandate to achieve
a final settlement of the outstanding issues between the parties, and
the specific mandate to protect the Palestinian refugees,[14] inter alia
by facilitating their repatriation and the payment of compensation
to them—were incompatible and represented a conflict of
interest[15] due to Israel's unalterable opposition to more than token
repatriation. Moreover, it became increasingly clear that the United
States and other Western powers, despite their endorsement of UN
General Assembly Resolution 194 (III), were not at all prepared
to insist on the "firm political decisions" that Bernadotte had said
were indispensable to securing a fair settlement.

Making little headway in the political realm, the UNCCP in June
1949 established a technical committee to investigate practical
ways of resolving the refugee problem. This included investigating
how to determine refugee choices and collecting information on
repatriation, resettlement, and compensation. The committee's
report assumed as a given the resettlement of large numbers
of refugees outside Israel. It also concluded that the idea of
determining *individual* refugee choices, called for by Bernadotte
and implied in UN General Assembly Resolution 194 (III) (i.e.,
"the refugees *wishing* to return . . .") was "premature," because
repatriation, unlike resettlement, was a "political decision."[16]

In August, a second committee, the Economic Survey Mission—
also known as the Clapp Commission, after its chairman, Gordon
Clapp—was established by the UNCCP to pursue another track,
this one emphasizing the improvement of the refugees' situation
through an integrated economic program. The word "repatriation"
was still used in its statement of purpose, but its real focus was
resettlement. Specifically, its mandate was to investigate ways
to "reintegrate the refugees into the economic life of the area on
a self-sustaining basis within a minimum period of time; and to
promote economic conditions conducive to the maintenance
of peace and stability in the area."[17] To this end, the Economic
Survey Mission undertook a tour of Arab countries to study their
economic situations and absorptive capacities. In its report to the
General Assembly in November, the Economic Survey Mission
showed a sympathetic understanding of the refugees' plight, but

its conclusions were determined by its mandate and the political realities of the time:

> Why do not the refugees return to their homes and solve their own problems? That is what the great majority of them want to do. They believe, as a matter of right and justice, [that] they should be permitted to return to their homes, their farms . . . They are encouraged to believe this remedy open to them because the General Assembly of the United Nations said so in its resolution of 11 December 1948. For purely psychological reasons, easily understandable, the refugees set great store by the assurances contained in this resolution . . . *But repatriation of Arab refugees requires political decisions outside the competence of the Economic Survey Mission.*

The report went on to ask rhetorically, "Why do not the refugees go somewhere else? Why not resettle them in less congested lands?" After providing several answers to this question, the report declared: "In these circumstances, the only immediate constructive step in sight is to give the refugees an opportunity to work *where they now are*."[18] Among its recommendations was the creation of a public works program to rehabilitate the refugees; it was out of this that UNRWA was established in December 1949 under UN General Assembly Resolution 302 (IV).

In fact, the right of return clause of UN General Assembly Resolution 194 (III) was doomed from the start, not only because of the realities on the ground but also because of the very composition of the UNCCP charged with implementing it. The UNCCP comprised representatives of the United States, France, and Turkey (both close U.S. allies), and it was this three-nation body that formulated UNCCP policy and carried out initiatives through the subcommittees responsible to it. According to historian Michael Fischbach, a leading expert in land issues,

> Washington was able to make sure that the commission's policy and initiatives did not cross the "red lines" it had established for resolving the conflict. Among the most important of these were that repatriation was not feasible and that refugee compensation must be in lieu of repatriation. These undeclared parameters were to guide the UNCCP's efforts throughout its entire existence, even though, for political reasons having to do with its mandate from the

UNGA, the commission continued to press for at least token
repatriation of some of the refugees.[19]

In this regard, Israel, under strong U.S. pressure, did agree in
September 1949 to repatriate 100,000 refugees if they could be
settled in areas Israel would determine by itself and in accordance
with its security needs, and if the Arab states would at the same
time agree to a general peace settlement. Neither the Arabs nor the
United Nations and the United States found the offer acceptable,
and Israel itself soon withdrew its offer.[20] Nonetheless, the UNCCP
forged ahead with attempts to facilitate the repatriation of refugees
who wanted to return to Israeli-controlled areas. For example, it
approached the government of Israel to secure the return of the
former inhabitants of the no-man's land in the north Gaza region,
refugees in Egyptian-administered Gaza, and refugees in the Gaza
zone who were from the Beersheba area. Only small groups were
returned, however. Refugees from the areas of Abasan and Akhzah
in Palestine were permitted to return to cultivate their lands.
Others were permitted to return if the family breadwinner had
remained in Israel. In December 1948, a total of 800 dependents
from Lebanon and Jordan rejoined their families in Israel, and 115
came back from Gaza.[21]

Early on, the UNCCP had begun to move away from its larger
mandate of mediation between the parties aimed at reaching
a final settlement in order to concentrate on more technical
matters.[22] Increasingly, it turned its attention to refugee properties.
Its demands that Israel abrogate its 1950 Absentee Property Law,
which gave a legal veneer to the seizure of refugee properties, led
nowhere, and the transfer of refugee land to the state continued
unabated, as did the demolition of mosques and other religious
buildings. The UNCCP also called for the suspension of all measures
of requisition and occupation of Arab houses and for the unfreezing
of *Waqf* (religious endowment) property.[23] In 1950, it established a
Refugee Office to determine the ownership, interest, and nature
of each refugee property. The office also prepared an initial plan
for the individual assessment of refugee properties relying on
detailed information collected from refugees. By 1964, the office
had collected 453,000 records amounting to 1,500,000 individual
refugee holdings.[24] The UNCCP maintains the most comprehensive
records in existence of Palestinian refugee properties. As for the
protection of the refugees' broader rights and interests, however,
within four years of its formation, the UNCCP had become little

more than a symbol of UN concern for the unresolved Arab-Israeli conflict.[25]

The 1951 Refugee Convention and Article 1D

Meanwhile, in December 1950, exactly a year after the establishment of UNRWA, the United Nations created the office of the High Commissioner for Refugees (UNHCR) as the principal international instrument responsible for protecting refugees worldwide and charged it with overseeing international refugee conventions. Several months later, in July 1951, a conference convened by the UN in Geneva approved the landmark Convention Relating to the Status of Refugees, which in turn mandated the UNHCR to represent refugees, intervening with state governments on their behalf, if necessary, in order to ensure their protection.[26] The 1951 refugee convention is the most comprehensive legal document ever issued on refugee rights: It defines who is considered a refugee, what rights refugees have, and the legal obligations of the countries in which they reside. According to the 1951 convention, a refugee is a person who,

> owing to a well-founded fear of being persecuted for reasons of race, religion, nationality, membership of a particular social group or political opinion, is outside the country of his nationality and is unable, or owing to such fear, is unwilling to avail himself to the protection of that country; or who, not having a nationality and being outside the country of former habitual, is unable or, owing to such fear, is unwilling to return to it.[27]

Contracting states are called upon to grant refugees "treatment as favorable as possible and, in any event, not less favorable than that accorded to aliens generally in the same circumstances." The protection and rights provided under the convention include the right to education, to free movement, to own and dispose of movable and immovable property, to form associations, to earn wage employment, and to have access to the courts.

Palestinian refugees, however, are not covered by this important convention. Article 1D states:

> This Convention shall not apply to persons who are at present receiving from organs or agencies of the United Nations other

than the United Nations High Commissioner for Refugees
protection or assistance.

Nowhere are Palestinians mentioned specifically in the 1951
convention, but there is no doubt that the exclusion referred to
them, since in principle they were already being served by two
UN bodies. The UNCCP had been expected to provide for their
protection based on UN General Assembly Resolution 194(III),[28]
and UNRWA had been created expressly to provide them with
assistance and relief. The Statute of the UNHCR contains a similar
clause excluding from its mandate the Palestinian refugees,[29]
as does the 1954 Convention Relating to the Status of Stateless
Persons.

Article 1D of the 1951 Convention does, however, contain a
qualifying clause. Its second paragraph reads as follows:

> When such protection or assistance has ceased for any reason,
> without the position of such persons being definitively settled
> in accordance with the relevant resolutions adopted by the
> General Assembly of the UN, these persons shall *ipso facto*
> be entitled to the benefits of this convention.

Commenting on the exclusion clauses of the 1951 Convention,
the UNHCR Statute, and other such instruments, legal scholar
Susan Akram writes:

> Almost all states and international entities have interpreted
> the relevant provisions . . . as severely restricting the rights [of
> Palestinian refugees] in comparison to the rights guaranteed
> every other refugee group in the world. As a result, Palestinian
> refugees have been treated as ineligible for the most basic
> protection rights guaranteed under international law to
> refugees in general . . .[30]

Akram, however, focuses on Article 1D's "protection or
assistance" and "*ipso facto*" phrases, arguing that that they
were intended to provide Palestinian refugees with continuity of
protection under various organizations and instruments. Basing
her analysis on the drafting histories of the various instruments,
she further maintains that the original intention of the international
community was not *less* protection for the Palestinian refugees but
a special "*heightened* protection regime" because of international
recognition of responsibility for the disaster that befell them.[31]

This being the case, according to Akram, Article 1D should be interpreted not as an exclusion clause but as a "contingent *inclusion* clause," ensuring that if, for whatever reason, *either* protection (provided by the UNCCP) *or* assistance (provided by UNRWA) should cease before a final resolution of the refugee situation, that agency's function should be transferred to the UNHCR, and the refugee convention would fully and immediately apply without preconditions to the Palestinian refugees.[32]

According to the 1951 convention's drafting history, as detailed in *Les Travaux Préparatoires*, "the shared intention of the Arab and Western states was to deny Palestinians access to the Convention-based regime so long as the United Nations continues to assist them in their own region."[33] Indeed, the Arab states led by Egypt are on record as favoring the Palestinian refugee exclusion clause of the 1951 convention and the UNHCR statute. Takkenberg states that the main reason that emerged from an examination of the *Travaux Préparatoires* was their concern that if the Palestinians were included under the UNHCR, they "would become submerged [within other categories of refugees] and would be relegated to a position of minor importance," which could have a negative impact on the refugees' chances of repatriation.[278] Takkenberg further notes that while the Arab states believed that funding the relief efforts was the responsibility of the Western states that had supported partition and the creation of Israel, they (the Arab states) "were concerned that assistance or protection be extended to the Palestinian refugees irrespective of whether [UN] relief would continue to be provided." As such, the Arab states made it clear that the "exclusion" provision was to be only temporary.[35]

Whatever the intentions of the United Nations and other concerned parties, it became increasingly obvious as years passed that Palestinian refugees were not receiving adequate protection, as was dramatically illustrated in the 1990–91 Gulf crisis that left tens of thousands of stateless Palestinians stranded in Kuwait and elsewhere, and in the Libyan expulsion episode of 1995–97. Apparently responding to concerns about the vulnerability of the Palestinian refugees, in October 2002 the UNHCR issued a "Note on the Applicability of Article 1D of the 1951 Convention relating to the Status of Refugees to Palestinian Refugees." (The text of the note is provided in Appendix 4.) After noting in its first paragraph that the convention "contains certain provisions whereby persons otherwise having the characteristics of refugees, as defined in Article 1A, are excluded from the benefits of this Convention" and summarizing paragraph 2 of Article 1D, the note's second paragraph reads as follows:

> While paragraph 1 of Article 1D is in effect an exclusion clause, this does not mean that certain groups of Palestinian refugees can never benefit from the protection of the 1951 Convention. Paragraph 2 of Article 1D contains an inclusion clause ensuring the automatic entitlement of such refugees to the protection of the 1951 Convention if, without their position being definitively settled in accordance with the relevant UN General Assembly resolutions, protection or assistance from UNRWA has ceased for any reason. The 1951 Convention hence avoids overlapping competencies between UNRWA and UNHCR, but also, in conjunction with UNHCR's Statute, ensures the continuity of protection and assistance of Palestinian refugees as necessary.[36]

Because the Palestinians living in Egypt do not receive assistance from UNRWA, it would seem obvious that they should fall under the "inclusion clause" in paragraph 2 of Article 1D. As such, it is logical that they would automatically be entitled to the benefits of the 1951 convention and fall within the mandate of the UNHCR, "providing of course that Article 1C, 1E and 1F do not apply,"[37] none of which in fact do apply to the great majority of the community. Yet the UNHCR has clearly not acted on what appears to open the door to extending protection under the 1951 convention to the Palestinians in Egypt, among other places.

The reason for the UNHCR's continuing failure to extend protection to the Palestinians in Egypt is not difficult to ascertain. Egypt ratified the 1951 convention in 1981 but at the same time placed reservations on a number of key articles.[38] These include articles 12, 22, 23, and 24, which address, respectively, personal status, access to public education, access to public relief and assistance, and labor legislation and social security. In other words, even though it ratified the convention, Egypt, by virtue of its formal reservations, is not obligated to provide even those refugees in Egypt who are registered with UNHCR (such as the Sudanese and the Somalis) permanent residence, the unqualified right to work, or education. Takkenberg suggests that Egypt's stance may derive from a "perceived conflict between the status favored by the Arab League and that of the Convention, and also because for many years the PLO had opposed providing individual Palestinian refugees with the status of the 1951 Convention because this was considered prejudicial to the inalienable rights of the Palestinian people as a whole."[39]

Other Conventions

Three other international conventions have potential relevance to the Palestinians in Egypt: the Convention Relating to the Status of Stateless Persons, the Convention on the Reduction of Statelessness, and the Convention on the Elimination of all Forms of Racism.

The 1954 Convention on the Status of Stateless Persons, passed on 28 September of that year at a conference convened by the UN Economic and Social Council, follows almost exactly the model of the 1951 convention. Using almost identical language, it applies to stateless persons (who are not necessarily refugees[40]) the rights accorded by the 1951 convention to the refugees covered by the UNHCR mandate. A stateless person is defined as one "who is not considered as national by any state under the operation of its laws."[41] It should be noted that Article 1.2 (i) of the 1954 convention contains the same exclusionary clause as the 1951 convention on refugees—that is, that it does not apply to persons who at present are receiving from UN organs or agencies other than the UNHCR "protection or assistance so long as they are receiving such protection or assistance." No further qualification is provided in the exclusion.

The 1961 Convention on the Reduction of Statelessness requires the contracting states to grant nationality to stateless persons meeting certain conditions, the most prominent of which is that the persons are born in that state's territory. Aside from listing the other qualifying conditions (besides birth in the country of residence), the convention spells out the modalities under which stateless persons should be naturalized.

Palestinians meeting the UNRWA definition of refugees (see Introduction) who have not been granted citizenship by any country are stateless as well as being refugees. However, the international community distinguishes between Palestinian refugees (who left Palestine as a result of the 1948 war) and those who left the West Bank and Gaza as a result of the 1967 war, who are "displaced persons" (except for those who were already registered as refugees with UNRWA—the "twice displaced"). Displaced persons who have not received citizenship in any country definitely qualify as being stateless. This category includes all Palestinians, whether or not they fit the legal definition of refugee, who hold Egyptian, Lebanese, and Syrian travel documents, "temporary" Jordanian passports (Gazans residing in Jordan and West Bankers), or Palestinian passports, which are in fact only travel documents, or *laissez-passer*.

Unfortunately, however, neither Egypt nor any of the Arab countries primarily concerned signed either of the two statelessness convention and therefore are not bound by their provisions. Only Algeria, Libya, and Tunisia signed the 1954 convention, and only Libya and Tunisia signed the 1961 convention. Moreover, Libya's ratification of both statelessness conventions did not prevent it from expelling its Palestinians in the mid-1990s.

A final convention with provisions relevant to Palestinians, the UN Convention on the Elimination of all Forms of Discrimination against Women, was adopted by the UN General Assembly in 1979. This convention potentially has enormous importance for Palestinians in Egypt, where thousands of Egyptian women married to Palestinians have been unable to pass Egyptian citizenship on to their children, who therefore remain stateless.[42] Paragraph 2 of Article 9 of the convention reads as follows: "States Parties shall grant women equal rights with men with respect to the nationality of their children." Egypt in fact did ratify the convention in 1981, but as in the case of the 1951 refugee convention, it ratified it with specific reservations, one of which was Article 9.

Regional Protection: Arab League Resolutions

Early Arab League resolutions concerning Palestinian refugees emphasize solutions based on "ensuring their return to their homes and confirming the preservation of their properties, their money, their life, and their freedom" (Resolution 205 of 17 March 1949). Statements on the treatment of Palestinian refugees in the host states were less committal: Resolution 391 of October 1951, for example, affirms that "The Council of the League approves the Political Committee's decision with reference to the decision of the Palestinian Permanent Council to *discuss* all refugee affairs thoroughly and to *consider* their need to work, travel, and remain in the host countries. The Council requests the committee to prepare a financial report on the needs for Palestinian refugees" (emphasis added).

In 1952, the Arab League established the Administrative Office of Palestine, with two sections, one for political and legal matters and another for refugee affairs. From then on, resolutions began to deal more substantively with practical issues pertaining to the refugees, often reiterating political positions as well. Resolution 462 of 23 September 1952 is a good example. In Article 1, the Political Committee advises Arab governments to defer efforts to settle Palestinian refugees and calls on the UN to implement the resolutions concerning the return of Palestinian refugees to Palestine and their compensation for damages and property losses. In Article 2, it recommends that the Arab host countries endeavor to improve the refugees' living conditions and coordinate with UNRWA to create work projects for Palestinians, though it confirms that these projects should not aim at settling Palestinians permanently and should preserve their right of return and compensation. In Article 3, the committee requires Arab governments to coordinate efforts to facilitate the travel of Palestinians and to cooperate in accommodating their temporary stay in host countries.

Several years later, Resolution 714 of 27 January 1954 unanimously approved the issuance of travel documents for Palestinian refugees. According to Article 1, "The governments of member states of the League have agreed that each government should issue the Palestinian refugees residing in its territory, or coming under its jurisdiction, temporary travel documents upon their request" and in accordance with the certain provisions that are spelled out. Of particular significance are Article 3, which stipulates that the bearer is subject to the residency rules of the issuing state (i.e., does not derive residency rights from the document), and Article 6, which stipulates that the member states "shall accord to the holders of these travel documents the same treatment with respect to visas and residence as is accorded to their own nationals."[43]

By far the most significant of the Arab League efforts with regard to the Palestinians is the Casablanca Protocol on the Treatment of Palestinians, adopted in 1965. (An unofficial translation of the Casablanca Protocol is provided in Appendix 3.) The protocol emphasizes the importance of preserving Palestinian identity and maintaining Palestinian refugee status (in anticipation of their eventual return). The Arab states that signed the Casablanca Protocol agreed to grant Palestinians living in their territories residence permits, the right to work, and the right to travel on a par with their nationals.[44] Article 3 states, "When their interests so require, Palestinians presently residing in the territory of [name of country] shall have the right to leave the territory of this state and return to it." The protocol does not, however, cover rights to own property, to access courts, or to education. Takkenberg points out that, in contrast to earlier resolutions, the protocol does not mention Palestinian *refugees* but rather refers simply to the treatment of "Palestinians," implying recognition that all Palestinians regardless of their *de jure* status require protection.[45]

Unfortunately, the observance of these basic rights has varied greatly from host state to host state, as well as within the same state at different times. (Egypt is a prime example of the latter.) As early as 1969, the League's Conference of Supervisors of Palestinian Affairs studied the actual treatment of Palestinians in various Arab countries and concluded that it was far below standard and urged member states to implement the Protocol in full.[46]

Realizing that the rights outlined in the Protocol were not being adequately upheld in the host states, and in view of various problems facing Palestinian refugees, the Arab League called a meeting of the Council of Arab Interior Ministers in December 1982, which adopted a "special resolution on the treatment of Palestinians in the Arab countries" designed to clarify and confirm the Protocol's provisions. Paragraph 1 confirmed that the travel documents issued to Palestinians by any Arab country must be granted on an equal basis with the national passports issued to its own citizens. Paragraph 2 stipulated that bearers of such documents "shall be accorded the same treatment as nationals of the state issuing this document, as regards freedom of residence, work, and movement." In addition, "special measures needed for the implementation" of the first two paragraphs were to be coordinated with the PLO. Paragraph 4 contained a provision that had not been included in the Casablanca Protocol nor in any previous resolution: "If a Palestinian perpetrates a crime in any Arab country, the laws of the country of his residence will be applicable."[47]

Despite efforts to promote compliance, the Casablanca Protocol has at best been implemented partially and intermittently in a number of Arab states, and the situation of Palestinians in these countries has remained precarious. The 1990–91 Gulf crisis, in particular, had a devastating impact on the treatment of Palestinians in the Arab world. It was in the shadow of this crisis that the forty-sixth session of the Conference of Supervisors of Palestinian Affairs in the host countries was held in August 1991. As a result of the intense anger in the Gulf over Palestinian support for Saddam Hussein during Iraq's invasion of Kuwait, one of the resolutions passed at the conference was amended at the request of Kuwait and Saudi Arabia in such a way as to considerably compromise the force of the Casablanca Protocol. As amended, paragraph 7 of Resolution 5093 dated 12 September 1991 reads as follows (the added clause being in italics):

> Having taken notice of the memorandum presented by the delegation of Palestine, the Conference expresses the hope that all Arab states, in a spirit of brotherhood and solidarity, will seek to abide by the Protocol relating to the Treatment of Palestinians *in accordance with the rules and laws in force in each state*, and calls upon the Arab states to overcome the negative impact of the Gulf crisis, as regards the implementation of this Protocol in respect of the Palestinian people.[48]

Shiblak interprets the added phrase "in accordance with the rules and laws in force in each state" as essentially releasing the signatories from their obligations under the Casablanca Protocol and leaving treatment of the Palestinians up to their discretion.[49] Others, including Takkenberg, question whether the obligations of member states under an officially ratified international agreement can be nullified on the basis of a recommendation of the Council.[50] It is true that a number of the signatories, including Egypt as of the late 1970s, have always applied the Protocol's provisions "at their discretion." Nonetheless, the fact that the Arab states can now claim justification for their failure to comply with the treaty they ratified constitutes a very severe blow to Palestinian rights in those states.

Politics and the Casablanca Protocol

Despite the obvious good will of the United Nations (and, at least in the early years, its lingering sense of responsibility for the plight of the Palestinians), and despite a spontaneous sympathy for and identification with the Palestinian refugees in the Arab countries, Palestinians remain unprotected both under international law and under Arab League protocols.

Egypt is a signatory to the Universal Declaration of Human Rights and has ratified both the 1951 Convention on Refugee Status (albeit with reservations) and the Arab League's Casablanca Protocol (without reservations). Accepting Takkenberg's interpretation that Egypt has by policy given priority to the Arab League protection regime—and leaving aside the above-mentioned amendment to the 1991 Arab League Council resolution—why has Egypt not implemented the provisions of the Casablanca Protocol, of which it was the chief backer and drafter? Shiblak has suggested that the Arab states' treatment of Palestinians is determined by two main factors: the absence of clear and well-defined legislation regulating the Palestinians' status, and the influence of shifting local politics and concerns.[51] The refugee rights organization BADIL expresses the same idea in different terms: "Political considerations and domestic law often trump the standards set forth in Arab League resolutions and the Casablanca Protocol."[52]

There is no doubt that *"raison d'état"* and considerations of domestic politics almost always take precedence over considerations of justice and human rights. As regards the Palestinians in Egypt, however, a good case can be made that flouting the provisions of the Casablanca Protocol does not serve state interests. During the Nasser years, the provisions of the Casablanca Protocol were effectively observed for the most part even before the Protocol was actually formulated, and they continued to be observed for a decade thereafter, with no discernible hardship to Egypt. What those years demonstrated was that when Palestinians are allowed to work unhindered, they are not a burden on the economy but productive members of society.

The virtually overnight change in Palestinian legal status in 1978 was politically, not economically, motivated. In a sense, it was aimed as much at the Egyptian as at the Palestinian population insofar as it sent a dramatic signal that an entire era of Egyptian policy had ended, that a page had been turned, and that a new chapter (which climaxed with the signing of the peace treaty with Israel two years later) had begun. Thirty years have passed since then, and there seems little political reason for continuing to maintain the tight restrictions then imposed, especially given the high degree of integration of the community.

Egypt has never invoked economic reasons for its continuing denial of rights to the Palestinian community and its ongoing nonobservance of the Casablanca Protocol. But even from the economic standpoint, despite the undeniable problems of overpopulation and the huge pressures on scarce jobs and resources, Palestinian numbers are too small to make a difference or add to Egypt's economic burden. The initial policy change was political; a new political decision reflecting new political realities can be taken to reverse it.

Notes

1. See, for example, Ahmad Beydoun, "The South Lebanon Border Zone: A Local Perspective," *Journal of Palestine Studies* 21, no 3 (Spring 1992), pp. 35–53, and Elias Srouji, "The Fall of a Galilean Village during the 1948 Palestine War: An Eyewitness Account," *Journal of Palestine Studies* 33, no. 2 (Winter 2004), pp. 71–80.

2. UN General Assembly Resolution 186 (S-2) of 14 May 1948.

3. David Hirst, *The Gun and the Olive Branch: The Roots of Violence in the Middle East* (New York: Harcourt Brace Jovanovich, 1977), pp. 147, 149.

4. *Progress Report of the United Nations Mediator on Palestine*, UN General Assembly Official Records: Third Session, Supplement no. 11 (A/648), 16 September 1948.

5. *Progress Report*, Part I, section V.3.

6. Ibid., Section V.6.

7. Ibid., Section V.7.

8. Ibid., Section V.8.

9. Ibid., Section I.10.

10. Ibid., Section VIII.4 (I).

11. Ibid., Section VIII.4.k (I-II).

12. Veteran British journalist and Middle East expert David Hirst notes that "compared with what Bernadotte had sought, the resolution was weak and imprecise; its enforcement was made contingent on Israel's goodwill; and it failed to specify by what agency the refugees would return." Hirst, *The Gun and the Olive Branch*, p. 263.

13. United Nations General Assembly Resolution 194(III), 5 and 6 (emphasis added).

14. Regarding the protection function, the mediator's role, which the UNCCP was instructed to assume, emphasizes assurance of the "safety and well being of the population of Palestine" and promoting the "welfare of the inhabitants of Palestine."

15. Rempel, *United Nations Conciliation Commission for Palestine*, p. 3.

16. Ibid., pp. 2, 4.

17. UNCCP Historical Survey 1961 report cited by Takkenberg, *The Status of Palestinian Refugees in International Law*, p. 25.

18. First interim report of the Economic Survey Mission, quoted by Takkenberg, *The Status of Palestinian Refugees in International Law*, p. 26 (emphasis added).

19. Michael Fischbach, "The United Nations and Palestinian Refugee Property Compensation," *Journal of Palestine Studies* 31, no. 2 (Winter 2002), p. 36.

20. Fred J. Khouri, *The Arab-Israeli Dilemma*, 2d ed. (Syracuse, N.Y.: Syracuse University Press, 1976), p. 128.

21. Rempel, *United Nations Conciliation Commission for Palestine*, p. 4.

22. According to Fischbach, the United States had been arguing within the UNCCP as early as January 1950 that the commission drop active conciliation efforts and concentrate on secondary issues. "The United Nations and Palestinian Refugee Property Compensation," p. 39.

23. Rempel, *United Nations Conciliation Commission for Palestine.*

24. The office estimated that a total of 17,167 square kilometers out of 26,320 square kilometers (the total area of pre-1948 Palestine) were determined to be refugee lands. Salman Abu Sitta, "The Right of Return: Sacred, Legal and Possible," in Naseer Aruri, ed. *Palestinian Refugees: The Right of Return* (London: Pluto Press, 2001), pp. 195–207.

25. Susan Akram, *Protection and Its Applicability to the Palestinian Refugee Case*, Information and Discussion Brief No. 4 (Bethlehem, West Bank: BADIL, 2000), p. 3.

26. Ibid., p. 2.

27. Article 1A (2) of the convention, as amended under the 1967 Protocol. The amended protocol also removes from the 1951 convention any geographical limitation.

28. According to Akram, the protection intended by UNCCP went beyond standard refugee rights to involve focused intervention in effort to secure a long-term solution based on repatriation and compensation. "Temporary Protection and its Applicability to the Palestinian Refugee Case," p. 5.

29. Paragraph 7(c) of the UNHCR Statute states that "the competence of the High Commissioner . . . shall not extend to a person . . . who continues to receive from other organs or agencies of the UN protection or assistance."

30. Akram, "Temporary Protection and its Applicability to the Palestinian Refugee Case," p. 1.

31. Ibid., p. 4.

32. Ibid., pp. 3, 4.

33. Hathaway in Takkenberg, *The Status of Palestinian Refugees in International Law*, p. 90.

34. According to Akram, the Arab states argued that the Palestinian refugee problem was to be resolved in accordance with UN General Assembly Resolution 194 (III), that is, on the basis of a special formula of repatriation and compensation, rather than the formula commonly accepted for refugees at the time, which was resettlement in a third country. Susan Akram, "Reinterpretating Palestinian Refugee Rights under International Law and a Framework for Durable

Solutions," in Naseer Aruri, ed., *Palestinian Refugees: The Right of Return* (London: Pluto Press, 2001), p. 173.

35. Takkenberg, *The Status of Palestinian Refugees in International Law*, p. 66.

36. The Note on Applicability carries here the following footnote: "A similar provision to Article 1D of the 1951 Convention is continued in UNHCR's Statute, paragraph 7(c) of which stipulated that the competence of the High Commissioner shall not extend to a person who 'continues to receive from other organs or agencies of the United Nations protection or assistance'."

37. Paragraph C.7 of the Note on Applicability. Article 1C of the 1951 Convention has a number of provisions, mainly involving acquiring a new nationality (and therefore the protection of that country) or being able to return to his original country. Article 1E excludes persons recognized by the host state as having the rights and obligations of that country's nationals. Article 1F excludes person who have committed major crimes before admission to the host state.

38. See the UNHCR Web site (www.unhcr.org) under 1951 convention, reservations by country.

39. Takkenberg, *The Status of Palestinian Refugees in International Law*, p. 125.

40. In its preamble, the 1954 convention notes that the "only those stateless persons who are also refugees are covered by the [1951] Convention . . . and there are many stateless persons who are not covered by that Convention."

41. Article 1 of the 1954 UN Convention Relating to the Status of Stateless Persons.

42. As noted elsewhere, the 2004 Nationality Law in principle allows Egyptian women married to foreigners to pass their nationality on to their children, but its implementation with regard to Palestinians has been uneven.

43. The text of Resolution 714 is reproduced in full in Takkenberg, *The Status of Palestinian Refugees in International Law*, pp. 372–74.

44. The Arab States that ratified the protocol without reservation are Jordan, Algeria, Sudan, Iraq, Syria, Egypt, and North Yemen. Kuwait and Lebanon ratified the protocol with reservations. Morocco and Saudi Arabia did not ratify the protocol. Other Arab states were not yet independent.

45. Takkenberg, *The Status of Palestinian Refugees in International Law*, p. 141.

46. Ibid., p. 145.

47. Ibid., p. 147.

48. Quoted in Takkenberg, *The Status of Palestinian Refugees in International Law*, p. 149.

49. Shiblak, "Living in Limbo," p. 5.

50. Takkenberg, *The Status of Palestinian Refugees in International Law*, p. 149.

51. Shiblak, "Living in Limbo," pp. 3, 4.

52. See the section "Protection: League of Arab States" on BADIL's Web site: www.badil.org.

Conclusion

Reflections on Identity
and the Future

*Few in number and scattered throughout the country,
Palestinians in Egypt were virtually engulfed by
overwhelming numbers of Egyptians. In order to blend
in with their surroundings, many Palestinians in Egypt
adapted their dialect and customs to those of Egypt; and
marriage to Egyptians, often the only sure route to a more
secure residency, was most common. Many people lost
track of where their former compatriots were and often,
at least in terms of outward indicators, became virtually
indistinguishable from their Egyptian hosts.*

—Laurie Brand, *Palestinians in the Arab World*, p. 85

In the twenty years since these words were written by American researcher Laurie Brand, another generation of Palestinians in Egypt has been raised, yet another born. The Oslo agreement was signed; the PA was established in Gaza and parts of the West Bank. Starting from the mid-1990s, tens of thousands of Palestinians have left Egypt for Palestine (though some have returned to Egypt under the impact of the second intifada), further fragmenting the already fragmented community. With Israel's closure regime drastically tightened since 2002, the back-and-forth movement between Gaza and Egypt for family visits that had continued almost uninterrupted since 1967, and which helped keep the Palestinian identity alive for many young people, has all but stopped. The ongoing tragedy of the intifada, the deep divisions within Palestine, and the fast-receding prospects of a Palestinian state with any semblance of sovereignty or viability have all taken a toll on the community's hopes for the future. Meanwhile, intermarriage with Egyptians has continued unabated (if not accelerated), having become all the more necessary as a means of survival.

174

In light of these developments, it seems an appropriate way to conclude this study by reflecting briefly on the state of Palestinian identity in Egypt, the factors affecting it, and on where the community might be headed in the future.

Factors Affecting Identity and the Pull of Assimilation

As has been clear throughout this study, Palestinians in the *ghurba* have always been pulled between two poles—assimilation and separateness. The pull toward assimilation is great. Factors that facilitate assimilation include the community's small numbers; its dispersal; the absence of any kind of "center" such as a single relief institution around which Palestinians could gather; the lack of civil society institutions or clubs; and, most important, the sense that Palestinians must blend in if they are to have any chance of getting ahead. On the "separateness" side are the distrust, fear, and suspicion fostered by the Emergency Laws and the experience of sudden shifts in political climate and local attitudes.

John Berry has labeled the changes refugees or migrants are forced to make when coming to a new country as *acculturation*, or the change resulting from continuous, firsthand contact between two "distinct cultural groups." What differs from case to case, according to Berry, is the amount of time it takes to move along the "continuum of integration" and the reversibility of the changes undergone by both the new arrivals and their hosts.[1] In the case of Egyptians and Palestinians, of course, we are not dealing with two distinct cultural groups, so in principle the similarities should shorten the distance to integration. Indeed, the very absence of distinctive characteristics or beliefs between new arrivals and the host community not only makes eventual integration almost inevitable, but also makes the long-term maintenance of a separate identity more difficult to sustain.

The following remarks by a young Palestinian typify the pull of assimilation tempered by ambivalence:

> I do not feel different from Egyptians. My brothers and I have lived here all our lives. We have definitely been affected by the Egyptian way of life. To a certain extent, we differ from our parents in the way we talk, the way we live. We differ also from the young people in Palestine. I went to live in Gaza

and I felt a great difference. The men there are strong and stubborn. They do not talk much and do not make jokes. Their lives are serious and hard, the exact opposite of here. Yet they are very kind people, and [it may take me time to adapt but] I like living in Palestine. (8/13, Shubra al-Khayma, 11 June 2002)

Many factors have contributed to shaping the identity of Palestinians in Egypt. The more obvious ones are discussed briefly below.

Political Environment

Over time and through intermarriage, it has become difficult to distinguish between Palestinians and Egyptians based on physical appearance, manners, and speech. Part of this is a natural consequence of living intermingled with a population whose ethnicity, customs, religion, and language were similar to begin with. But there is also no doubt that the impulse (conscious or otherwise) to "blend in" and adopt the manners of the host population is encouraged by the community's political insecurity and vulnerability. Since the mid-1970s, the volatile swings of Egyptian opinion with regard to Palestinians, not to mention the search campaigns, arrests, and deportations that increased during periods of aggravated political tension, contributed to the widespread tendency to de-emphasize or conceal characteristics readily identifiable as Palestinian. Most obviously, the insecurity speeded up the adoption (at least in public) of the Egyptian dialect, which the majority of Palestinians in Egypt now speak. This linguistic assimilation is a means of becoming accepted within the host community and avoiding scrutiny. Some interviewees reported that their own family members ask them to lower their voices in public when talking about Palestine or Palestinian relatives. Time and again we heard things like "I never emphasize who I am" or "I try not to say I am Palestinian." Many told us that "no one knows" they are Palestinian, or that "not many people can tell whether I am Palestinian or Egyptian." It should be noted that a number of these quotations and others in the same vein are from persons who are deeply attached to their Palestinian identity. For many, assimilation, even at an unconscious level, is a measure of self-defense or even a strategy for survival.

The Generational Factor

As might be expected, we found sharp differences between, on the one hand, first-generation Palestinians who had lived in Palestine and witnessed the Nakba (the 1948 arrivals) or who came of age in its aftermath (the 1967 arrivals) and, on the other hand, the generations born and raised in Egypt. Members of the first generation very often "looked" more Palestinian and were more easily identifiable as such by speech and manner. Their identity for the most part was clearly and unambiguously "Palestinian," even if they had close relations with their Egyptian neighbors or even had married into Egyptian families. They also tended to be more engaged and preoccupied with things Palestinian, expressing nostalgia for the homeland and bitterness at Arab and international betrayal, and sometimes still entertaining dreams of liberation.

In our interviews with the second and third generations, by contrast, we often found considerable ambivalence. Many were torn between their loyalty to Palestine and their Palestinian identity on the one hand and a sense of being comfortable in— and even, to an extent, part of—Egyptian society on the other. Beyond ambivalence, we also frequently found identity confusion. The younger brother of the young man quoted above (who said he does "not feel different from Egyptians" but who was also attracted by the idea of living in Palestine) is a good example of this confusion:

> Here in Egypt I am known as 'Arif al-*Filistini* [Arif the Palestinian]. In Palestine, when I went to visit, I was known as 'Arif al-*Masri* [Arif the Egyptian]. I am quite confused about who I should be. Anyway, I am proud of being Palestinian and at the same time, I do not hate being Egyptian. Like it or not, I live the way they live. Some of them keep making us feel different and accuse us of having sold our lands. I try to convince them that this isn't true, but they have rigid ideas and don't want to discuss it. (8/13, Shubra al-Khayma, 11 June 2002)

We also found second- or third-generation Palestinians who expressed indifference to Palestine or even identified more strongly with Egypt. More than one person told us that they felt Palestinian only when they were reminded of it by having to go to the *Mugamma'* to renew their residencies or travel documents. How much of this identification with Egypt or turning away from the Palestinian identity is deeply felt, and how much is an unconscious response to the uncertain environment is impossible to gauge, but in the final analysis the result is the same.

Education

Palestinian children in Egypt receive no information about the Palestine issue unless they get it from their parents. Under the Emergency Law, Palestinians are not permitted to hold public meetings or to have clubs where Palestinian history and events can be discussed. Private schools for Palestinians are not allowed.[2] Those who benefited from PLO exemptions enabling them to attend Egyptian public schools learned nothing about Palestine. Arab identity itself has been strongly de-emphasized in Egypt's post-Nasser school curriculum. A 1981 study of the political education of Egyptian children through their school textbooks (history, geography, and civic education) noted that "only 16 percent of instruction was aimed at promoting the sense of belonging to the Arab nation, whereas 54 percent was devoted to Pharaonic Egypt and 30 percent to the Egyptian identity per se, above and beyond the stress placed on Egyptian citizenship considered independently of the Arab or Islamic nation."[3] The result is that most Palestinians of the second and third generations have little knowledge of their own history. This was demonstrated during the training sessions for the five research assistants who worked on this project. All were Palestinian, all had university degrees, but in discussions about the readings they were given it became clear that except for the team member from Gaza, the researchers had no idea about the history of the Palestine problem and were not even familiar with UNRWA.

The situation in the UNRWA-run schools in the refugee camps of Jordan, Syria, and Lebanon is very different. Jason Hart,[4] an anthropologist who worked as a volunteer English teacher at UNRWA schools in the Jabal al-Hussein refugee camp in Jordan, remarked that the teaching staff, most of whom were Palestinian refugees themselves, taught the children about Palestine and about their villages of origin. Furthermore, the very fact that the children live in refugee camps that are frequently divided into sections named after the towns where their parents originated encourages them to express their feelings and sense of belonging and strengthens their Palestinian identity. Palestinian children in Egypt have no such opportunities to learn their history.

Family

In every culture, the "education" or "upbringing" by the parents has a profound influence on their children's sense of who they are. The correlation between the parents' attitudes toward Palestine and the extent to which their children identified with Palestine was striking in our field research. For example, a man who told us that his father had refused to apply for Saudi or Egyptian nationality because he worried that the occupied homeland could not be liberated if Palestinians took other nationalities, himself showed a real attachment to Palestine and tried to participate in whatever Palestine-related activities he could find (7/37, Faqus, 14 July 2002). On the other hand, those whose parents did not talk much about Palestine tended to express little interest in their country of origin ("Palestine is a place I have never thought of in my life." 7/44, Hehya, 15 July 2002). We also found that in families where the father was a PLO fighter who spent long periods away from his family, or where the father had to work at several jobs in the informal sector and came home only to sleep, memories of Palestine or the family history were not passed on. Traditional authoritarian relations between the father and the children also limit the friendly, participatory home environment through which an exchange of ideas, stories, and questions can take place to teach children about the homeland.

Close ties to relatives in Palestine generally made for a stronger Palestinian identity; exchanges of visits were particularly significant. Conversely, negative experiences with family members in Palestine (for example, disputes over inheritance) caused alienation and a turning away not only from the family but from Palestine in general. Disrupted marriages also had a powerful influence on attitudes about Palestine. Many Egyptian women were abandoned or divorced by their husbands when they left for Gaza after the establishment of the PA, sometimes even taking second wives, and this inevitably affected their children.

Marriage

In general, mixed marriage, especially when the mother is Egyptian, has an impact on the child's identity formation. An Egyptian mother, whether or not she has an appreciation of Palestinian traditions, naturally tends to pass her own Egyptian sense of belonging on to her children. In most of the families interviewed, second- or third-generation Palestinians expressed stronger ties with their Egyptian family than with their Palestinian relations because they knew them better and saw them more often. When such marriages end in divorce, especially in the case of Palestinian fathers who went back to Gaza in the mid-1990s, the identification with the Egyptian side of the family was even stronger.

By the same token, a preference for marrying within the Palestinian community is often in itself an indicator of a strong Palestinian identity having been transmitted to the children. When both parents have a shared history as Palestinians and are able to expose their children to Palestinian customs and traditions, the identity is naturally reinforced.

The few factors mentioned above point to some of the reasons why Palestinians in Egypt choose either to emphasize or to de-emphasize their identity as Palestinians. However, even those who feel strongly about their identity often conceal their "Palestinianism." Revealing one's Palestinian identity is not always prudent, particularly during times of political tension. The fact that in many cases Palestinians feel compelled to hide their identity in turn affects the construction of social networks and the sense of community among Palestinians, and it distorts their feelings of belonging to Palestine.

Whither the Community?

One of the defining characteristics of Palestinian life in Egypt, as we have seen throughout this study, is that there is no cohesive Palestinian community as such. There are many reasons for this, some of which have already been discussed (especially in chapter 3). What has perhaps not been sufficiently addressed is a subtle "split," or at least differentiation, between the 1948 Palestinians and the 1967 Palestinians—the two principal waves of Palestinian influx into Egypt.

1948 and 1967: Community Divides

Without doubt, all Palestinians who came to Egypt, whether as refugees, "displaced persons," or socioeconomic migrants, share the common experience of dispossession, a central element of Palestinian identity. Notwithstanding this shared core identity, however, the 1948 and 1967 waves were shaped by very different experiences. The 1948 arrivals, while they had lived in an all-Palestinian environment until the Nakba, were mostly from villages or rural areas; despite their strong feelings about what had happened to their country, they had not been politicized. Once in Egypt, the absence of permanent camps or any centralizing agency meant that they more or less had to fend for themselves and find their own way. This led to an almost haphazard self-settlement based on social and family networks and chance, contributing to their wide dispersal. By the time the second great wave arrived in 1967, and although the anti-Palestinian backlash was still a decade in the future, most of the young people born or brought up in Egypt had already undergone some assimilation.

By contrast, those who arrived in 1967 (both "displaced" and "twice displaced") had lived for two decades or come of age in the intensely and self-consciously Palestinian environment of the Gaza Strip, often in refugee camps, in very different conditions from those experienced by their compatriots in Egypt. Many had been involved in resistance activities against Israel and/or had joined the PLO military forces established a few years before the 1967 war. For these reasons, it is hardly surprising that for the most part they were far more politicized than the Palestinians who had spent the last twenty years in Egypt as a small, widely scattered community totally intermingled with Egyptians in all spheres of life.

Also significant is that most of those who came with the PLO or who had served under Egyptian military command were helped to settle by the Egyptian government, which meant that they tended to live in the same neighborhoods, which then drew other 1967 arrivals through family and social networks. Thus, by and large, the 1967 influx was less dispersed than the earlier wave. Even more important in differentiating the 1948 and 1967 communities, however, was an effect of Egypt's changed legislation regarding the Palestinians in 1978. From then on, those with PLO connections benefited from privileges not enjoyed by other Palestinians. Even though many of the 1967 arrivals were by no means privileged, the widely perceived association between PLO/privilege and the 1967 community in general continued to stick,[5] adding another layer to the wider Palestinian community's fragmentation.

As discussed in chapter 6, virtually all the post-1995 "returnees" to Gaza had been part of the 1967 wave, and most of them were able to return thanks to their PLO connections. There had always been a tendency among PLO fighters and former fighters in Egypt to form a group unto themselves; mingling with other groups was limited. Still, their departure in large numbers as of 1995 could only have had a demoralizing effect on the community as a whole, especially in Cairo, where the greatest number of the 1967 group had lived. The impact of their "return to Palestine" and the thinning out of certain neighborhoods was compounded by the dramatic reduction of the formerly vast PLO apparatus to little more than an embassy occupied primarily with catering to the needs of the PA. While the PLO had done little for the community at large, its presence up to the 1990s nonetheless provided, by virtue of its high visibility, a kind of focal point and even a semblance of protection that has since all but disappeared.

While the 1948/1967 divide forms the principal "fault line" within the fragmented and dispersed Palestinian community, others can be added. Most importantly, the 2004 revision in the Nationality Law—which guarantees automatic Egyptian citizenship to all children of mixed Palestinian-Egyptian marriages born *after* the law's passage—promises to develop into a major "divide" as years go by, this one cutting across families, with younger siblings having Egyptian citizenship and the privileges that go with it, and older ones consigned to statelessness.

Rights, Not Citizenship

Under an unwritten policy, Palestinians were the only foreigners in Egypt systematically excluded from full coverage under the 2004 Nationality Law. Without doubt, this has stirred resentment, but it is important to emphasize that citizenship has never been a collective Palestinian demand. Neither has *tawtin*—permanent resettlement in Arab host countries. No Palestinian human rights group has ever declared either naturalization or permanent resettlement as a goal. Palestinians are the first to want their right of return to Palestine protected and acknowledged.[6] The issue for Palestinians in the host countries has always been *rights*.

In fact, citizenship for Palestinians is not even an issue in most Arab host countries. Yet too often in Egypt (and certain other Arab countries as well) there is a conflation between citizenship and/ or *tawtin*, on the one hand, and the provision of basic rights and protections on the other. An argument frequently heard in Egyptian intellectual and official circles is that granting Palestinians basic rights and improving their living conditions would jeopardize their right of return (or at the very least, diminish Israel's responsibility for the refugees' plight). Improving Palestinian conditions and giving them basic rights, it is reasoned, would facilitate their full integration into Egyptian society and weaken their Palestinian identity, leading them to forget Palestine. In other words, Palestinians must be deprived of their rights in order to preserve their Palestinian identity.

This is a relatively new argument, and it flies in the face of the historical record of the Arab states' Palestine policy. Certainly, insistence on the repatriation of refugees to their lands in Palestine has always been a cornerstone of Arab policy, regularly expressed by individual Arab governments and by the Arab League (including in the 1959 protocol cited by Egyptian interior ministry officials as an explanation as to why Palestinian applications for citizenship under the 2004 Nationality Law are not accepted[7]). But at least in theory, the demand for repatriation has always been entirely separate from the issue of Palestinian rights in host countries. In tandem with the calls for repatriation, an unbroken stream of Arab League resolutions from the early 1950s onward, culminating in the Casablanca Protocol, has been issued called on Arab governments to grant Palestinians residing within their borders a wide range of basic rights. It is clear that for the Arab League, at least, there is no contradiction between the two policies.

More to the point, the falsity of the supposed linkage between the provision of basic rights and the loss or weakening of Palestinian identity is perhaps nowhere better illustrated than in Egypt itself. Our field research demonstrated beyond any doubt that the major factor encouraging Palestinians to hide or even *lose* their sense of Palestinian identity is precisely the deprivation of basic rights and the uncertainties arising from the precariousness of their legal status. Conversely, the small number of wealthy Palestinians located mainly in Cairo and Alexandria who are utterly secure, thanks to their connections, money, and power in Egyptian society (and sometimes having Egyptian nationality from pre-1948 days), do not hesitate to speak volubly of their Palestinian identity at important Egyptian official functions, to warm applause.[8]

Looking Ahead

As the first generations (1948 and 1967 arrivals) gradually pass from the scene, it is inevitable (assuming the ongoing denial of basic rights to Palestinians in Egypt) that assimilation, already pronounced among the younger generations five years ago when we conducted our research, will not only continue but accelerate, especially in light of the 2004 Nationality Law. Indeed, it is impossible to reflect on the future of the Palestinians in Egypt without considering the long-term implications of this law. Because it involves the automatic naturalization of children born after 2004 to Palestinian-Egyptian couples, the incentive for intermarriage in present conditions far exceeds anything known to date. Thus, with the number of children being born with Egyptian nationality (who formerly would have been Palestinian) expanding, and with older Palestinians dying off, it does not take a demographer to predict that over the next three generations or so, Egypt's "Palestinian problem" will in all likelihood "solve itself."

One can legitimately ask, however: Is this the best "solution"?

Three generations is a very long time for persons suffering the humiliation and hardships of living on goodwill in the only country they know. And in the intervening decades before such a long-term demographic "solution" works itself out, it is not difficult to imagine what the Palestinian "community" in Egypt will look like: still scattered, dwindling in number, rent by the 2004 cross-family dividing line between citizenship and statelessness, more and more indistinguishable from Egyptians, having an increasingly diffuse Palestinian identity, but living in a legal limbo. Indeed, the very extent of the community's assimilation only accentuates the anomaly of their statelessness. Thus, no matter how "Egyptian" Palestinians may appear—and indeed, how "Egyptian" many of those born before 2004 (and therefore not covered by the new Nationality Law) actually are[9]—they are on their own, without protection. Under current laws, their residencies must be renewed regularly; young people no longer in school can be legally deported if they have not found work by the time they turn 18 or, if they pursued higher education, by the time they turn 21. Even though the state tends to turn a blind eye to expired residencies—at least in the sense that it does not actively search for persons in that situation—any mishap or casual brush with the law can activate deportation proceedings. There are unquestionably thousands of Palestinian "illegals" in Egypt, many of whom were born there and know no other home. Such people can never leave the country unless they are prepared to leave for good, and they must live with the constant fear of being discovered. This situation is exceedingly painful for the Palestinians. It also does no credit to Egypt.

In seeking a more just and palatable alternative to the painfully slow "absorption through intermarriage" solution, it might be useful to look briefly at what must have been Egypt's calculations in determining its stance on the Nationality Law. It seems clear that the law was enacted in order to bring the country in step with internationally accepted norms of gender equality. Its passage presented the country with a dilemma, however: The law's provision mandating that Egyptian nationality be granted to the children born of Egyptian women married to foreigners went against long-stated national policy concerning Palestinian residents. To cut through this dilemma, the government appears to have resorted to a compromise. On the one hand, it apparently made the conscious decision that it could not decently exclude Palestinians from benefitting from the *automatic* portion of the law (Article 2). On the other hand, in an attempt at balance, it simultaneously excluded Palestinians from coverage in the law's *non*-automatic Article 3.[10] In this way, Egypt could maintain at least the appearance of upholding what has been a core ideological position ever since 1948.

In a sense, Egypt's adherence to official Arab policy on the Palestinian right of return could suggest a way out of the current impasse with regard to its Palestinian residents. Having formally upheld the political commitment, it can now honor another commitment almost as old: granting Palestinians basic rights as enshrined in numerous Arab League resolutions and the Casablanca Protocol. As mentioned above, citizenship has traditionally not been a Palestinian demand; if mixed Palestinian-Egyptian couples want their children to have Egyptian nationality, it is only because their children, as Palestinians in Egypt, do not at present have even minimal legal protections. If Palestinians enjoyed such rights—valid travel documents allowing them to enter and leave, education, the right to work—the lure of citizenship would surely fade, assimilation (real or simulated) would no longer be a coping mechanism, and the push to intermarriage (at least as a key strategy for survival) would disappear. Continuing to withhold basic rights seems all the more pointless and illogical given the long-term prospects of legal absorption that appear inevitable as a result of the 2004 Nationality Law.

Among the Arab host populations, there has always been a dualism between Palestine, the *cause*, and the Palestinian *individuals* living in their midst. This dualism, which has been especially evident in Egypt, forms an important underlying theme of this study. Thus, for all the ups and downs and complexities of Egypt's relationship with Palestine—the enthusiasm and recriminations, the passionate support in some periods and bitterness at "unacknowledged sacrifices" in others—Palestine continues to have the potential for tapping into a huge reservoir of emotion. In the popular Egyptian psyche, however, passion for Palestine concerns the larger *cause:* Palestine as the embodiment of the struggle against Israel; Palestine as a symbol of injustice against the Arab nation aided and abetted by foreign powers; Palestine as stubborn resistance in the face of terrible odds.

What this study has tried to do is to refocus attention on the "smaller," more human, and ultimately more easily resolvable issue: the plight of the Palestinians in Egypt. Given Egypt's long involvement with and championship of the Palestinian cause, its central role in the formation and consolidation of the PLO, and its political pre-eminence in the Arab world, it would seem especially appropriate for Egypt to take this step. Even leaving aside this rich past history, Egypt continues to work closely with the Palestinians at the political level, sponsoring efforts to heal rifts between factions and acting as mediator between the PA and Israel, not to mention the Egyptian media's role in rallying popular opinion against Israeli incursions and actions since the outbreak of the second intifada. These factors, coupled with the minuscule size of the Palestinian community (eliminating any possibility of threat to state interests) and the long-term inevitabilities mentioned above, give reason to hope that Egypt may decide at last to put an end to the dualism between cause and community and to lead the way in reviving the Casablanca Protocol. Such a decision would do honor to Egypt, and restore its pre-eminence in the Palestinian issue at little cost to itself.

Notes

1. John Berry, "Acculturation and Adaptation in a New Society," *International Migration* 30 (1992), p. 87.

2. A Palestinian school, funded by the Palestinian Businessmen's Association and the PA Ministry of Education, was established in al-'Arish in the 1990s. After it was built, however, it was not allowed to serve Palestinians students exclusively. It now shelters sheep belonging to Bedouin in the area. Interview with Ali Jawhar, 22 October 2001.

3. Yehia, "The Image of Palestinians in Egypt, 1982–1985," p. 48.

4. Jason Hart, "UNRWA and Children: Some Thoughts on an Uneasy Relationship," paper presented at UNRWA, A History within History Workshop, Amman, Jordan, 1998.

5. It might bear emphasis that most of the PLO groups in the last analysis were also vulnerable and unprotected, as became particularly clear for those who returned from Gaza following the outbreak of the second intifada.

6. Surveys conducted among refugees across the diaspora have repeatedly demonstrated that the "right of return" for large numbers of Palestinians is not just a symbolic demand. Consistently, refugees have been shown to oppose a rhetorical recognition of the *principle* of return with *actual* return limited to a "Palestinian state" in parts of the West Bank in Gaza. What they want is *actual* return to their lands.

7. As explained elsewhere, children born after the passage of the 2004 law obtain citizenship automatically, whereas formal applications need to be filed for those born before the law was passed. See especially chapter 2.

8. It might also be noted that Palestinian identity has shown no signs of abating either in Jordan, where most of the Palestinians have citizenship, or in Syria, where their rights do not differ significantly from those of Syrian nationals and where they have the same access to education and government services.

9. In our field research, three-quarters of our sample had at least one Egyptian grandparent, and many in the younger generations had two or even three.

10. See chapter 2.

Appendix 1

Research Sources and Methodology

Initial Interviews

Many sources of information have been used for this research. Initially, Palestinian officials were interviewed in Cairo, including those working on the Palestinian issue at the Arab League, diplomats at the Palestinian embassy and the PLO office, members of the Palestinian Women's Union (General Union of Palestinian Women—GUPWom), the Palestinian Labor Union (General Union of Palestinian Workers—GUPW), and the heads of the Palestinian Charitable Association and the Association of Martyred and Injured Palestinians. These interviews were used to collect general information on the socioeconomic situation and legal status of Palestinians in Egypt. Because of the unavailability of official demographic information, the interviews provided various "guesstimates" and impressionistic information on geographic areas of Palestinian concentration and employment.

In addition to interviewing officials, the research team met with scholars who had themselves conducted research on Palestinians in Egypt. These included Abdul Qader Yassin, who provided a number of articles about Palestinians in Egypt; Mohamed Khalid al-Az'ar, who studied the conditions of women and children with a team of researchers in 1995[1] and provided a copy of his work on the community published in 1986[2]; Sari Hanafi, who shared his findings on Palestinian businesspeople in the diaspora, including Egypt; and Lamia Raie, who wrote a master's thesis on the legal status of the Palestinians in 1995.

Demographic Information

Reliable sources of information concerning the geographical distribution and social and demographic characteristics of the Palestinians in Egypt are hard to come by. In the years following

189

the 1948 war, limited information on the numbers of Palestinians entering the country as well the population in Gaza was made available to the public through the semi-official daily *al-Ahram*. But in recent decades, the government has not released overall population data on the Palestinians in Egypt, much less the number of Palestinians living in the various governorates.

Unofficially and off the record, an Egyptian foreign ministry source estimated that 70,000 Palestinians lived in Egypt in 2000. The estimate for that same year given by the Palestinian ambassador to Egypt was 53,000.[3] Meanwhile, according to the 2002 report of the United States Committee for Refugees and Immigrants, the Palestinian population in Egypt "was believed to number 50,000 or more persons at the end of 2001, with some estimates placing the number as high as 70,000."[4] Earlier estimates varied just as widely: The 1988 figure given by the PLO's Central Bureau of Statistics and Natural Resources, using projections based on figures from a 1976 Egyptian census, was 41,279.[5] A mere six years later, the results of a 1995 census conducted by the Egyptian Ministry of Interior, as reported in *al-Wafd* (7 July 1995), was more than twice that number: approximately 89,000.[6]

Information concerning the number of foreign employees in the Egyptian public sector does exist: The Egyptian Central Agency for Public Mobilization and Statistics (CAPMAS), the government body responsible for census data, publishes such data in regularly issued reports. However, as the figures are amalgamated, combining Palestinians and other Arab foreigners, we found the CAPMAS documents to be of little use.

Attempts to arrange interviews with government officials for the purpose of obtaining further information on Palestinian demographics (as well as government policies toward the community) were not successful. A meeting with the director of the Administrative Office of the Governor of Gaza (AOGG), Gen. Mohammad Mahmoud Marzouk, resulted in promises to "look into the matter" of the Palestinian population in Egypt. General Marzouk claimed that the figures requested, such as the number of Palestinians in Egypt and the number of Palestinian students in public schools, were not available and that authorities were trying to collect more information and make it available. No figures were provided after that meeting.[7]

Secondary Sources

Libraries at the AUC, the *Centre des Etudes et de Recherches de Moyen Orient Contemporain* (CERMOC) in Amman, the Documentation Centre of the Refugee Studies Centre at Oxford University, and the British Library in London, among others, were visited to collect material on the Palestinians in Egypt. Although there were not many references, some articles did offer perspectives on Egypt's political and national positions and actions during and after the 1948 and 1967 wars, and how these shaped Egyptian attitudes toward Palestinians and the PLO.[8] Palestinian diaspora studies have only rarely investigated the Palestinians in Egypt, though several sources provided estimates of their numbers without investigating their socioeconomic conditions.[9] In many studies, the period of Egypt's administration of Gaza was examined, including the economic and social conditions of the region.[10] The manner in which Egypt administered the Gaza Strip was seldom examined.

Few scholars have investigated the status of Palestinians in Egypt, and most of the studies that do exist date to the second half of the 1980s. Nadera al-Sarraj described their situation from 1948 until 1986, including the demographic, socioeconomic, historical, and political dimensions.[11] An in-depth study of Palestinian organizations in Egypt (and of the Egyptian government's attitude toward them) was written by Maha Dajani. She analyzed how Palestinian identity, which she calls "Palestinianism," generated institutions within the Palestinian community in Egypt, viewing the formation of these groups as an embodiment of social and national consciousness among stateless Palestinians.[12] Laurie Brand devoted the three chapters of her book on Palestinians in the Arab world to Egypt, examining the policy changes of successive Egyptian governments toward Palestinians, particularly relevant legislation in the fields of employment, business, and education, and how it affected them. Brand also analyzed the role of the Palestinian unions, the construction of Palestinian community in Egypt, and the struggle for a Palestinian national identity.[13] Lamia Raie, in her master's dissertation at AUC, studied the legal status of some twenty Palestinian families in Egypt and the effects of their legal status on their socioeconomic conditions.[14] Abdul Qader Yassin, a Palestinian refugee who experienced displacement firsthand through a series of deportations from Haifa, Gaza, and Egypt, has studied several aspects of Palestinian life in Egypt, including the economic, demographic, political, educational, and legal factors affecting their survival.[15] Basing many of his statistics and figures on Sarraj's study, he updated the data with concrete events and stories about Palestinians in Egyptian universities and markets. Sari Hanafi wrote about Palestinian businesspeople in the diaspora. He discussed Egypt's policies toward Palestinians during two periods: the Golden Era, (1962–78) and the end of the "'honeymoon" (i.e., 1978 to the present). He briefly explains the effects of these two eras on the employment of Palestinians in Egypt.[16]

The British Public Records Office at Kew Gardens, London, was visited to collect material written on Palestinians in Egypt. There, the most useful material for our purposes was found in the correspondence file of the Foreign Office (File 371). Most of it concerned Egypt's administration of Gaza, with a few letters shedding light on the conditions of Palestinians in Egypt and agreements reached by the Egyptian government to accommodate refugees. The majority of the letters were about the influxes of Palestinians during 1948, 1950, and 1952 as a result of the military manoeuvres between the Egyptian and Israeli armies. Correspondence also discussed the situation of Palestinians in Gaza and UNRWA's large-scale projects.

Internet Web sites were searched for articles about Palestinian refugees and the livelihoods of refugees. In addition, periodicals such as the *Journal of Palestine Studies, American Anthropologist,* and the *Journal of Refugee Studies* were reviewed. Correspondence was conducted with representatives from the American Friends Service Committee (Quakers), who were unable to provide details concerning their emergency operations in Egypt during 1948 and 1949. Correspondence with USAID was also unsatisfactory, with the agency claiming to have no record of the humanitarian aid they provided in Egypt from 1948–50. The only document obtained described aid provided to the Egyptian government as a whole and not to a particular community of Palestinians in an emergency situation.

Visits were made to the major universities in Egypt to review dissertations on the subject. The works found dealt with general issues related to Palestinian refugees; none focused on Palestinians in Egypt. Although some dealt with the creation of the Palestinian refugee problem and its effect on the Middle East, they did not focus on Egypt. A study on general theories regarding the right to seek asylum in international law analyzed asylum-seeking in general, again with no reference to Palestinians in Egypt. Although we did find a dissertation about the health, education, and social services provided to Palestinians in refugee camps in Jordan, Syria, and Lebanon from 1948 through 1956, it did not refer to Palestinians in Egypt.

Articles on Palestinians in Egypt from 1948 until July 2002 in the Egyptian newspaper *al-Ahram* depicted the living conditions of Palestinians and the administrative regulations concerning them. Many of the articles were found in the *al-Ahram* archives; however, page numbers were not always available. Several articles were found in the French language *al-Ahram Hebdo* and the English-language *al-Ahram Weekly*. Articles from other newspapers, including *al-Akhbar* and *al-Usbu'*, were also collected. Legal and administrative regulations in the government's monthly official gazette *Jaridah Rasmiyyah* and from *Waqa'e' Yawmieh* (Daily Decisions) were also gathered, as were Arab League resolutions concerning Palestinian refugees in Arab countries.

For the purpose of this research, unofficial translations were made of documents, resolutions, and articles from Arabic and French originals. I also translated interviews conducted in Arabic into English. While translating, I tried to preserve the voice of the interviewee as much as possible. Certain Arabic phrases and proverbs have been included in italics with an English translation.

Fieldwork Preparation

A qualitative case-study approach was used in this study. This approach was necessary because statistical sampling and quantitative data collection would have been impossible given that the exact number of Palestinian refugees in Egypt is unknown and the results of the government's 1995 census are not available.[17] I therefore used a combination of data collection methods, including interviews, personal experience and observations, and written texts.

The general geographical distribution of Palestinians in rural and in urban areas was identified based on readings and referrals from social workers at the Palestinian Women's Union and the Labor Union. Because I decided to rely on interviews with Palestinians in their homes and workplaces, I intended to interview a sample from each village, city, and district visited. An attempt was made to interview Palestinians from both genders and from a range of age groups, types of households, educational backgrounds, types of residency, and social classes. According to the initial work plan, some 300 households, including 15 out of the 27 governorates in Egypt, were to be covered in the research.[18] In fact, as a result of the interruption of the research by Egyptian security (see below), only 80 households comprising 401 persons in six governorates were visited; full interviews were conducted in only three governorates (Cairo, Sharqiyyah, and Qalyubiyyah). Of the 401 persons interviewed, 215 were men and 186 were women.

Research Assistants

Conducting fieldwork is a challenging responsibility that raises a number of moral and methodological questions. How is the researcher perceived by the studied community, and how is the community perceived by the researcher? Are the subjects, as Narayan has suggested, viewed as mere fodder for professionally self-serving statements about a generalized "other"? Or are they accepted as subjects with their own voices, views, and dilemmas?[19] Keeping in mind these kinds of questions and the complex relationship between the studied community and the researcher, careful attention was paid to selecting research assistants from the Palestinian community in Cairo. By word of mouth, potential research assistants were located and interviewed with the help of several Palestinian scholars and the Women's Union.

The hope (and expectation) was that the interviewers, being Palestinian, would be able to establish a rapport with those being interviewed and to build enough trust to solicit detailed information about Palestinian livelihoods and the ways Palestinians manage to overcome obstacles. It was hoped that interviewees, talking to compatriots, would feel more at ease in discussions about the difficulties they face in Egypt, especially if the interviewers shared and were familiar with their experiences. Thus, interviewers with Palestinian backgrounds and a legal status similar to that of the interviewees were preferred as candidates. It should be noted, however, that this type of selection also has disadvantages. If the interviewer is Palestinian, the Palestinian interviewee may feel that he or she should emphasize his/her Palestinian identity in order to please the interviewer. Interviewers were instructed to do what they could to create an open and comfortable atmosphere, including providing examples themselves so as to stimulate ideas and permit the interviewees to answer without fear of being judged.

Five research assistants—four women and one man, aged 22 to 28 years, all Palestinians—were selected from among many applicants. Of the four women, three had Egyptian mothers, and although both parents of the fourth were Palestinian, the father had been employed by the Egyptian government and in many ways had been treated like an Egyptian national until 1978. The male researcher, a master's student at the Institute of Arab Research and Studies in Cairo, was from Khan Yunis in the Gaza Strip. He and I, the principal researcher, were the only ones who had not lived primarily in Egypt. I am Palestinian-Jordanian, born to Palestinian parents and brought up in Amman, Jordan.

All five researchers had university degrees. While I had taken care to select assistants from the community being studied for the reasons mentioned above, they differed from most of their interviewees in several ways. In particular, they had social and economic advantages that enabled them to get university degrees and employment. Even so, emphasizing similarities rather than the social or economic differences was an important way in which to gain an "insider's" approach to the community, to gain trust, and to ensure a productive interview.

Training for Fieldwork

Because the primary criterion in choosing the team had been membership in and affinity with the community under study, the research assistants had little prior experience in social science research and none in fieldwork. The training period was therefore very important, and lasted for two months, during which time they were given readings about research methodology and schooled in issues concerning approaches to researching refugees. Background information about the Palestinian exodus and the legal status of Palestinians in Arab host countries were also discussed. Although the team members were Palestinian, they were unfamiliar with much of the historical background on Palestinian refugees. Their lack of background knowledge contrasts sharply with that of Palestinian refugees living in camps served by UNRWA, where the employees and teachers, generally Palestinian themselves, make a point of trying to instil in young people a sense of history of the homeland and their villages of origin. Apart from the young man from Gaza, none of the research assistants even knew about UNRWA. It was therefore essential to equip them with information about various international refugee conventions, details about the legal status of Palestinians, and the role of various United Nations bodies in serving Palestinians.

The ambiguous legal status of Palestinians in Egypt was illustrated in the lives of the research assistants. They were able to reflect on their own dreams that were collapsing as a result of this status and the opportunities they had lost in education and work due to bureaucratic impediments. For example, one research assistant, a musician who played the lute with a musical group, could not travel to another African state to perform with her colleagues because her Egyptian travel document was not recognized by the embassy of that state. The planned engagement of another team member to an Egyptian army lieutenant was called off when the young man learned that marriage to a Palestinian would affect his advancement within the Defense Ministry. A third research assistant was unable to apply for scholarships to continue her higher education because the application guidelines require that Palestinian candidates must be residents either of the West Bank or Gaza, and she was neither. These experiences helped in formulating the questionnaire.

Preparing the Questionnaire

In framing the questionnaire, we used many samples from previous studies. Several questionnaires used in projects by AUC's Social Research Center to study aspects of livelihood in Egypt were considered. The questionnaire used in the research that led to Barbara Harrell-Bond's *Imposing Aid* also provided guidelines for the work.[20]

Preliminary visits to Palestinian households were conducted with the assistance of social workers from the Women's Union. These visits brought home to me the major gaps in the research relating to the livelihoods of Palestinians in Egypt, and therefore helped in drafting the questionnaire. After the initial drafting, a brainstorming meeting was held. Community leaders, social service NGO members, and academics, including those with particular knowledge of Palestinian and Egyptian communities, were invited to discuss the questionnaire. During this meeting, some questions were added and others were removed to sharpen the focus and lay the ground for later quantitative and qualitative analysis.

The questionnaire covered twelve themes relating to livelihood: household composition; arrival in Egypt; social networks; family in Palestine and abroad; ownership (business, property, land); legal status; education; work (public and private sector); health; financial support; expenditures; and identity. Each theme included ten to fifteen questions (see Appendix 2). Answers to these questions enabled the researcher to trace changing state policies toward Palestinians, from the tight restrictions of the immediate post-1948 period through the loosening of restrictions as of the mid-1950s, to the important 1962 regulations placing Palestinians on a par with Egyptian nationals with regard to education, work, and property ownership, and finally to the abrupt reversal of policy in 1978 that made Palestinians in Egypt foreigners once again. Among the goals of the questionnaire was to explore the impact of these policy changes on Palestinian legal status, socioeconomic situation, education, work, health, financial status, and sources of income.

Another goal of the questionnaire was to highlight strategies deployed by Palestinians to circumvent the restrictions. To this end, the questions were open-ended to enable the interviewees to narrate their own ways of getting by (for example, in renewing residence permits). The questionnaires were constructed as a guide to help the researchers cover all the topics. Questionnaires were never distributed to interviewees, and questions were in no way restricted to those listed in the questionnaire. Wherever possible, the interviews were written up using the words of the interviewee.

Locating Palestinians

Palestinians in Egypt are not as easy to locate as they are in other host countries, where most tend to live either in Palestinian neighborhoods (including squatter areas) or refugee camps. In the absence of such patterns, finding them—especially in rural or urban areas outside of Cairo (where certain districts are known to have Palestinian residents)—is a challenge.

With information obtained from readings, and through discussions with the Women's Union and the Labor Union, we were able to map out where Palestinians could be found. Preliminary

visits to Palestinian households in Cairo were conducted with
the help of the Women's Union and the Association of Martyred
and Injured Palestinians. Two social workers accompanied me to
Cairo districts such as Wailey, Dar al-Salam, and Madinat al-Salam.
Meanwhile, the head of the Labor Union offered to put me in
touch with representatives of the union's branches outside Cairo.
However, the contacts had not materialized by the time we were
ready to begin the field research, and. I decided to go ahead anyway:
Although the contacts would have facilitated matters, reliance on
the PLO-affiliated union representatives to identify interviewees
could have resulted in disproporationate representation of a
particular population and the exclusion of circles outside these
networks.[21] Furthermore, our experience in Cairo had already
shown that some people appeared more reserved in their responses
if union representatives remained with the research assistants
during the interview. I therefore decided to depend on a snowball
method in searching for Palestinians.

In the course of our field research, we visited the following
districts and towns, arranged below by governorate:

Cairo

The Cairo Governorate, and especially the city of Cairo, has the
largest Palestinian population in Egypt, mainly in the following
areas: Shubra, 'Izbit al-Nakhal, al-Zawiyyah al-Hamra, Imbaba, Dar
al-Salam, 'Ayn Shams, Wailey, Helwan, and Hilmiyyat al-Zaytun.
Even in such neighborhoods, however, Palestinians are not easy
to find; as almost everywhere in Egypt, they are dispersed among
and intermingled with the local population. Moreover, many of the
Palestinians who used to live in Cairo, particularly in areas that
hosted many PLA officers or fighters from the Mustafa Hafiz forces
(for example, 'Ayn Shams, Wailey, Dar al-Salam), left in 1995 for
Palestine.

Giza

Giza is a separate governorate bordering on the Cairo
Governorate, with the city of Cairo spilling into it across the Nile.
Such integrally Cairene neighborhoods as Dokki are in fact in Giza
Governorate. Outside the "Cairo" part of Giza, we visited Faysal
and Bulak al-Dakrur.

Qalyubiyyah

Qalyubiyyah Governorate is a rural and agricultural area adjacent to the Cairo Governorate to the north. We located Palestinians in towns, but not in villages, in the districts (*marakez*) of Shibin al-Qanatir, Shubra al-Khayma, Khanka, Abu Za'bal, Banha, Bahtim, Kufr Shukr, and Qanatir al-Khairiyyah. Public services were available for Palestinians in the towns we visited, as were private *azhari* (religious) schools. Despite the fact that Qalyubiyyah is an agricultural area, very few Palestinians work in the agricultural sector, undoubtedly because of the tight restrictions on land ownership for Palestinians. Most are employed in the tertiary sector, especially in the transport business, with many driving heavy trucks and semi-tractor trailers.

Sharqiyyah

In Sharqiyyah Governorate, we visited Hehya, Kufr Saqi, Minya al-Qamah, Bani Ayub, Abu Hammad, Zaqaziq, Jazirat Abu Fadil, Qanayyat, Dyarb Nijim, Manshiyyah, Faqus, Bilbays, Hussiniyyah, Salhiyyah, and Abu Kabir. It was not difficult to locate Palestinians in the towns of Sharqiyyah because they are well known to the other residents and are well integrated socially. Many of the Palestinians in the governorate had an Egyptian grandparent from the pre-1948 period. It was in Sharqiyyah, on the other hand, that we encountered the most "isolated" Palestinian community of our experience, Jazirat Abu Fadil, which was discussed in chapter 3.

Northern Sinai

Al-'Arish and Rafah, the most important "Palestinian" areas in the Northern Sinai Governorate, were visited very briefly to get the "lay of the land," to see what general services were available, and to determine how the interviewing would best proceed. Al-'Arish, some 381 km from Cairo in the Sinai desert not far from the Gaza border, was said to host more than 8,000 Palestinians at the time of the research.[22] They are easily identifiable. During the visit, people often directed us to the *mukhtar*, al-Jawrani, who represents Palestinians in the region. The areas of al-'Arish with the largest numbers of Palestinians are Karm Abu Injileh, 'Izbit Mallim, Qarieyyat Atef al-Sadat, al-Mazra'a/al-Masmi (arable land), Hayy al-Safa, al-Dahiyyah, Birket Halimesh, and Salaiemah.

Not far from Palestine and overlooking the sea, al-'Arish at the time of our research had a booming economy, with Palestinians working mainly in trade and skilled professions. During the first decade or so of the Israeli occupation, Palestinians "were able to work and to travel inside Palestine to make some money" (PP 3, al-'Arish, 25 June 2001).

After 1978, when Palestinians lost their access to public schools, two private schools were built in al-'Arish—Sinai School near Busta Road and a school in Dahiyyah/'Izba. There was also a school that local residents said was "built by Arafat" (in fact it had been funded by the PLO education department), which is now closed. Apparently the idea of a school that would serve a non-Egyptian community was not welcomed: According to Ali Jawhar of the Palestinian Charitable Association, there had been a dispute with the Egyptian Ministry of Education about opening the school.[23] The building is still there and is used by Bedouin to shelter their animals. There are two university faculties in al-'Arish, a Faculty of Agriculture and a Faculty of Education, linked to the University of Suez. A branch of the Palestinian Labor Union is also located in al-'Arish.

We also visited the Rafah area on the Egyptian side of the border with Gaza. During the visit, the researcher met some 200 Bedouin from the Palestinian side who had been living there in tents without access to public services. Some had Egyptian travel documents and others Palestinian identity cards. At the time of our visit we were told that approximately 10,000 Palestinians lived in Rafah, Egypt.[24]

It should be noted that until 2000, Egyptian Rafah was the site of the so-called "Canada Camp"[25] for Palestinian refugees. The housing that came to constitute the "camp" was built by Israel in the early 1970s for the some 5,000 Palestinian refugees whose houses in Rafah camp, Gaza, had been bulldozed as part of street-widening operations to facilitate the passage of tanks during Ariel Sharon's "iron fist" counter-insurgency against Palestinian fedayeen in 1970. At that time, the entire Sinai Peninsula was under Israeli occupation, so even though the Palestinians had been moved to the Egyptian side of the border, no barrier separated them from their brethren on the Gaza side. But when Israel completed its withdrawal from the Sinai in April 1982 following its 1979 peace treaty with Egypt, a "Berlin-style" barrier of razor wire was erected, slicing the camp in half.[26] Though the agreement was that the Palestinians would be moved back to the Gaza side as quickly as possible to be reunited with their kinsmen, the relocation did not even begin until 1989, with thirty-five households to be moved at a time. After 1991, Egypt was unable to continue funding the relocation. The PLO provided some funds at first, but with the financial crisis after the Gulf war, Egypt sought help from outside donors. Kuwait and Canada both contributed, but it took until 2000 for the last ten households to be settled in their new houses at Tal al-Sultan.[27] In the meantime, the refugees had been receiving emergency relief from UNRWA. After the last households were transferred to Palestinian Rafah, the camp was demolished.

Isma'iliyyah and Port Said

Brief "reconnaissance" or exploratory visits were made to the Isma'iliyyah and Port Said governorates. In Isma'iliyyah, we were particularly interested to see whether we could find any Palestinians at Qantara Sharq on the Sinai side of the Suez Canal, where Egypt's largest temporary camp for Palestinian refugees had been set up by the Higher Committee for Palestinian Immigrant Affairs in 1948. While the camp was emptied in 1949, with most of its residents transferred to the Gaza Strip, a number of Palestinians were known to have remained in the area. However, the brief visit to Qantara was not sufficient to assess the extent of a Palestinian presence, if any, in the area, which had been occupied by Israel in 1967 and was on the front lines during the war of attrition that followed. Our visit to the large cities of Isma'iliyyah and Port Said were similarly inconclusive; to have an idea of the size of the Palestinian communities there, cooperation with members of the Labor Union would have been necessary. However, during the visit we did manage to meet several Palestinians who informed us of the general situation of their lives.

Minya

Minya is a three-hour train ride south of Cairo. Palestinians are said to have gone to the region for jobs with the Egyptian government from 1962 to 1967, and we were told that some Palestinians still teach in schools there. However, it was not possible to meet with any of them. Instead, we interviewed several Egyptian families who had lived in Palestine before 1948. Local residents referred to them as Palestinian because their parents had been among those fleeing Jaffa in 1948.

Locating Palestinian Households

The pilot visits targeted households in the Cairo Governorate (indicated by a "P" followed by the interview number). Feedback from these interviews was used to fine-tune the questionnaire. While conducting our research in Cairo, the team used several ways to locate Palestinian households, principally the snowball methodology. When arriving in the area, the researcher would ask a shopkeeper about a particular Palestinian who lived in the area. Because of close community ties, especially in *'ashwa'iyyat*, or unplanned housing settlements, it was usually easy to gain referrals to Palestinians. Vendors would often say, "I have never heard this name, but there is a Palestinian family that lives in the next block." One research assistant found Palestinian residents by asking at local barbershops, because barbers are known to have close relationships with their clients. In many areas, we were helped by people working in a *baqqal*s, or mini-markets, usually located on residential streets. In some cases, shopkeepers were suspicious of "outsiders" asking about Palestinian families. Shopkeepers occasionally denied knowing any Palestinians, perhaps in an attempt to protect neighbors. On the other hand, because Palestinians and Egyptians live intermingled and are often indistinguishable one from the other, a shopkeeper or a laundry man, for example, might not be aware that a client is Palestinian unless specifically told.

In towns outside Cairo, locating Palestinians was often easier, because many inhabitants remembered Palestinians joining the community in the late 1940s and early 1950s or in the 1960s and were more aware of the presence of non-Egyptians. In some cases, names provide a clue. Upon arriving in Abu Hammad, in Sharqiyyah Governorate, for example, when we asked a vegetable vendor if there were Palestinians in the town, he quickly identified Abu Hadi al-Shami. When arriving in Shubra al-Khayma, in Qalyubiyyah, we saw a big poster on the wall of the railway station advertising the shop of Said al-Falastini.

Ideally, the interviews should reflect the heterogeneity of the Palestinian community.[28] In this regard, the snowball approach has its limitations. First, it does not allow for the compilation of a complete and accurate sampling frame, as noted, and it may lead to respondents who are all or mostly part of the same social network. In an attempt to compensate, the six researchers, working in pairs, went to different areas. Even so, we sometimes discovered that two teams had met interviewees in different areas who knew each other. Or we learned that one household had talked about the team to a household that was visited the next day. Furthermore, areas such as Wailey and 'Ayn Shams in Cairo, which are near military bases, have large concentrations of former military personnel from the 'Ayn Jalut Brigade or Mustafa Hafiz forces, which meant that the people we met there had similar backgrounds and economic situations.

Conducting the Interviews

Face-to-face interviews were conducted using a series of open-ended questions structured to evoke descriptive qualitative data on the survival strategies of refugee households and to gain an understanding of the factors influencing their livelihoods. The fact that research team members were all of Palestinian origin and that some spoke the Palestinian dialect facilitated the interviews. We had no problem being invited into households to interview members. Often, we were quickly welcomed into the living room.

Introductions normally took 30 to 45 minutes. We openly answered any questions about the research and its objectives and explained why the study was important. Many interviewees were very concerned about our aims, worrying in particular about whose interests the research would serve. In general, the more educated the respondents, the longer the introductions would take. We also became accustomed to hearing rhetoric about U.S. and Israeli plans and intentions concerning the permanent settlement of Palestinians in Arab countries. These preliminary conversations were crucial to gaining the trust of those we were interviewing and to make sure that they fully understood why we would be asking about their personal experiences. On some occasions, particularly when I explained my background as a Palestinian from Jordan, the conversation would turn to the situation of Palestinians living in camps in Jordan. I tried to explain that just as we had learned about Palestinians in the camps in Jordan, Lebanon, Syria, the West Bank, and Gaza Strip, so was it important to learn about the survival mechanisms employed by Palestinians in Egypt. Frequently, we would talk about the interviewees' relatives in Jordan. Through these introductions, we tried to allay any suspicions or misgivings that interviewees may initially have had concerning our visit, and we ensured that they gave their consent to the interview.

On four or five occasions, after long introductions had been made, members of the household declined to be interviewed. This can be understood in view of Egypt's security situation, in which people are often suspicious of newcomers and do not easily trust others.

In order to maintain confidentiality, we tried to record nicknames rather than proper last names, even in our field notes. For instance, we would refer to a father not by his own name but by reference to his oldest son. Thus, a man whose oldest son was named Ali would be called "Abu Ali," or "father of Ali." Likewise, in households headed by a woman, we would refer to the mother as "Um Ali," or "mother of Ali." For other people in the household, we recorded first names only. For security reasons, even in our field notes we preferred to use numbers both for the researchers and the families to ensure that the interview remained confidential. It should be noted that in the few instances in this work where an interviewee's name is mentioned, it is not the real name; aliases have been adopted to protect the speaker's privacy.

The interviews quoted in the text are referenced by code. Basically, the interviews/visits fall into three categories: the preliminary or pilot interviews and visits both by the author individually and the research team; the regular interviews; and the handful of interviews conducted by the author after the research was interrupted. The "regular" interviews were all carried out in the Sharqiyyah and Qalyubiyyah governorates; almost all the pilot visits by the research team were in the Cairo Governorate. The codes for the various categories are as follows:

PP: Pilot visits/interviews by the author
P: Pilot visits/interviews by research team (author and assistants) in the Cairo Governorate
AP: Visits/interviews conducted after termination of fieldwork
7:     Regular interviews (i.e., part of the main body of the fieldwork), conducted in Sharqiyyah Governorate
8:     Regular interviews conducted in Qalyubiyyah Governorate

The category designation in the code is followed by the number within that category of the household visited, the governorate in which the interview took place (if not already subsumed in the category designation), the name of the district or locale within the governorate, and the date of the interview. For example, the code "8/8, Abu Za'bal, 2 July 2002" would mean that the interview took place in the Qalyubiyyah Governorate, that the household was the eighth visited by the research team during the main body of the fieldwork (i.e., it was not a pilot), and that it was conducted in the town of Abu Za'bal on 2 July 2002. "P12, 'Izbit al-Nakhal, 29 May 2002," would indicate a pilot interview conducted by the research team in the Cairo Governorate (unless otherwise indicated), that the household was the twelfth visited by the team in the pilot phase, that the household was located in the district of 'Izbit al-Nakhal, and that the interview took place on 29 May 2002. "PP9, Port Said, 18 June 2002" would indicate the ninth preliminary visit by the author, which took place in the governorate of Port Said, the city of Port Said, on 18 June 2002. In a few exceptional cases where the interviewee shared particularly sensitive information, the name of the city or area within the governorate was omitted. It bears emphasis that the interviews conducted in Cairo, even though they were pilots, were full interviews covering the entire range of issues indicated on the questionnaire.

It is important to note that each interview code covers the entire household. If, for example, five members are interviewed, they do not have separate numbers; the only indication that a different person is talking is the context.

After the introductions and preliminaries were completed, we asked the members of the household to sit with us and share their experiences. In some cases, neighbors would join us. Because the questionnaire had many open-ended questions, we tried to have all the family members share their experiences with us individually. This was not always possible, however. In some households, it became obvious that as long as the father was speaking the rest of the family did not feel free to express their views. In other cases, the mother would answer the questions from her own perspective. Still, we did our best to involve as many people as possible when asking questions about life in Egypt. Questions relating to education were directed primarily at children. We found that young people often had difficulty answering questions relating to identity and knowledge about or interest in Palestine. In many situations, we sensed that we were introducing topics that had never before been discussed in the home. In some cases, the parent took the lead and answered the questions on behalf of their children.

Using maximum discretion, we often had to follow up on questions pertaining to coping strategies in order to uncover the various means used to overcome administrative obstacles. Livelihood strategies may involve the illegal processing of papers, for example, a fact that might not be revealed without some subtle prompting from the researcher.

The interviews were usually conducted by two researchers, both taking notes, but only one asking questions. No tape recorders were used so as not to intimidate interviewees. Even writing in notebooks sometimes had an inhibiting effect, and in such cases we would stop taking notes and simply continue the discussion with household members. Conducting interviews in pairs was also useful because we could discuss the case after leaving the house and record each researcher's detailed impressions of the interview.

Interview sessions generally lasted from two to six hours. The time spent with the household sometimes prompted discussions of other issues, including the intifada and reactions to events in Palestine. In rural areas especially, interviews sometimes included lunch breaks, with the family often insisting on sharing their food with the researchers. As only one interview was conducted with each household, the more time we spent with the family, the more we learned about their lives.

Meetings after the interviews among the researchers offered a chance to discuss each case. Many factors influence household interviews, such as the relationship between the researcher and the research community, or what Rosemary Sayigh calls "intersubjectivity"[29]: the age and cultural background of the researchers; the political-cultural worlds to which each belongs; and the ultimate purposes of the research project. The researcher's identity and subjectivity cannot be abstracted from the research process.[30]

Intersubjectivity is a particularly important consideration for researchers who are not from the same community as their interviewees, even if both are Palestinian. How are the researchers' motivations understood by the communities they study? How does their own sense of identity influence their fieldwork?[31] Conversely, how are the researcher's personality, beliefs, and sense of Palestinian identity influenced by the interviewees and their answers? Although the researchers took pains to emphasize the importance of the data that the interviewee would reveal as a means of focusing attention on their difficult situations, people often engaged in self-censorship in their replies. Sari Hanafi has noted that this is often evident in countries where the government discourages researchers from addressing topics perceived as sensitive on a national or regional level and where discussion of such issues may cause problems with state security authorities.[32] This self-censorship can also be imposed by other social and political bodies, such as the Palestinian unions.

The Perils of Research

My original intention had been to plan the fieldwork jointly with the unions so the research findings could be shared as the basis for discussing and exploring the problems and needs of Palestinians in Egypt. The hope was that the findings would eventually be useful in designing development projects addressing needs not being met by NGOS or the host state. The project faced a number of difficulties, however.

The study as conceived involved considerable travel throughout Egypt by research teams made up of Palestinians with Egyptian travel documents seeking to interview Palestinians in their homes. The field research required coordination with Palestinian unions and officials, and, most crucially, proper authorization from officials to avoid misunderstandings with security personnel in the field.

As already mentioned, the research was conducted under the umbrella of the Forced Migration Refugee Studies Program (FMRS) of the AUC. Colleagues at the university who had done fieldwork in Egypt warned me of the difficulties faced by non-Egyptians working at American institutions in obtaining security clearance. Inquiring about procedures, I learned from the AUC director of security that a letter from FMRS, as overseer of the work, should be sent to him for forwarding to the state security and to CAPMAS to get clearance for the fieldwork.

Two months before starting the fieldwork, a document in Arabic based on the research proposal and explaining its objectives was duly sent to the AUC office of security. Copies of the document were sent to the state security and to CAPMAS. In order to issue the clearance, copies of the passports and travel documents of all of the members of the research team were sent to these bodies.

When the team was ready to begin the interviews, the university security office informed us by telephone that we had received approval from the state security. Accordingly, a letter for use during fieldwork was written by FMRS clarifying the purpose of the research and introducing the members of the research team. As the principal researcher, I signed the letter, as did the AUC director of security. Copies of the letter were distributed to the research team to use when necessary.

The letter of permission from the university security office provided us with credibility in conducting our fieldwork. We showed it whenever we were questioned by interviewees about the objectives of the research and why we were focusing only on Palestinians, and it helped allay whatever concerns people may have had. This procedure worked well until the team arrived in a village whose inhabitants were originally from Beersheba. The *mukhtar* did not welcome our visit. He took the copy of the letter we showed him, and although he permitted us to remain for some time in the village while accompanied, he told us we were expected to leave immediately afterward.

Upon our return to Cairo, I was summoned to the office of the state security. The security official asked three main questions. The first concerned the "true objectives" of my research; I was told that Security had not found the objectives set out in my previous correspondence convincing. Second, I was asked on what basis our team was conducting the fieldwork. Third, I was asked who had given me permission to work in the field.

Understandably, fieldwork on topics considered sensitive is suspect in Egypt.[33] Qualitative data can be politicized and used to serve various agendas. The analysis of livelihoods, studies of the problems of Palestinians in relation to changing state policies, and the depiction of poverty and service provision can all serve political purposes. In this particular case, there was concern that the information collected could be used in ways that might conflict with Egypt's national interests, especially since the research reveals the need for improvements in the legal and socioeconomic status of Egypt's Palestinian community. In light of this, security officials could have construed the research as serving Western or Israeli interests. Security officials may also have feared that we would take advantage of the time spent with interviewees to spread political ideas seen as subversive.

I was impressed by the fact that the security officer who questioned me had read all the letters and papers I had sent to obtain the permission. He also knew where my assistants and I had visited while conducting fieldwork. The meeting lasted an hour and a half and ended with an order that the fieldwork be stopped until written approval from Security was obtained. Such approval never was granted. My short visit with this officer helped me understand why Palestinians feared to speak freely.

Timing

Our initial plan was to conduct a trial run of the questionnaire for one month, from mid-May till mid-June, and then to conduct home interviews for the next six months, from mid-June until mid-December. We hoped to cover 15 governorates, mainly in the north where most Palestinians live. By mid-July 2002, when the security services halted the fieldwork, we had visited 26 households in the Cairo Governorate and 44 households in Qalyubiyyah and Sharqiyyah, in addition to five cases in Port Said and Isma'iliyyah.

The research took place during a period of heightened political tension in the Middle East. The al-Aqsa intifada was a highly emotional time not only for the Palestinians in Egypt but also for Egyptians. Israel "reoccupied" the West Bank in spring 2002, with massive destruction in towns and villages and great loss of life. With over 40,000 Palestinians having returned to Palestine after the establishment of the PA, many of the households we interviewed had family members in the territories, especially Gaza, and feared that Gaza would be next. In such conditions, Security may have been even more skeptical about a study claiming to focus on legal status and socioeconomic circumstances of Palestinians in Egypt.

Moreover, during the preparation for the fieldwork, Saad Eddin Ibrahim, the former director of the Ibn Khaldoun Center and a professor of political sociology at AUC, was convicted of charges of embezzlement believed to have been linked to the center's acceptance of an allegedly "illegal" grant from the European Commission used to produce a film depicting voter intimidation in the 1995 Egyptian parliamentary election.[34] Ibrahim's connection to AUC, and the fact that he had been funded by international donors, had made an impact. For example, several of our interviewees, particularly professionals, mentioned him in discussions about the livelihood project. Ibrahim's case strengthened suspicions about the objectives and intentions of our study on the part of representatives of the Palestinian unions. I was once told by a representative of the development projects for Palestine at the Arab League that as a Palestinian, I should be ashamed of myself for serving imperialist agencies in the Arab world. During the research period, the attitudes of many Egyptians and Palestinians in Egypt became increasingly anti-American, though fortunately we rarely encountered such attitudes in our interviews; even when they existed initially, we were able to establish trust. But at the more "official" level, the backlash from the Saad Eddin Ibrahim case without doubt affected the reception of the research project and the researchers.

Indeed, several people stated directly that that the project was poorly timed. A lawyer from the Hisham Mubarak Human Rights Center told me, "I would have accepted this research had it been done two years ago." Politics are intertwined with discussions of basic human rights of Palestinians. Academics, professionals, diplomats, and Palestinian representatives openly suggested that a project on Palestinian livelihoods would serve Israel's agenda of ending the Palestinian refugee issue; efforts to improve the living conditions of Palestinians in Egypt were seen by many as promoting *tawtin*, the permanent resettlement of Palestinians outside their homeland.

Lamia Raie, who conducted her fieldwork on the Palestinians in Egypt in 1993, commented: "It was not the right time. Oslo was underway and any approach to the Palestinians was badly interpreted."[35] The question can be asked as to whether there will ever be a "right time" to talk about the conditions of Palestinians in Egypt.

Notes

1. UNICEF, "Analysis of the Conditions of Palestinian Women and Children in Egypt," [in Arabic], unpublished draft, 1996.

2. Sarraj et al., *Arab Palestinians in Egypt*.

3. Interview with Palestinian ambassador Zuhdi al-Qudwah, 23 September 2001.

4. U.S. Committee for Refugees and Immigrants, *World Refugee Survey 2002: An Annual Assessment to Conditions Affecting Refugees, Asylum Seekers, and Internally Displaced Persons* (Arlington, VA: USCRI, 2002).

5. PLO, *Palestinian Statistical Abstract*. Central Bureau of Statistics and Natural Resources, 1987 and 1988, no. 8, Damascus, Syria (1989).

6. Yassin, "Palestinians in Egypt," *Samed al-Iqtisadi*.

7. General Marzouk expressed his disappointment with my affiliation with the AUC. In an interview held on 29 April 2003, he told me, "I would have preferred to look for the figures and give them to a researcher at Cairo University."

8. See Brand, "Nasir's Egypt and the Re-emergence of the Palestinian National Movement"; Fawaz Gerges, "Egypt and the 1948 War: Internal Conflict and Regional Ambition," in *The War for Palestine, Rewriting the History of 1948*, Eugene Rogan and Avi Shlaim, eds. (Cambridge, England: Cambridge University Press, 2001), pp. 151–77; Miller *Arab States and the Palestine Question*; Ilan Pappé, *Making of the Arab-Israeli Conflict 1947–1951*(London: I.B. Tauris,

1992); Avi Shlaim, "The Rise and Fall of the All-Palestine Government in Gaza," *Journal of Palestine Studies* 20, no. 1 (Autumn 1990), pp. 37–63; and Avi Shlaim, *The Politics of Partition, King Abdullah, the Zionists and Palestine 1921–1951* (Oxford: Oxford University Press, 1998).

9. Abdullatif Ata Akel, "Sociopsychological Analysis of the Palestinian Response to Homelessness," (master's thesis, U.S. International University, 1979); Said et al., *A Profile of the Palestinian People* (Chicago: Palestine Human Rights Campaign, 1988); Janet Abu-Lughod, "Palestinians: Exiles at Home and Abroad," *Current Sociology* 36, no. 2 (Summer 1988), 61–69.

10. Sara Roy, "Gaza: New Dynamics of Civic Disintegration." *Journal of Palestine Studies* 22, no. 4 (1993), pp. 20–31; William H. Haddad, Ghada H. Talhami, and Janice J. Terry, *The June 1967 War after Three Decades* (Washington, DC: Association of Arab American University Graduates, 1999).

11. Sarraj et al., *Arab Palestinians in Egypt.*

12. Dajani, *Institutionalisation of Palestinian Identity in Egypt.*

13. Brand, *Palestinians in the Arab World.*

14. Raie, "Forgotten Population."

15. Yassin, "Palestinians in Egypt," *Samed al-Iqtisadi.*

16. Sari Hanafi, *Entre Deux Mondes.*

17. Raie, "Forgotten Population"; Hanafi, *Entre Deux Mondes.*

18. A governorate is the equivalent of a state (as in the United States) or a province, with a capital city and other towns and villages. The fieldwork was to take place in the following governorates: Cairo, Giza, Alexandria, Port Said, Suez, Damyat, Daqahliyyah, Sharqiyyah, Qalyubiyyah, Gharbiyyah, Buhayrah, Isma'iliyyah, North Sinai, Minya, and Marsa Matruh.

19. Kirin Narayan, "How Native is a 'Native' Anthropologist?" *American Anthropologist* 95, no. 3 (1993), pp. 671–86.

20. Barbara Harrell-Bond, *Imposing Aid: Emergency Assistance to Refugees* (Oxford: Oxford University Press, 1986).

21. Alice Bloch, "Carrying out a Survey of Refugees: Some Methodological Considerations and Guidelines," *Journal of Refugee Studies* 12, no. 4 (1999), p. 371.

22. Interview with Adel Attiyah, 24 September 2001.

23. Interview with Ali Jawhar, 22 October 2001.

24. Interview with Abu Mustafa al-Jabur, the *mukhtar* of the Palestinians in Rafah, 25 June 2001.

25. The name comes from the fact that the camp was near the site of a military base where Canadian UNEF soldiers were stationed from 1956 to 1967. In Rafah, Gaza, there is a similar housing project called Brazil Camp after the Brazilian UNEF Contingent (Wilkinson, "Initial Review: Canada Camp Location").

26. Dick Doughty and Mohammed El Aydi, *Gaza: Legacy of Occupation* (West Hartford, CT: Kumarian Press, 1995), p. xxvi.

27. Wilkinson, "Initial Review: Canada Camp Location."

28. Wilson, Ken B. "Thinking about the Ethics of Fieldwork," in *Fieldwork in Developing Countries*, Stephen Devereux and John Hoddinott, eds. (Boulder, CO: Lynne Rienner, 1993), pp. 179–99.

29. Rosemary Sayigh, "Researching Gender in a Palestinian Camp: Political, Theoretical and Methodological Issues," in Denis Kandiyoti, ed., *Gendering the Middle East, Emerging Perspectives* (London and New York: I.B. Tauris, 1996), p. 146.

30. Ibid.

31. Seteney Shami and Linda Herrera, "Introduction," in *Between Field and Text: Emerging Voices in Egyptian Social Science*, Seteney Shami and Linda Herrera, eds., Cairo Papers in Social Science, Vol. 22, no 2 (Cairo: American Univeristy of Cairo Press, 1999), p. 5.

32. Sari Hanafi, "Between Arab and French Agendas: Defining the Palestinian Diaspora and the Image of the Other," in *Between Field and Text*, Seteney Shami and Linda Herrera, eds., pp. 139–59.

33. Sholkamy, "Why Is Anthropology so Hard in Egypt?" in *Between Field and Text*, Seteney Shami and Linda Herrera, eds., pp. 119–38.

34. To read more about this, see http://www.mesa.arizona.edu/about/cafmenaletters. htm.

35. Raie, "Forgotten Population."

Appendix 2

Questionnaire for the Study on the Livelihood of Palestinians in Egypt

Interview

Code of interviewer

Interview Number / Region/

Region _____ City_____ Area_____
District_____Street name_____

Interview Date (indicate if it is a holiday)

Time of the interview (from ___ to ___)

Number of visits per interviewer per day (until the time this interview was conducted).

Anyone refuse to conduct this interview?

1. Household composition (Answer in the table for household composition)

1.1   How many people normally live in the household?
1.2   How many units (families)?
1.3   How many men/women are in this household?
1.4   Who is the head in this household (in making decisions, breadwinner)?
1.5   Number in household now present at the interview?

213

1.6   Where are the absentees?

1.7   Who is the oldest in this household?

2. Arrival in Egypt

2.1   When did the first person [member of the family] first arrive in Egypt?

2.2   What were you doing before coming to Egypt? What was the main source of income for you/your family while you were in Palestine? (Specify how rural/urban-oriented their life in Palestine had been.)

2.3   What happened to the house of the family back in Palestine? (Specify in what village/area it was.)

2.4   How did you arrive in Egypt (via Gaza, West Bank, Jordan, Syria, Lebanon, or elsewhere; by bus, train, car, camel, on foot)? How long did you stay in the last country/city you were in before your arrival in Egypt (in camps, outside camps)?

2.5   Have you settled in Egypt since that date (either because you could not go back, got married, were in university, or were working)?

3. Social networks

3.1   Tell me about your relatives or neighbors who migrated with you from Palestine. Are you still in contact with them?

3.2   Do any of these relatives or neighbors live nearby?

3.2   For how long have you been living in this neighborhood? Where were you before? How often do/did you change houses/areas? Why?

3.4   Are there any Palestinians living in your neighborhood? Where?

3.5   Do you meet with them? How often do you see each other? Do you arrange activities together?

3.6   How are your relations with the Egyptian neighbors? Do you see each other often? Do you borrow food items or anything you may need at home from them?

3.7   On whom do you rely in case you were in need of urgent help or support? (Elaborate on examples at sickness, funerals, need to borrow money or even weddings.)

3.8   On whom do you count for bureaucratic issues (renewal of residency, travel documents, papers for schooling or for health, registration of property)? If it happens to be someone in an influential positions (owners of companies, shops, work in the government or the embassies), clarify if you have a *wasta* that facilitates your paper processing. (When was last time you had a problem with bureaucracy, and how did you solve it?)

3.9   If you have any membership in clubs, cultural or social forums, unions, political parties: What are the benefits you get out of this membership? If you are not a member, why not? Is there a membership fee that you feel you cannot afford?

4. Family in Palestine and abroad

4.1   Are you in contact with relatives residing in Palestine/Israel?

4.2   During the most recent events [second intifada], have you been able to check on your family in Palestine? (Do you call them? Send messages, via Internet?)

4.3   Do you have relatives living in the Gulf, Libya, Yemen, Jordan, or in the West?

4.4   Have your relatives ever come to Egypt? How often do they come? Where do they stay?

4.5   Through their contacts and work relations, did your relatives help any of your family members to visit them (where they are)? How? (Describe the procedures of travel, of getting a contract for work, of issuing a Palestinian ID.)

4.6   Do you know of people who went to Palestine and applied for passports or overstayed in Palestine? Were they able to come back to Egypt?

4.7   Do you know what happened to their house in Egypt? Did they sell it, rent it, or was it taken away from them?

4.8   Have you ever applied to go and live/work in Gaza? Tell me about this experience.

4.9   Would you like to apply for a Palestinian passport yourself? Why?

5. Ownership

5.1   Does anyone take care of your property in Palestine?

5.2   How much do you pay for the rent of your house in Egypt? Does a contract exist between you and the owner?

5.3   How did you pay for the property you have in Egypt (e.g., in credits, cash, based on your seasonal income)? How did you register your property (in your name or the name of any other member of the family)? When did you register the property? (Indicate the year.)

5.4   How many houses do you or any member of your family own in Egypt? How were they registered?

5.5   Do you own a car, taxi, bus, boat, donkey, horse, water buffalo, or any other means of transportation/livelihood?

5.6   Do you have a machine that helps you in your work (e.g., sewing machine)?

5.7   Do you have a business of your own (pushcart, street stand, company, shop)? How did you purchase this business (paid cash, borrowed money, remittances from abroad, a friend helped, etc.)?

Questions directed to each member in the household:

6. Legal status

6.1   Tell me about the procedures you go through when you renew your travel document. Do you do it yourself or do you count on someone to help you out? What difficulties do you face in renewing it?

6.2   How often do you need to renew your residency? (Clarify the category of the document.) How much do you pay for renewal? (Indicate if the mother is Egyptian.)

6.3   What are the procedures for renewing the residency? What are the procedures for men age 21 or older? What is the basis for your residency (work, mother, husband, pension, driving licence for public transport)?

6.4   Were you ever late in renewing these documents? What did you do to get them back again? Did you pay a fine?

6.5   Have you ever needed to borrow money to renew your papers or the papers of your family?

6.6   Can you travel with the travel document you now hold? Have you ever used it to travel? Where to? When?

6.7   If you have traveled, what were the reasons: for work, education, or for any other opportunity? How did you pay the travel expenses?

6.8   Did the Gulf war (1990–91) or other political events in the region (e.g., the 1982 war in Lebanon, the first intifada of 1987, the Libya-Egypt standoff in 1995) affect any members of your family?

6.9   Do you have any problems applying for visas to go abroad?

6.10 Where you (or any members of the family) ever deported and managed to sort it out? How? Where to?

6.11 Do you need a return visa to come back to Egypt? Did you have any difficulties getting one?

6.12 Do you think you are entitled to an UNRWA registration card? Were your parents registered with UNRWA when they were in Gaza or the West Bank, before coming to Egypt?

6.13 Do you know of UNHCR? Have you ever tried to seek help or protection from them?

6.14 Have you ever been stopped by the Egyptian police? Why?

6.15 Were you ever in dispute with an Egyptian person who tried to sue you where you had to go to court (e.g., for rent)?

6.16 Were you ever in need of suing someone but you felt you couldn't because you are Palestinian?

6.17 Have you ever been arrested? Why?

Socioeconomic conditions

7.1 Education

7.1.1 Talk about any difficulties you had in your education: paying fees, being unable to catch up with the level of the class, being in need of money, having to leave in order to work, e.g.

7.1.2 Have you ever attended vocational training/short skill courses?

7.1.3 What was your parents' role in your attending school? What are your parents' plans for your education?

7.1.4 Were/are you paying fees? How did you manage to pay the fees?

7.1.5 What is the importance of education, in your opinion?

7.1.6 Have you ever been discriminated against in the Egyptian educational system (e.g., deprived of an award, scholarship, book fees, social class, ID, food ration)? How did this discrimination affect you?

7.1.7 Do you have any plans to go for further education? Did you ever try to apply for scholarships reserved for Palestinians?

7.1.8 How did you choose your university major (if applicable)?

7.2 Work

7.2.1 How old were you when you first became employed? What did you do?

7.2.2   How many times have you changed the type work you do?

7.2.3   What was your main activity in the last five years (part time job/full time job)?

7.2.4   In the past 12 months, how did you search for a job?

7.2.5   Did your qualifications, skills, background help/ prevent you from finding a job?

7.2.6   What were the available jobs for you (in terms of your qualifications; as a Palestinian)?

7.2.7   How easy/difficult is it to obtain a work permit? For how long does it last? (Regarding residency:) How much does it cost to renew the permit? Tell me about the procedures to get it.

7.2.8   Have you had any experiences with the work permit issuance and your residency permit?

7.2.9   Have you ever lost a job opportunity because of the work permit procedures?

7.2.10 Have you ever stopped working for more than a week for an illness? How were you treated at your work for this (granted sick leave, penaized for not coming to work)?

7.2.11 In your opinion, are you disadvantaged at work (for example, paid less, not given insurance, badly treated) because you are Palestinian?

7.2.12 Have you worked/ever applied to work in the Gulf market?

7.3   Government/PLO/Army employees

7.3.1   Where do/did you work? When?

7.3.2   How were you recruited? (Under what conditions did you start your job?)

7.3.3   What is/was your job?

7.3.4   Do/did you have a contract? Is it regular or on work basis?

7.3.5   Do you get any pension/award at the end of the period of your service? Do you receive any medical insurance from the Palestine Red Crescent Society or government health services?

7.3.6   Do/did you have another job, in addition to your government job?

7.3.7   What do you think are the advantages of working in the government?

7.4 Private work, wage labor, seasonal work (table to help in specifying the work)

Self-employed income	a. Profit from household nonagricultural enterprise
	b. Profit from hh agricultural enterprise (sale of eggs, meat produced at hh)
	c. Payment from home production for sale such as embroidery, food preparation, and so on
	d. Income from street vending such as lottery or cigarettes
	e. Income of informal taxi or other transport services, building repair, work painting, plumbing, and so on

7.4.1 What is your work?

7.4.2 Where do you work?

7.4.3 How did you find this work?

7.4.4 How many hours do you work a week? How much do you make?

7.4.5 Do you expect to have your children take over the same work you are currently doing when they grow up?

7.4.6 Have you ever been stopped by the police and asked for a work permit?

7.4.7 Do you know of any Palestinian businessmen who recruited fellow Palestinians? Did you try to approach any of them for a job?

7.4.8 How are you able to make use of your skills and resources (that you have acquired or inherited) or the potentials of your house or location to make a living?

7.4.9 What do you do to improve your income? What other informal jobs do you do?

7.4.10 Do you own any livestock here? How does it affect your revenue?

7.5   Health and chronic illnesses

7.5.1   Do you have any health problems?

7.5.2   (If so:) How did this health problem affect your life: going to school, getting married, choice of work, expenses?

7.5.3   Has there ever been a need for a family member to stay beside an ill person to take care of her or him? How did this affect the caregiver (schooling, work, aspirations)?

7.5.4   Do you benefit from medical insurance? (Elaborate.)

7.5.5   Where do you go for medical exams or consultations?

7.5.6   Are there appropriate medical facilities nearby?

7.5.7   How much do you pay per doctor's visit?

7.5.8   How much do you spend on medicine?

7.5.9   Have you ever treated yourself with traditional methods?

7.5.10 Questions for mothers:

7.5.11 For child delivery: Where did you deliver your children? Do you remember how much it cost?

7.5.12 Is there any child and maternity care in your area? Were you taking vitamins and going for regular visits during the pregnancy?

7.5.13 How many miscarriages/abortions have you had in your life?

8. Financial support

8.1   Do all those in your household who work contribute to covering household expenses?

8.2   How long does the income last?

8.3   Do you have a ration card and/or subsidy from the Ministry of Social Development? (Is it full subsidized or half subsidized?)

8.4   Are you part of any financial cooperative among neighbors or relatives? What do you do with the money? (Emphasize planning/sustainability.)

8.5   Do you save money? If so, how (bank, postal savings, gold, livestock, stock market)?

8.6   Did you have any problems opening an account at the bank?

8.7   Do you get any financial support from *zakat* committees or charity people during seasonal feasts or other occasions? Talk about this.

8.8 Have you ever had a major financial problem? Have you ever needed to sell your properties, gold, or anything else?

8.9 What do you do when you are in financial trouble? (Arrange according to the priority of approach.)

8.10 If you have family in the Gulf/Libya/Palestine, how did adverse events there affect your family, from a financial perspective? (Elaborate on the effect of the recent intifada/war.)

8.11 How do you develop your skills to make your income better?

8.12 Have you ever tried to approach an NGO, a charitable association, the Arab League, or the Palestinian embassy for help? What help do you expect from such bodies?

9. Expenses

9.1 Talk about how you spend your income.

9.2 How much do you spend on [household] expenses?[1]

9.3 Does your household ever run out of money to buy food to make a meal?

9.4 Do you reduce the size of meals or skip meals because there is not enough money for food?

9.5 What do you make or prepare at home to cut down on expenses (*zabadi*, pickles)?

9.6 Have you had any recent financial crisis that affected your expenses?

10. Marital status

10.1 How many times have you been married? How old were you when you first married?

10.2 Are you related to your spouse (cousin, neighbors, from the same village)?

10.3 How is your family's relationship with your in-laws? Talk about your relations with and support of one another.

10.4 When married to an Egyptian woman: How did the fact of your marrying an Egyptian woman helped you in your life in Egypt?

10.5 Does your wife work? How so?

10.6 Did she work before marriage?

10.7 Has your wife ever been obliged to work, e.g, if you have been sick, in prison, away, etc.?

10.8 How do you feel about your wife or daughters working?

10.9 What are methods of advancement for daughters and the wife who are not active in the labor market?

10.10 For women at home: What are your aspirations for the future? (Are any of your girls married/divorced/widowed/ living living in the same household?)

10.11 Why do you prefer to see your children marrying Egyptian or Palestinian?

10.12 Do you think it is difficult to have your sons marrying Egyptian women? Are there any obstacles for this kind of marriage?

10.13 Do you think your children feel part of the Egyptian society?

11. Identity

11.1 Do you feel it is better to appear Egyptian?

11.2 In what situations do you feel different from Egyptians?

11.3 Do you use a different dialect at home from what you use on the street?

11.4 Are there particularly Palestinian ceremonies, activities, communities that you like to be involved with?

11.5 Do you think Egyptians perceive you as an Egyptian, or do some make you feel different?

11.6 Do you follow Palestinian news (radio/TV)?

11.7 Do you read the newspaper? How often do you buy it?

11.8 What are your near plans for the future?

11.9 If you had a choice, would you prefer to spend the rest of your life back in Gaza/the West Bank or remain in Egypt as you now know it?

Notes

1. Question originally read: "How much do you spend on such expenses? How often do you buy them? (Use the table.)" The chart was not available for translation.

Appendix 3

The 1965 Casablanca Protocol on the Treatment of Palestinian Refugees

[This is an unofficial translation provided by Badil Resource Center for Palestinian Residency and Refugee Rights, available at http://www.badil.org/Documents/Protection/LAS/Casablanca-Protocol.htm]

On the basis of the Charter of the League of Arab States and its special annex pertaining to Palestine, and of the LAS Council resolution concerning the Palestinian issue, and, in particular, of the special resolution pertaining to safeguarding Palestinian existence,

The Council of Foreign Ministers of Member States agreed, in its meeting in Casablanca on 10 September 1965, upon the following regulations, and called upon member states to take the necessary measures to put them into the sphere of implementation:

(1) Whilst retaining their Palestinian nationality, Palestinians currently residing in the land of _____ have the right of employment on part with its citizens.

(2) Palestinians residing at the moment in _____, in accordance with the dictates of their interests, have the right to leave and return to this state.

(3) Palestinians residing in other Arab states have the right to enter the land of _____ and to depart from it, in accordance with their interests. Their right of entry only gives them the right to stay for the permitted period and for their declared purpose of entry, provided the authorities do not agree to the contrary.

(4) Palestinians who are at the moment in _____, as well as those who were residing and left to the Diaspora, are given, upon request, valid travel documents. The concerned authorities must, wherever they may be, issue these documents or renew them without delay.

(5) Bearers of these travel documents residing in LAS states receive the same treatment as all other LAS state citizens regarding visa and residency applications.

On behalf of: The Secretary General

Casablanca, 11 September 1965

Appendix 4

Note on the Applicability of Article 1D of the 1951 Convention Relating to the Status of Refugees To Palestinian Refugees

---

Article 1D of the 1951 Convention:

This Convention shall not apply to persons who are at present receiving from organs or agencies of the United Nations other than the United Nations High Commissioner for Refugees protection or assistance.

When such protection or assistance has ceased for any reason, without the position of such persons being definitively settled in accordance with the relevant resolutions adopted by the General Assembly of the United Nations, these persons shall *ipso facto* be entitled to the benefits of this Convention.

A. Introduction

1. The 1951 Convention relating to the Status of Refugees (hereinafter "the 1951 Convention") contains certain provisions whereby persons otherwise having the characteristics of refugees, as defined in Article 1A, are excluded from the benefits of this Convention.* One such provision, paragraph 1 of Article 1D, applies to a special category of refugees for whom separate arrangements have been made to receive protection or assistance from organs or agencies of the United Nations other than the United Nations High Commissioner for Refugees (UNHCR). In today's context, this excludes from the benefits of the 1951 Convention those Palestinians who are refugees as a result of the 1948 or 1967 Arab-Israeli conflicts,

*Available at http://www.unhchr.ch/html/menu3/b/o_c_ref.htm.

225

and who are receiving protection or assistance from the United Nations Relief and Works Agency for Palestine Refugees in the Near East (UNRWA).

2.   While paragraph 1 of Article 1D is in effect an exclusion clause, this does not mean that certain groups of Palestinian refugees can never benefit from the protection of the 1951 Convention. Paragraph 2 of Article 1D contains an inclusion clause ensuring the automatic entitlement of such refugees to the protection of the 1951 Convention if, without their position being definitively settled in accordance with the relevant UN General Assembly resolutions, protection or assistance from UNRWA has ceased for any reason. The 1951 Convention hence avoids overlapping competencies between UNRWA and UNHCR, but also, in conjunction with UNHCR's Statute, ensures the continuity of protection and assistance of Palestinian refugees as necessary.[1]

B. Palestinian Refugees within the Scope of Article 1D of the 1951 Convention

3.   UNHCR considers that two groups of Palestinian refugees fall within the scope of Article 1D of the 1951 Convention:

(i)   Palestinians who are "Palestine refugees" within the sense of UN General Assembly Resolution 194 (III) of 11 December 1948 and other UN General Assembly Resolutions,[2] who were displaced from that part of Palestine which became Israel, and who have been unable to return there.[3]

(ii)   Palestinians who are "displaced persons" within the sense of UN General Assembly Resolution 2252 (ES-V) of 4 July 1967 and subsequent UN General Assembly Resolutions, and who have been unable to return to the Palestinian territories occupied by Israel since 1967.[4]

For the purposes of the application of the 1951 Convention, both of these groups include persons who were displaced at the time of hostilities, plus the descendants of such persons.[5] On the other hand, those individuals to whom Articles 1C, 1E or 1F of the Convention apply do not fall within the scope of Article 1D, even if they remain "Palestine refugees" and/or "displaced persons" whose position is yet to be settled definitively in accordance with the relevant UN General Assembly resolutions.[6]

4.   A third category of Palestinian refugees includes individuals who are neither "Palestine refugees" nor "displaced persons," but who, owing to a well-founded fear of being persecuted for reasons of race, religion, nationality, membership of a particular social group or political opinion, are outside the Palestinian territories occupied by Israel since 1967 and are unable or, owing to such fear, are unwilling to return there. Such Palestinians do not fall within the scope of Article 1D of the 1951 Convention but qualify as refugees under Article 1A(2) of the Convention, providing that they have neither ceased to be refugees under Article 1C nor are excluded from refugee status under Articles 1E or 1F.[7]

C. The Application of Article 1D of the 1951 Convention

5.   If it is determined that a Palestinian refugee falls within the scope of Article 1D of the 1951 Convention, it needs to be assessed whether he or she falls within paragraph 1 or paragraph 2 of that Article.

6.   If the person concerned is inside UNRWA's area of operations and is registered, or is eligible to be registered, with UNRWA, he or she should be considered as receiving protection or assistance within the sense of paragraph 1 of Article 1D, and hence is excluded from the benefits of the 1951 Convention and from the protection and assistance of UNHCR.

7.   If, however, the person is outside UNRWA's area of operations, he or she no longer enjoys the protection or assistance of UNRWA and therefore falls within paragraph 2 of Article 1D, providing of course that Articles 1C, 1E and 1F do not apply. Such a person is automatically entitled to the benefits of the 1951 Convention and falls within the competence of UNHCR.

This would also be the case even if the person has never resided inside UNRWA's area of operations.[8]

8.   The fact that such a person falls within paragraph 2 of Article 1D does not necessarily mean that he or she cannot be returned to UNRWA's area of operations, in which case, once returned, the person would fall within paragraph 1 of Article 1D and thereby cease to benefit from the 1951 Convention. There may, however, be reasons why the person cannot be returned to UNRWA's area of operations. In particular:

   (i)   He or she may be *unwilling* to return to that area because of threats to his or her physical safety or freedom, or other serious protection-related problems; or

   (ii) He or she may be *unable* to return to that area because, for instance, the authorities of the country concerned refuse his or her re-admission or the renewal of his or her travel documents.

9.   The rationale behind "returnability" to effective protection has been developed in the context of addressing irregular movements of refugees, including through Executive Committee Conclusion No. 15 (XXX) (1979) on Refugees Without an Asylum Country and Executive Committee Conclusion No. 58 (XL) (1989) on the Problem of Refugees and Asylum-Seekers Who Move in an Irregular Manner from a Country in Which They Had Already Found Protection.

D. Registration with UNRWA

10.   UNRWA was established pursuant to UN General Assembly Resolution 302 (IV) of 8 December 1949 to "carry out in collaboration with local governments [. . .] direct relief and works programs" for Palestine refugees and to "consult with the interested Near Eastern Governments concerning measures to be taken by them preparatory to the time when international assistance for relief and works projects is no longer available."[9] Since 1967, UNRWA has also been authorized to assist certain other persons in addition to Palestine refugees. In particular,

UN General Assembly Resolution 2252 (ES-V) of 4 July 1967 endorsed the efforts of UNRWA to "provide humanitarian assistance, as far as practicable, on an emergency basis and as a temporary measure, to other persons in the area who are at present displaced and are in serious need of immediate assistance as a result of the recent hostilities". Subsequent UN General Assembly Resolutions have endorsed on an annual basis UNRWA's efforts to continue to provide such assistance.[10]

11. UNRWA has decided, for its working purposes, that a "Palestine refugee" is any person "whose normal place of residence was Palestine during the period 1 June 1946 to 15 May 1948 and who lost both home and means of livelihood as a result of the 1948 conflict."[11] This "working definition" has evolved over the years,[12] and is without prejudice to the implementation of relevant UN General Assembly Resolutions, in particular paragraph 11 of Resolution 194 (III) of 11 December 1948.[13]

12. Persons registered with UNRWA include: "Palestine refugees" as defined by the Agency for its working purposes; persons currently displaced and in serious need of continued assistance as a result of the June 1967 and subsequent hostilities; descendants by the male line of the aforementioned persons; and certain other persons.[14] UNRWA's operations are currently limited to five areas, namely, Jordan, Syria, Lebanon, the West Bank and the Gaza Strip.[15]

13. The question [of] whether a Palestinian is registered, or is eligible to be registered, with UNRWA will need to be determined individually. In cases where this is unclear, further information can be sought from UNRWA.[16]

E. Conclusion

14. UNHCR hopes that this Note clarifies some pertinent aspects of the position of Palestinian refugees under international refugee law, and that it serves as useful guidance for decision-makers in asylum proceedings.

Office of the United Nations High Commissioner for Refugees (UNHCR) October 2002

Notes

1. A similar provision to Article 1D of the 1951 Convention is contained in UNHCR's Statute, paragraph 7(c) of which stipulates that the competence of the High Commissioner shall not extend to a person who "continues to receive from other organs or agencies of the United Nations protection or assistance."

2. The term "Palestine refugees," while never explicitly defined by the UN General Assembly, almost certainly also encompasses what would nowadays be called internally displaced persons. See, for example, UN Doc. A/AC.25/W.45, Analysis of paragraph 11 of the General Assembly's Resolution of 11 December 1948, 15 May 1950, Part One, paragraph 1: "During the debate preceding the adoption of [UN General Assembly Resolution 194 (III) of 11 December 1948], the United Kingdom delegation, which had sponsored the draft resolution, stated in reply to a question that the term 'refugees' referred to all refugees, irrespective of race or nationality, provided they had been displaced from their homes in Palestine. That the General Assembly accepted this interpretation becomes almost certain if it is considered that the word 'Arab', which had preceded the word 'refugees' in the first two texts of the United Kingdom draft resolution [...] was omitted in the final text which was approved by the Assembly. [...] According to the above interpretation the term 'refugees' applies to all persons, Arabs, Jews and others who have been displaced from their homes in Palestine. This would include Arabs in Israel who have been shifted from their normal places of residence. It would also include Jews who had their homes in Arab Palestine, such as the inhabitants of the Jewish quarter of the Old City. It would not include Arabs who had lost their lands but not their houses, such as the inhabitants of Tulkarm." For further analysis of the term "Palestine refugees," see, for example, UN Doc. W/61/Add.1, Addendum to Definition of a "Refugee" Under paragraph 11 of the General Assembly Resolution of 11 December 1948, 29 May 1951; UN Doc. A/AC.25/W.81/Rev.2, Historical Survey of Efforts of the United Nations Commission for Palestine to secure the implementation of paragraph 11 of General Assembly resolution 194 (III). Question of Compensation, 2 October 1961, section III.

3. The UN General Assembly resolved in paragraph 11 of Resolution 194 (III) that "the refugees wishing to return to their homes and live at peace with their neighbors should be permitted to do so at the earliest practicable date" and that "compensation should be paid for the property of those choosing not to return and for loss of or damage to property." In the same paragraph, the General Assembly instructed the United Nations Conciliation Commission for Palestine (UNCCP) to "facilitate the repatriation, resettlement and economic and social rehabilitation of the refugees and the payment of compensation." The General Assembly has since noted on an annual basis that UNCCP has been unable to find a means of achieving progress in the implementation of paragraph 11 of Resolution 194 (III). See, most recently, General Assembly Resolution 56/52 of 10 December 2001, which notes that the situation of the Palestine refugees continues to be a matter of concern and requests UNCCP to exert continued efforts toward the implementation of that paragraph.

4. Essentially two groups of Palestinians have been displaced from the territories occupied by Israel in 1967: (i) Palestinians originating from East Jerusalem, the West Bank and the Gaza Strip; (ii) "Palestine refugees" who had taken refuge in East Jerusalem, the West Bank and Gaza Strip. UN General Assembly Resolution 2452 (XXIII) A of 19 December 1968 and subsequent General Assembly resolutions have called for the return of these "displaced persons." Most recently, General Assembly Resolution 56/54 of 10 December 2001 reaffirms the "right of all persons displaced as a result of the June 1967 and subsequent hostilities to return to their homes or former places of residence in the territories occupied by Israel since 1967," expresses deep concern that "the mechanism agreed upon by the parties in Article XII of the Declaration of Principles on Interim Self-Government Arrangements on the return of displaced persons has not been effected"; and expresses the hope for "an accelerated return of displaced persons."

5. The concern of the UN General Assembly with the descendants both of "Palestine refugees" and of "displaced persons" was expressed in UN General Assembly Resolution 37/120 I of 16 December 1982, which requested the UN Secretary-General, in cooperation with the Commissioner-General of UNRWA, to issue identity cards to "all Palestine refugees and their descendants [...] as well as to all displaced persons and to those who have been prevented from returning to their home as a result of the 1967 hostilities, and their descendants". In 1983, the UN Secretary-General reported on the steps that he had taken to implement this resolution, but said that he was "unable, at this stage, to proceed further with the implementation of the resolution" without "significant additional information [becoming] available through further replies from Governments" (paragraph 9, UN Doc. A/38/382, Special Identification cards for all Palestine refugees. Report of the Secretary-General, 12 September 1983).

6. For example, a Palestinian referred to in paragraph 3 of this Note may be considered by the competent authorities of the country in which he or she has taken residence as having the rights and obligations which are attached to the possession of the nationality of that country, in which case he or she would be excluded from the benefits of the 1951 Convention in accordance with Article 1E. Moreover, many Palestinians have acquired the nationality of a third country and any claim they make for recognition as a refugee should, therefore, be examined under Article 1A(2) of the 1951 Convention in relation to the country of their new nationality. In certain cases, the Palestinian origins of such persons may be relevant to the assessment of whether they are outside the country of their new nationality owing to well-founded fear of being persecuted "for reasons of" race, religion, nationality, membership of a particular social group, or political opinion.

7. There is no consensus whether Palestinians who have not acquired the nationality of a third country are stateless, but many States consider that such Palestinians are stateless in the sense of Article 1(1) of the 1954 Convention relating to the Status of Stateless Persons and assess their claims for refugee status under Article 1A(2) of the 1951 Convention accordingly. It should be noted that Article 1(2)(i) of the 1954 Statelessness Convention provides that the 1954 Convention shall not apply to "persons who are at present receiving from organs or agencies of the United Nations other than the United Nations High Commissioner for Refugees protection or assistance so long as they are receiving such protection or assistance."

8. For example, a descendant of a "Palestine refugee" or of a Palestinian "displaced person" may never have resided in UNRWA's area of operations, and also not fall under Articles 1C or 1E of the 1951 Convention.

9. UN General Assembly Resolution 302 (IV) of 8 December 1949 directs UNRWA to consult with the UNCCP "in the best interests of [UNRWA's and UNCCP's] respective tasks, with particular reference to paragraph 11 of General Assembly resolution 194 (III) of 11 December 1948." UN General Assembly Resolution 393 (V) of 2 December 1950 further instructed UNRWA to "establish a reintegration fund which shall be utilized for projects requested by any government in the Near East and approved by the Agency for the permanent re-establishment of refugees and their removal from relief." The same resolution authorized UNRWA, as circumstances permit, to "transfer funds available for the current relief and works programs [and for direct relief to Palestine refugees in need] to reintegration projects." Neither UN General Assembly Resolution 302 (IV) of 8 December 1949 nor any subsequent UN General Assembly Resolution has specifically limited the scope of UNRWA's mandate. Accordingly, UNRWA's mandate has evolved, over the years, with the endorsement of the UN General Assembly. For example, UN General Assembly resolutions between 1982 and 1993 on the Protection of Palestine refugees called upon UNRWA to play a protection role in the territories occupied by Israel since 1967. The last such resolution was Resolution 48/40 H of 10 December 1993, which urged "the [UN] Secretary-General and the Commissioner-General [of UNRWA] to continue their efforts in support of the upholding of the safety and security and the legal and human rights of the Palestine refugees in all the territories under Israeli occupation since 1967." Subsequent resolutions, including most recently UN General Assembly Resolution 56/56 of 10 December 2001, refer to the "valuable work done by the refugee affairs officers [of UNRWA] in providing protection to the Palestinian people, in particular Palestine refugees."

10. Most recently, UN General Assembly Resolution 56/54 of 10 December 2001 endorses the efforts of UNRWA to "continue to provide humanitarian assistance, as far as practicable, on an emergency basis and as a temporary measure, to persons in the area who are currently displaced and in serious need of continued assistance as a result of the June 1967 and subsequent hostilities."

11. Information provided by UNRWA. As mentioned in endnote 2 above, the UN General Assembly has never explicitly defined the term "Palestine refugees."

12. See, for example, UN Doc. A/1451/Rev.1, Interim Report of the Director of the United Nations Relief and Works Agency for Palestine Refugees in the Near East, 6 October 1950, paragraph 15: "For working purposes, the Agency has decided that a refugee is a needy person, who, as a result of the war in Palestine, has lost his home and his means of livelihood"; UN Doc. A/2717/Add.1, Special Report of the Director of the Advisory Commission of the United Nations Relief and Works Agency for Palestine Refugees in the Near East, 30 June 1954, paragraph 19: "The definition of a person eligible for relief, as used by the Agency for some years, is one 'whose normal residence was Palestine for a minimum period of two years preceding the outbreak of the conflict in 1948 and who, as a result of this conflict, has lost both his home and means of livelihood'"; UN Doc. A/8413, Report of the Commissioner-General of the United Nations Relief and Works Agency for Palestine Refugees in the Near East, 30 June 1971, footnote 1: "A Palestine refugee, by UNRWA's working definition, is a person whose normal

residence was Palestine for a minimum of two years preceding the conflict in 1948 and who, as a result of this conflict, lost both his home and means of livelihood and took refuge, in 1948, in one of the countries where UNRWA provides relief."

13. In establishing UNRWA and in prolonging its mandate, the UN General Assembly has consistently specified that the Agency's activities are without prejudice to the provisions of paragraph 11 of Resolution 194 (III) of 11 December 1948. See, most recently, UN General Assembly Resolution 56/52 of 10 December 2001, extending the mandate of UNRWA until 30 June 2005.

14. Information provided by UNRWA.

15. Currently, UNRWA's operations are limited to the five areas listed in paragraph 12 of this Note. However, at times, UNRWA has provided assistance to Palestine refugees and other Palestinians registered with the Agency in additional areas of the Near East, including Kuwait, the Gulf States, and Egypt.

16. It should be noted that not all "Palestine refugees" residing in UNRWA's area of operations are registered with UNRWA. It should also be noted that Palestinians satisfying UNRWA's eligibility criteria do not necessarily cease to be eligible for UNRWA services if they acquire the nationality of a third country. In fact, many such persons continue to receive UNRWA services, particularly in Jordan.

Bibliography

Archival and Government Sources

Egypt:
> Central Agency for Public Mobilization and Statistics (CAPMAS)
> Letters from the Information Office of the Minister of Higher Education to the Palestinian Cultural Attaché

Palestine:
> Palestinian Central Bureau of Statistics

United Kingdom:
> Foreign Office
> Public Records Office

Other:
> Australian Bureau of Statistics
> UN Office Records of the General Assembly
> UNRWA Public Records Office, Gaza

Interviews

Adel Attiyah, head of the PLO Labor Union, 24 September 2001.

Barakat al-Farra, representative of Fatah and director of Association of Martyred and Injured Palestinians in Egypt, 25 October 2001.

Karim al-Iraqi, head of the social affairs section of the PLO Labor Union, 17 July 2002.

Abu Mustafa al-Jabur, *mukhtar* of the Palestinians in Rafah, Egypt, 25 June 2001.

Ali Jawhar, head of the Palestinian Charitable Association, 22 October 2001.

Fathi Kuttab, education office of the Palestinian Embassy in Egypt, 8 July 2003.

Muhammad Mahmud Marzouk, director of the Administrative Office of the Governor of Gaza (AOGG), 29 April 2003.

Zuhdi al-Qudwah, PLO ambassador to Egypt, 23 September 2001.

Ron Wilkinson, UNRWA official, December 2003.

Muhammad Zaghlul, director of the Palestine Red Crescent Society Hospital—Palestine, 29 April 2003.

Unpublished Works

Abdel-Qader, Hala. "Statelessness in Egypt." Paper presented at the Statelessness in Arab World regional workshop, Ayia Napa, Cyprus, 2001.

El-Abed, Oroub. "An Analysis of the Economic Integration of Palestinian Refugees in Jordan and Its Impact of Economic Growth." Master's thesis, SOAS, University of London, 1999.

Akel, Abdullatif Ata. "Sociopsychological Analysis of the Palestinian Response to Homelessness." Master's thesis, U.S. International University, 1979.

Australian Bureau of Statistics. "Measuring Social Capital: Current Collections and Future Directions," Discussion Paper, November 2000. Available at: http://www.abs.gov.au/852563C30080E02A/0/6CD8B1F3F270566ACA25699F0015A02A?Open.

Frechette, Ann. "Notes Towards the Development of a Multi-Disciplinary Model for Comparative Research on 'Integration'." Unpublished manuscript, 1994.

Hart, Jason. "UNRWA and Children: Some Thoughts on an Uneasy Relationship." Paper presented at UNRWA: A History within History Workshop, Amman, Jordan, 1998.

———. "Whose Future is it Anyway? Children, UNRWA and 'The Nation'." Paper presented at an International Symposium on The Palestinian Refugees and UNRWA in Jordan, the West Bank and Gaza, 1949–1999, Dead Sea, Jordan, 1999.

Kaenel, Yvan Von. "Exil, Reconstruction et Reseaux, Les Refugiés Palestiniens du Liban, de Syrie et de Jordanie, 1948-1991." PhD diss., IUED [Graduate Institute for Development Studies], Geneva University, 1995.

McGregor, J., B. Harrell-Bond and R. Mazur. "Mozambicans in Swaziland: Livelihood and Integration." Paper prepared for World Food Program and EEC, Refugee Studies Program, 1991.

Pollock, Alex. "The Potential of Microfinance and Microcredit in UNRWA: Developing Outreach and Self-sufficiency." Paper presented at an International Symposium on The Palestinian Refugees and UNRWA in Jordan, the West Bank and Gaza, 1949–1999, CERMOC, Dead Sea, Jordan, 1999.

Raie, Lamia. "Forgotten Population: A Case Study of Palestinians in Cairo." Master's thesis, American University in Cairo, 1995.

Saleh, Rima Yusuf. "The Changing Roles of Palestinian Women in Refugee Camps in Jordan." PhD diss., University of Michigan, 1986.

Shiblak, Abbas. "Living in Limbo: Preliminary Observations on Canada Refugee Camp." Paper for Refugee Studies Program, 1995.

UNICEF. "Analysis of the Conditions of Palestinian Women and Children in Egypt" [in Arabic]. Unpublished draft, 1996.

Wilkinson, Ron. "Initial Review: Canada Camp Location." Prepared for the International Development Research Centre, 2001. Available at: http://www.dfait-maeci.gc.ca/middle_east/peaceprocess/cdacamp_review-en.asp.

Published Works

Abdel Shakur, Mohamed, Sohair Mehanna, and Nicholas Hopkins. "War and Forced Migration in Egypt: The Experience of Evacuation from the Suez Canal Cities (1967–1976)." *Arab Studies Quarterly* 27, no. 3 (2005). Available at http://findarticles.com/p/articles/mi_m2501/is_3_27/ai_n15795980.

Abu Iyad (Salah Khalaf) with Eric Rouleau. *My Home, My Land: A Narrative of the Palestinian Struggle.* Translated by Linda Butler Koseoglu. New York: Times Books, 1981.

Abu-Lughod, Janet. "Palestinians: Exiles at Home and Abroad." *Current Sociology* 36 (Summer 1988): 61–69.

Abu Sitta, Salman. 2001. "The Right of Return: Sacred, Legal and Possible." In *Palestinian Refugees: The Right of Return*, edited by Naseer Aruri, 195–207. London: Pluto Press, 2001.

Akram, Susan. *Temporary Protection and Its Applicability to the Palestinian Refugee Case.* Information and Discussion Brief No. 4. Bethlehem, West Bank: BADIL, 2000.

———. "Reinterpretating Palestinian Refugee Rights under International Law and a Framework for Durable Solutions." In *Palestinian Refugees: The Right of Return*, edited by Naseer Aruri, 165–94. London: Pluto Press, 2001.

Azar, Khaled. *Hukamat Umum Falastin fi Thikraha al-Khamin* [Government of All Palestine on its Fiftieth Anniversary]. Dar al-Horouq, 1998.

Berry, John. "Acculturation and Adaptation in a New Society." *International Migration* 30 (1992): 69–95.

Beydoun, Ahmad. "The South Lebanon Border Zone: A Local Perspective." *Journal of Palestine Studies* 21, no. 3 (Spring 1992): 35-53.

Bloch, Alice. "Carrying out a Survey of Refugees: Some Methodological Considerations and Guidelines." *Journal of Refugee Studies* 12, no. 4 (1999): 367–83.

Brand, Laurie. "Nasir's Egypt and the Re-emergence of the Palestinian National Movement." *Journal of Palestine Studies* 17, no. 2 (Winter 1988): 29–45.

———. *Palestinians in the Arab World: Institution Building and the Search for a State.* New York: Columbia University Press, 1988.

Buehrig, Edward H. *The UN and the Palestinian Refugees: A Study in Nonterritorial Administration.* Bloomington, IN: Indiana University Press, 1971.

Calhoun, Ricky-Dale. "Arming David: Haganah's Arms Procurement Network in the United States, 1945–49." *Journal of Palestine Studies* 36, no. 4 (Summer 2007): 22–32.

Chambers, Robert. *Poverty and Livelihoods: Whose Reality Counts?* Brighton, U.K.: Institute of Development Studies, University of Sussex, 1995.

————. *Whose Reality Counts? Putting the First Last.* London: Intermediate Technology Publications, 1997.

Coleman, James S. *Foundations of Social Theory.* Cambridge, MA: Harvard University Press, 1990.

Dajani, Maha. *The Institutionalisation of Palestinian Identity in Egypt.* Cairo Papers in Social Science, American University in Cairo, 1986.

Dorai, Mohamed Kamel. "The Meaning of Homeland for the Palestinian Diaspora, Revival and Transformation." In *New Approaches to Migration? Transnational Communities and the Transformation of Home,* edited by Nadje Al Ali and Khalid Koser, 87–95. New York: Routledge, 2002.

Doughty, Dick and Mohammed El Aydi. *Gaza: Legacy of Occupation.* West Hartford, CT: Kumarian Press, 1995.

Ennab Wael R. *Population and Demographic Developments in the West Bank and Gaza Strip until 1990.* Geneva: UNCTAD, 1994.

Farah, Randa. "Crossing Boundaries: Reconstruction of Palestinian Identities in Al-Baqa Refugee Camp, Jordan." In *Palestine, Palestiniens, Territoire National, Espaces Communitaires.* Amman, Jordan: CERMOC, 1997.

————. "UNRWA in Popular Memory al-Baq'a Refugee Camp." In *CERMOC: A History within History: Humanitarian Aid and Development.* Amman: CERMOC, October, 1998.

Fetterman, David. *Ethnography, Step by Step.* Vol. 17, *Applied Social Research Methods Series.* Thousand Oaks, CA: Sage, 1989.

Fischbach, Michael. "The United Nations and Palestinian Refugee Property Compensation." *Journal of Palestine Studies* 31, no 2 (Winter 2002): 34–50.

————. *Records of Dispossession: Palestinian Refugee Property and the Arab-Israeli Conflict.* Institute for Palestine Studies Series. New York: Columbia University Press, 2003.

Gerges, Fawaz. "Egypt and the 1948 War: Internal Conflict and Regional Ambition." In Rogan and Shlaim, *The War for Palestine,* 151–77.

Geyer, Felix, ed. *Alienation, Ethnicity, and Postmodernism.* Westport, CT: Greenwood Press, 1996.

Ghabra, Shafeeq. *Palestinians in Kuwait.* Boulder, CO: Westview Press, 1987.

Gilen, Signe, Are Hovedenak, Rania Maktabi, Jon Pedersen, and Dag Tuastad. *Finding Ways: Palestinian Coping Strategies in Changing Environments.* Oslo: Fafo Institute for Applied Social Science, 1994.

Gilmour, David. *Dispossessed: The Ordeal of the Palestinians.* London and Sydney: Sphere Books, 1980.

Goodwin-Gill, Guy. *The Refugee in International Law.* Oxford: Clarendon Press, 1996.

Grabska, Katarzyna. "Living on the Margins: The Analyses of the Livelihood Strategies of Sudanese Refugees with Closed Files in Egypt," Working Paper no. 6, Cairo: AUC, 2005.

Griffith, David. "Lasting Firsts." *American Anthropologist* 99, no. 1 (March 1997): 23–29.

Gupta, Akhil and James Ferguson. "Beyond 'Culture': Space, Identity, and the Politics of Difference." *Cultural Anthropology* 7, no. 1 (February 1992): 6–23.

Hadawi, Sami. *Bitter Harvest: A Modern History of Palestine.* New York: Olive Branch Press, 1989.

Haddad, William H., Ghada H. Talhami, and Janice J. Terry. *The June 1967 War after Three Decades.* Washington, DC: Association of Arab American University Graduates, 1999.

Hallaj, Muhammad. "The Challenge of Life." *Journal of Refugee Studies* 2, no 1 (1989): 11–19.

Hamid, Rashid. "What is the PLO?" *Journal of Palestine Studies* 4, no. 4 (1975): 90–109.

Hanafi, Sari. *Entre Deux Mondes: Les Hommes d'Affaires Palestiniens de la Diaspora et la Construction de l'Entité Palestinienne.* Cairo: CEDEJ (Centre d'Etudes et de Documentations Economique, Juridique et Sociale), 1997.

———. "Between Arab and French Agendas: Defining the Palestinian Diaspora and the Image of the Other." In *Between Field and Text: Emerging Voices in Egyptian Social Science,* edited by Seteney Shami and Linda Herrera, 139–59. Cairo Papers in Social Science. Vol. 22, no 2. Cairo: AUC Press, 1999.

Hanafi, Sari, and Olivier Saint-Martin. "The Problematic of Border-Dwellers: The Condition of Palestinians in North Sinai" [in Arabic]. In *Palestinians in Egypt.* Ramallah, Palestinian Authority: Shaml, 1996.

Harik, Iliya. "The Palestinians in the Diaspora." In *Modern Diasporas in International Politics,* edited by G. Sheffer, 315–32. London: Croom Helm, 1986.

Harrell-Bond, Barbara. *Imposing Aid: Emergency Assistance to Refugees.* Oxford: Oxford University Press, 1986.

Hart, Alan. *Arafat: Terrorist or Peacemaker?* London: Sidgwick & Jackson, 1984.

Hathaway, James. *The Law of Refugee Status.* Toronto: Butterworth-Heinemann, 1991.

Hirst, David. *The Gun and the Olive Branch: The Roots of Violence in the Middle East.* New York: Harcourt Brace Jovanovich, 1977.

Hovdenak, Are, Jon Pedersen, Dag H. Tuastad, and Elia Zureik. *Constructing Order: Palestinian Adaptations to Refugee Life.* Oslo: Fafo Institute for Applied Social Science, 1997.

Husseini, Jalal. "The Future of UNRWA: A Palestinian Perspective." In *The Final Status Negotiations on the Refugee Issue: Positions and Strategies,* 101–112. Department of Refugee Affairs, PLO, 2000.

Jacobs-Huey, Lanita. "The Natives are Gazing and Talking Back: Reviewing the Problematics of Positionality, Voice, and Accountability among 'Native' Anthropologists." *American Anthropologist* 104, no. 3 (2002): 791–804.

Khalidi, Walid. "Plan Dalet: Master Plan for the Conquest of Palestine." *Journal of Palestine Studies* 18, no. 1 (Autumn 1988): 4–33.

———. *Before Their Diaspora: A Photographic History of the Palestinians, 1876–1948.* Washington, DC: Institute for Palestine Studies, 1991.

———. *All That Remains: The Palestinian Villages Occupied and Depopulated by Israel in 1948.* Washington, DC: Institute for Palestine Studies, 1992.

———. "Revisiting the UNGA Partition Resolution." *Journal of Palestine Studies* 27, no. 1 (Autumn 1997): 5–21.

Khouri, Fred J. *The Arab-Israeli Dilemma.* 2d ed. New York: Syracuse University Press, 1977.

Le Sage, André, and Nisar Majid. "The Livelihoods Gap: Responding to the Economic Dynamics of Vulnerability in Somalia." *Disasters: The Journal of Disaster Studies, Policy and Management* 26, no. 1 (2002): 10–27.

Luciani, Giacomo, and Ghassan Salamé. *The Politics of Arab Integration.* London: Croom Helm, 1988.

Lynd, Staughton, Sam Bahour, and Alice Lynd, eds. *Homeland: Oral Histories of Palestine and Palestinians.* New York: Olive Branch Press, 1994.

Masalha, Nur. "The 1967 Palestinian Exodus." In *Palestinian Exodus, 1948–1998,* edited by Ghada Karmi and Eugene Cotran, 63–109. Reading, U.K.: Ithaca Press, 1999.

Mattar, Philip, ed. *Encyclopedia of the Palestinians.* New York: Fitzhenry and Whiteside, 2000.

Miller, Aaron D. *The Arab States and the Palestine Question: Between Ideology and Self-Interest.* Washington, DC: Center for Strategic and International Studies, Georgetown University, 1986.

Miller, Ylana. *Government and Society in Rural Palestine 1920–1948.* Austin, TX: University of Texas Press, 1985.

Morris, Benny. *Israel's Border Wars 1949–1956.* Oxford: Clarendon Press, 1993.

————. *1948 and After: Israel and the Palestinians.* Oxford: Clarendon Press, 1994.

————. "Critical Analysis of the Birth of the Palestinian Refugee Problem," 2001. Available at http://www.palestineremembered.com/Acre/Palestine-Remembered/Story562.html.

————. *The Birth of the Palestinian Refugee Problem Revisited.* Cambridge: Cambridge University Press, 2004.

Morrow, Betty. "Identifying and Mapping Community Vulnerability." *Disasters: The Journal of Disaster Studies, Policy and Management* 23, no. 1 (1999): 1–18.

Narayan, Deepa, Robert Chambers, Meera K. Shah, and Patti Petesch. *Crying Out for Change (Voices of the Poor).* Washington, DC: Oxford University Press, 2000.

Narayan, Kirin. "How Native is a 'Native' Anthropologist?" *American Anthropologist* 95, no. 3 (1993): 671–86.

Nasser, Gamal Abdul. "Memoirs of the First Palestine War." *Journal of Palestine Studies* 2, no. 2 (Winter 1973): 3–32.

O'Balance, Edgar. *The Arab-Israeli War 1948.* Westport, CT: Hyperion Press, 1981.

Pappé, Ilan. *The Making of the Arab-Israeli Conflict 1947–1951.* London: I.B. Tauris, 1992.

————. "Were They Expelled? The History, Historiography and Relevance of the Palestinian Refugee Problem." In *Palestinian Exodus, 1948–1998,* edited by Ghada Karmi and Eugene Cotran, 37–61. Reading, U.K.: Ithaca Press, 1999.

Peteet, Julie. "The AFSC Refugee Archives on Palestine, 1948–1950." In *Reinterpreting the Historical Record: The Uses of Palestinian Refugee Archives for Social Science Research and Policy Analysis,* edited by Salim Tamari and Elia Zureik, 109–128. Jerusalem and Washington, DC: Institute for Jerusalem Studies and Institute for Palestine Studies, 2001.

Rempel, Terry. *The United Nations Conciliation Commission for Palestine, Protection, and a Durable Solution for Palestinian Refugees.* Information and Discussion Brief No. 5. Bethlehem, West Bank: BADIL, 2000.

Rogan, Eugene and Avi Shlaim, eds. *The War for Palestine: Rewriting the History of 1948.* Cambridge: Cambridge University Press, 2001.

Roy, Sara. "Gaza: New Dynamics of Civic Disintegration." *Journal of Palestine Studies* 22, no. 4 (1993): 20–31.

————. *The Gaza Strip: The Political Economy of De-Development.* 2d ed. Washington, DC: Institute for Palestine Studies, 2001.

Said, Edward. *A Profile of the Palestinian People.* Chicago: Palestine Human Rights Campaign, 1983

Sarraj, Nadera al-, et al., *Arab Palestinians in Egypt* [in Arabic]. Cairo: Dar El Mustakbal, 1986.

El Sayed, Mustapha "Egyptian Popular Attitudes toward the Palestinians since 1977." *Journal of Palestine Studies* 18, no. 4 (Summer 1989): 37–51.

Sayigh, Rosemary. "Researching Gender in a Palestinian Camp: Political, Theoretical and Methodological Issues." In *Gendering the Middle East: Emerging Perspectives*, edited by Deniz Kandiyoti, 145–69. New York: I.B. Tauris, 1996.

Sayigh, Yezid. *Armed Struggle and the Search for State: The Palestinian National Movement, 1949–1993*. Oxford and Washington, DC: Oxford University Press and the Institute for Palestine Studies, 1997.

Seale, Patrick. *Abu Nidal: A Gun for Hire*. New York: Random House, 1992.

Segev, Tom. *1967: Israel, the War, and the Year that Transformed the Middle East*. New York: Metropolitan Books, 2007.

Shami, Seteney. "The Social Implications of Population Displacement and Resettlement: An Overview with a Focus on the Arab Middle East." *International Migration Review* 27, no. 101 (1993): 4–33.

Shami, Seteney and Linda Herrera, eds., *Between Field and Text: Emerging Voices in Egyptian Social Science*. Cairo Papers in Social Science, Vol. 22, no 2. Cairo: AUC Press, 1999.

Sharmani, Mulki al-. *Livelihood and Identity Constructions of Somali Refugees in Cairo*. Cairo: AUC Press, 2003.

Shemesh, Moshe. *The Palestinian Entity 1959–1974: Arab Politics and the PLO*. London: Frank Cass, 1996.

Shiblak, Abbas. "Residency Status and Civil Rights of Palestinian Refugees in Arab Countries." *Journal of Palestine Studies* 25, no. 3 (Spring 1996): 36–45.

————. *The League of Arab States and Palestinian Refugees' Residency Rights* [in Arabic]. Shaml Monograph Series. Ramallah: Palestinian Authority, 1998.

Shlaim, Avi. "The Rise and Fall of the All-Palestine Government in Gaza." *Journal of Palestine Studies* 20, no. 1 (Autumn 1990): 37–63.

————. *The Politics of Partition, King Abdullah, the Zionists and Palestine 1921–1951*. Oxford: Oxford University Press, 1998.

Sholkamy, Hania. "Why Is Anthropology so Hard in Egypt?" In *Between Field and Text: Emerging Voices in Egyptian Social Science*, edited by Seteney Shami and Linda Herrera, 119–38. Cairo: AUC Press, 1999.

Shukrallah, Hani. "Egypt: Rediscovering Palestine." *Journal of Palestine Studies* 31, no. 4 (Summer 2002): 44–65.

Smith, Pamela Ann. "The Palestinian Diaspora, 1948-1985." *Journal of Palestine Studies* 15, no. 3 (Spring 1986): 90–108.

————. "Palestine and the Palestinians." In *Power and Stability in the Middle East*, edited by Berch Berberoglu, 157–72. London: Zed Books, 1989.

Spradley, James. *The Ethnographic Interview*. New York: Holt, Rinehart and Winston, 1979.

Srouji, Elias. "The Fall of a Galilean Village during the 1948 Palestine War: An Eyewitness Account." *Journal of Palestine Studies* 33, no. 2 (Winter 2004): 71–80.

Takkenberg, Lex. *The Status of Palestinian Refugees in International Law*. Oxford: Clarendon Press, 1998.

Todaro, Michael. *Economic Development*. 6th ed. London: Longman, 1997.

UNHCR, Note on the Applicability of Article 1D of the 1951 Convention relating to the Status of Refugees to Palestinian Refugees *International Journal of Refugee Law* 14, nos. 2–3 (2002): 450–56.

UNRWA. *UNRWA Past, Present and Future: A Briefing Document*. Vienna: United Nations Relief and Works Agency for Palestine Refugees in the Near East, 1986.

U.S. Committee for Refugees and Immigrants, *World Refugee Survey 2002: An Annual Assessment to Conditions Affecting Refugees, Asylum Seekers, and Internally Displaced Persons*. Arlington, VA: USCRI, 2002.

Waldron, Sidney. "Anthropologists as 'Experts Witnesses'." In *Engendering Forced Migration, Theory and Practice*, edited by Indra Doreen, 342–49. New York: Berghahn Books, 1999.

Weis, Paul. *Nationality and Statelessness in International Law*. 2d ed. Dordrecht, Netherlands: Kluwer Academic, 1979.

Wilson, Ken B. "Thinking about the Ethics of Fieldwork." In *Fieldwork in Developing Countries*, edited by Stephen Devereux and John Hoddinott, 179–99. Boulder, CO: Lynne Rienner, 1993.

Wishah, Um Jabr. "The 1948 War and its Aftermath." *Journal of Palestine Studies* 35, no. 4 (Summer 2006): 54–62.

Yassin, Abdul Qader. "Palestinians in Egypt" [in Arabic]. *Samed al-Iqtisadi Magazine* 18, no. 106 (1996).

———. *Palestinians in Egypt* [in Arabic]. Ramallah, West Bank: Shaml, 1996.

———. *Between Two Worlds: Palestinian Businessmen in the Diaspora and the Build up of the Palestinian Entity* [in Arabic]. Cairo: Dar El Mustakbal, 2000.

Yehia, Karem. "The Image of the Palestinians in Egypt, 1982–1985." *Journal of Palestine Studies* 16, no. 2 (Winter 1987): 45–63.

Zureik, Elia. *Palestinian Refugees and the Peace Process*. Washington, DC: Institute for Palestine Studies, 1996.

Zureik, Elia. "The Trek Back Home: Palestinians Returning Home and their problems of Adaptations." In *Constructing Order: Palestinian Adaptations to Refugee Life*, edited by Are Hovdenak, Jon Pedersen, Dag Tuastad, and Elia Zureik, 79–102. Oslo: FAFO Institute for Applied Social Science, 1997.

Newspapers

Al-Ahali
Al-Ahram
Al-Ahram Hebdo
Al-Akhbar
Akhbar al-Yawm
Al-Fajr
Al-Hayat
An-Nahar
Cairo Times
Egyptian Weekly Magazine
Jaridah Rasmiyyah
Al-Sha'b
Al-Usbu'
Al-Wafd
Waqa'e' Yawmieh

Web Sites

http://www.badil.org	BADIL Resource Center for Palestinian Residency and Refugee's Rights
http://www.shaml.org	Shaml: The Palestinian Diaspora and Refugee Center
http://www.undp.org.eg	United Nations Development Program— Egypt
http://www.unhcr.org	Office of the UN High Commissioner for Refugees
http://www.pcbs.gov.ps	Palestinian Central Bureau of Statistics
http://www.refugees.org	U.S. Committee for Refugees and Immigrants

Index

'Abbasiyyah, xvi, xxvii, 17–18, 59, 61, 134
Abdallah, King of Jordan, 31n25, 38
Absentee Property Law (Israel 1950), 160
Abu Ghazalah, Samirah, 134, 151n27
Abu Hammad, xxv, 90, 199, 202
Abu Iyad (Salah Khalaf), xvii–xviii, 129, 150n11, 150n12
Abu Jihad (Khalil Wazir), 129
Abu Kabir, 28, 59, 61, 90, 122, 199
Abu Nidal Faction, xx, 46
Abu Nidal (Sabri al-Banna), 56n30, 46
Abu Za'bal, xxv, 27, 199
Acre, xxviii, 15
Administration Office of the Governor of Gaza (AOGG), ix, xxvii, 24, 54, 62, 79–80, 82, 85, 90, 92, 106, 114, 120–21, 134, 137, 190
Ahram, al-, 19, 28, 33n66, 48, 55n12, 56n29, 190, 193
Ahram Hebdo, al-, 65, 90, 193
Ahram Weekly, al-, 53, 193
aid/relief:
  1948 relief efforts, 154.
  See also American Friends Service Committee, Higher Committee of Palestinian Immigrant Affairs, Disaster Relief Project, UN Relief for Palestinian Refugees, UNRWA
aims of study, 4–5
Akhbar, al-, 47, 193
Akhbar al-Yawm, 50
Akram, Susan, 162–63, 172n28, 172n34
Alexandria, xxv–xxvi, 14, 107, 136, 183, 211n18
Algeria , xix, xx, 130, 166, 173n44
American Friends Service Committee (AFSC, Quakers), ix, xvii, 20, 31n35, 38–39, 192
AOGG. *See* Administration Office of the Governor of Gaza

al-Aqsa intifada. *See* intifada (second)
al-Aqsa mosque, 12
Arab-Israeli wars:
  1948 war, 14–15, 17, 155–56;
  1956 Suez war (tripartite invasion of Egypt) , 19, 21–22, 32n51n53, 91, 33n55, 42, 91;
  1967 war, xix, 23–27, 33n68;
  1973 war, xx, 46–47, 141
Arab League, 6, 31n28, 189, 209, 221:
  Administrative Office of Palestine, xvii, 167;
  and the Casablanca Protocol, xix, xxii, 89, 167–70, 183, 185;
  and Palestinian governance, 38;
  and the PLO, xix, 127–29, 140;
  policy toward Palestinians, 53, 155, 183, 185, 193;
  policy vs. implementation, 2, 155, 164, 166–73, 183;
  resolutions on Palestinian rights in host countries, 2, 16, 89, 166–68, 183, 185;
  resolutions on the right of return, 53, 166;
  summits, xix, xx, 128–30
Arab nationalism (pan-Arabism), xix, 22, 42, 128–29, 150n6, 150n10, 150n12
Arab rebellion of 1936–39, xv, 13
Arab state policy:
  dualism between Palestinian cause and local Palestinian populations, 185;
  factors affecting Palestinian rights, 170;
  repatriation/right of return, 163, 183
Arafat, Yasir, xvii–xxi, 45, 46, 129, 132, 150n3, 150n4, 150n11, 150n12, 200
'Arish, al-, xxv–xxvi, xxviii, 60–61, 90, 93, 133, 139, 186n2, 199–200
armistice agreements, xvi–xvii, 4, 16,19, 30n22, 36, 38, 54